BUSTER KEATON

INTERVIEWS

CONVERSATIONS WITH FILMMAKERS SERIES
PETER BRUNETTE, GENERAL EDITOR

Courtesy of Photofest

BUSTER KEATON

INTERVIEWS

EDITED BY KEVIN W. SWEENEY

UNIVERSITY PRESS OF MISSISSIPPI/JACKSON

www.upress.state.ms.us

The University Press of Mississippi is a member of the
Association of American University Presses.

Copyright © 2007 by University Press of Mississippi

Manufactured in the United States of America

First Edition 2007

∞

Library of Congress Cataloging-in-Publication Data

Keaton, Buster, 1895–1966.
 Buster Keaton : interviews / edited by Kevin W. Sweeney.
  p. cm. — (Conversations with filmmakers series)
 Includes index.
 ISBN-13: 978-1-57806-962-0 (cloth : alk. paper)
 ISBN-10: 1-57806-962-9 (cloth : alk. paper)
 ISBN-13: 978-1-57806-963-7 (pbk. : alk. paper)
 ISBN-10: 1-57806-963-7 (pbk. : alk. paper) 1. Keaton, Buster, 1895–1966—
Interviews. 2. Motion picture actors and actresses—United States—Interviews.
3. Comedians—United States—Interviews. I. Sweeney, Kevin W., 1945–
II. Title.
 PN2287.K4A3 2007
 791.4302'8092—dc22   2006033949
 [B]

British Library Cataloging-in-Publication Data available

CONTENTS

INTRODUCTION

OFF SCREEN, BUSTER KEATON was a shy man, fearful of crowds, and suspicious of public attention, particularly a woolly adulation of his "genius." "How can you be a genius in slapshoes?" was his response to such fawning. His public comedic persona with the famous "deadpan" countenance, the "great stone face," was often interpreted—not quite accurately, I believe—as an attempt to mute feeling, a reluctance to show the world his reactions. In view of this purported psychological distance from the world and suspicion of critical attention, one might be surprised to learn that Keaton gave so many interviews and that the interviews took place throughout almost his entire working life, from his teenage vaudeville days up until Rex Reed's interview of October 1965, just several months before his death.

In the early days, studio publicity certainly was a major motivation behind his agreeing to be interviewed, and in his later days in some of the longer interviews, he was interested in drawing public attention to his project of reissuing his classic silent two-reel and feature-length comedies. Yet the later interviews also convey his pride—justifiable, to be sure—in his accomplishments. He wants to let people know that he is still professionally active. "I work more than Doris Day," he tells Rex Reed. He is also particularly interested in discussing his own filmmaking in the 1920s, revealing how innovative and masterful it was and conveying how much fun he had in making his films.

Nevertheless, perhaps employing a psychological strategy in keeping with his deadpan reputation, Keaton in the interviews often presents himself in a rather legendary guise. A basic aspect of this legendary identity comes out in the tale Keaton repeatedly tells about how he acquired his name, "Buster." No less a celebrity than Harry Houdini, the great escape artist and master showman, on seeing the infant Keaton fall down a flight of stairs unharmed, exclaims that such an amazing fall was a "buster." The name takes, and Keaton assumes a mantle of future showmanship, one that warrants his recognition as a prodigy on the vaudeville stage and augurs a destiny of greatness. In her biography of Keaton, Marion Meade assembles considerable evidence to deflate this myth of Houdini's prophetic naming. Most likely, she claims, it was Keaton's father or one of his associates who gave the infant Keaton his nickname.[1]

Another legendary tale in the interviews concerns Keaton's introduction to filmmaking in March 1917. In that year the family vaudeville act, "The Three Keatons" (father, mother, and Buster), had broken up, and Keaton had gone to New York to look for work on Broadway. In the interviews, Keaton repeatedly claims that walking down the street in midtown Manhattan he had run into an old vaudeville friend, Lou Anger, who was with Roscoe "Fatty" Arbuckle. Right there, Anger introduced Keaton to Arbuckle. Arbuckle had recently been lured away from Mack Sennett by Joseph Schenck who had set him up in his own production company, the Comique Film Corporation, where he was just starting to make two-reel comedies. Arbuckle invited Keaton to come by the Colony Studio on East Forty-eighth Street and do a scene with him. The next day Keaton does the scene with Arbuckle and decides to work in pictures with Arbuckle, giving up a lucrative Broadway contract. The story might very well be true, although it has that fortuitous air about it like other stories that make up the Keaton legend. Was Keaton's meeting Arbuckle on the street just an accident? Film historian Peter Krämer finds the story of this coincidental meeting suspicious and notes the powerful economic reasons that might have been at work in Keaton's teaming up with Arbuckle.[2]

In pondering how Keaton came to join Arbuckle at Comique, one should keep in mind that in the late 1910s, American film comedy had a penchant for pairing comedians with contrasting body types and characters. In his 1916–17 Mutual films, diminutive, crafty Chaplin played brilliantly against hulking, at times ruthless, Eric Campbell.

In his own two-reelers, Keaton used the principle of comic contrast in frequently pairing himself with Big Joe Roberts. In his 1921 interview with Keaton, W. E. Mulligan notices the comic contrast between Arbuckle and Keaton. He points out that not only were they contrasts in body type, but they were also contrasts in expressive attitude. Arbuckle was known for his broad smile and frequent laughter, as was Al St. John, while Keaton fulfilled the role of the one who didn't smile or laugh. Even so, Kevin Brownlow in his interview with Keaton draws attention to the shot of Buster's broad grin in Arbuckle's 1917 *Coney Island*.[3] This invites the question of whether the contrastive pairing of Arbuckle and Keaton was still being developed in the fall of 1917. Thus, one can wonder about whether the pairing of Arbuckle and Keaton was simply fortuitous or whether it might have been planned by Schenck or others, anticipating that the two would make a good comedic team.

In the interviews Keaton describes his comedic style of deadpan response as originating in his vaudeville days. He points to two sources. On the vaudeville stage, he explains, it was *natural* for him to develop such a comedic style of restrained affect. He tells Arthur Friedman: "You just simply worked your natural way. I developed the 'Stone Face' thing quite naturally. I just happened to be, even as a small kid, I happened to be the type of comic that couldn't laugh at his own material. I soon learned at an awful early age that when I laughed the audience didn't. So, by the time I got into pictures, that was a natural way of working." His claim is that his deadpan reaction was naturally encouraged by how the audience responded.

Secondly, his father monitored Buster's developing comedic style, even whispering to him on stage to freeze his facial expression. Yet the father and son's stage interactions were so knockabout and boisterous that it seems hard to imagine the young Keaton as always being facially disaffected on stage. In Meade's biography, there is a photograph of The Three Keatons, staged to be sure, in which Buster is smiling while his father clings precariously to a table. Also, as the Markle interview shows, there was at least one other Three Keatons gag that required Buster to wear an exaggerated facial expression: Standing by the side of the stage, Buster had to look as if someone were choking him and trying to pull him off stage. In addition, Buster regularly parodied other acts and stage personalities. He even performed melodramatic roles in playlets. The variety of stage roles would seem to have allowed Keaton to express several different acting styles.

While crediting Arbuckle as one of the best comedy directors at the time and a brilliant teacher, Keaton says very little about how he developed a comedic persona that complemented Arbuckle's. When Robert Franklin asks Keaton to recall and describe Arbuckle's and his making of *Coney Island* out at the Long Island amusement park, Keaton replies: "I remember making it very well—nothing to write about. We just went down there, went on the concessions at Luna Park, and got in trouble— that was all there was to that." The impression given by Keaton's reply is that his and Arbuckle's interactions were in some way *natural* behavior. Both had a natural penchant for getting "in trouble," a talent the films exploited.

Of course, there was more to it than that. This tendency to downplay the skill and artifice behind filmmaking extended to the way Keaton sometimes described his own films. Recognizing the brilliance of the extended chase scene at the end of *Cops*, Studs Terkel asks him to talk about this amazing achievement. Keaton modestly replies: "Oh, just doing a hit-or-miss routine there, just ducking cops in all directions. Just a common ordinary chase sequence." Sure, sure, and the Taj Mahal is just a bunch of stones piled on top of each other!

Nevertheless, Keaton had a firm idea about how he thought his films should be made. He held very definite views about acting style in his feature-length films. For example, he tells Kevin Brownlow that one of his criticisms of Donald Crisp, whom he had hired initially to co-direct *The Navigator* with him, was that Crisp allowed the actors to overact. Referring to an early scene in the film in which spies confer about the need to sink the ship in order to prevent it from being used to aid their enemies, Keaton says that he had to reshoot the scene because Crisp "let them do a little overacting. I was always a little fussy about that. I didn't like overacting."

Given Keaton's deadpan countenance and his characteristic comic behaviors (e.g., his labored pacing, his bending way over at the waist to look at something), one can question Keaton's commitment to presenting human activity in some natural way. James Agee thought that American silent comedy had developed a special vocabulary of exaggerated comic actions. Yet there is no question that Keaton's interest in natural deportment and restrained acting informs his view about the presentation of comedy in his films, particularly the sequencing of gags. The interviews show his concern for the appropriateness and coherent fit of comic structures. He mentions some problems that he had with several gags: he had to modify or eliminate certain pieces of comic business in the underwater sequence of *The Navigator* and in the Tong war in *The Cameraman*. If a gag did not work in a particular sequence, however funny the gag might be as a single piece of comedy, Keaton insisted that it not be used. He was also not averse to giving the inappropriate gag to other comedians to use in their films.

Keaton's insistence on the appropriateness of the gag and its natural coherence with the narrative also extended to his thoughts on the construction of the comic narrative. Several times he discusses the procedure he and his usual three-person comedy team would use for developing comic material. He tells Friedman: "So, the minute somebody had an idea—we said what is it going to lead to? We don't go to the middle of the story; we jump right to the finish. So the finish—this would be the natural finish—says now does that give us any opportunities for gags? Make it exciting, fast action sometimes, and a couple of outstanding gags. We've got to be able to place those naturally, 'cause one of the worst mistakes you could make in those pictures was dragging in a gag by the heels. A misplaced gag, even though it's good, it's wrong to do." The middle of the narrative or comic sequence, Keaton thought, would be worked on later. He told Robert Franklin: "We always figured the middle would take care of itself." In skipping the middle until later, Keaton envisions that there will be a natural way to link the beginning with the finish.

Despite this particular form of comic scenario construction, Keaton in several interviews stresses that he never used a script for his two-reel and even his feature-length comedies. He tells Friedman: "We never had a script; we never did have one." To which Friedman responds, "And you'd go out and shoot this and let the cameras grind and see what they could pick up. Is that the idea?" Keaton rejects that perspective, saying: "Well, we didn't need a script. I knew in my mind what we were going to do, because with our way of working, there was always the unexpected happened." Of course, he had to do considerable planning even if there were no "script." Kevin Brownlow asks Keaton to explain how he knew what to take on location if there were no script: "But if you hadn't written anything, how did you know what props to take?" Keaton replies: "Oh, they all knew. The prop man, he'd know everything you needed. Wardrobe department would too. Gabourie knew what to build. Didn't need anything on paper."

Although it doesn't settle this issue, part of the problem might have to do with not using the right term to describe the plan for the film narrative. As derived from the theater, a script would list the successive speeches of the actors and integrate them with the development of the narrative. Of course, in the silent era the narrative wasn't presented in terms of dialogue. What dialogue there was in the film was presented in inter-titles, which were usually written after the scenes had been shot. In fact, in the silent era, the common term for the plan of the film narrative was "the continuity," not the script. One set out the scenario in "the continuity." In a telling remark about making *The General*, Keaton tells Brownlow: "Now, I wrote my own story, my own continuity. I directed it and cut it and titled it. So actually it was a pet."

However, in his rejection of the script, Keaton is emphasizing the role that spontaneity played in the filmmaking process. As he later saw when at MGM in the 1930s, big studios used a script as a fixed recipe for exactly what was to be included in the film narrative. The script was to be rigidly adhered to; no deviations were to be allowed. Keaton welcomed the unexpected and unrehearsed. In his autobiography, he says that "I always preferred working on location because more good gags suggested themselves in new and unfamiliar surroundings."[4] The Terkel and the Friedman interviews have examples from *Three Ages* and *Seven Chances* which show how Keaton and crew were able to take advantage of unexpected occurrences while in the process of shooting. Even in editing the film, Keaton, who did his own editing, gives the impression that he wanted to reserve the right to make later changes in the narrative, to reshoot scenes if he thought necessary. After all, he points out, the whole production crew was on salary; his studio owned the cameras and equipment. If he wanted to reshoot a scene, the only cost was the expense of the film and gasoline for transportation.

Nevertheless, Keaton's view of filmmaking was not completely centered on exploiting coincidences that occurred while filming. If he had a particular gag in mind, if there were a comic effect that he wanted to achieve, he was tireless in working to realize it. Perhaps the best example from the interviews is Keaton's description of how he and his crew overcame numerous obstacles to perfect the gag in *The Boat* in which Buster at the prow of his little craft slides down the slipway and disappears under the water leaving only his porkpie floating on the surface.

Time and again in the interviews Keaton reveals the techniques he and his crew used in the 1920s to create his comedies. He tells Kevin Brownlow about the innovative means he used to make the montage of changing scenes in *Sherlock Jr.* and how he used surveyor's instruments to match shots in *Seven Chances*. The great traveling shots of *The General* are also discussed, as is the underwater sequence in *The Navigator*. Keaton is informative about the contributions of his crew, pointing out how one of his top-notch cameramen, Elgin Lessley, shot certain scenes in *Sherlock Jr.*, and how Fred Gabourie, his brilliant technical and art director, constructed some of the sets.

In supplying details about the ways that he solved problems involved in making his films, Keaton reveals how frequently the films themselves are based on scenarios of problem solving. This is not to say that the films reflexively comment on Keaton's filmmaking, but that Keaton has an interest in technical problem solving. He explains that what drew him to filmmaking was his fascination with the mechanics of producing a film. He frequently said that if he hadn't been a filmmaker and entertainer he would have liked to have been an engineer. This interest comes out in how he made his films, the scenarios he used, and the roles he played in the films. As a protagonist in his films Keaton often exhibits an agency and an energy that overcome any melodramatic positioning of his character as a victim. One of my favorite lines in the interviews is Keaton's response to a comment that Herbert Feinstein makes in discussing the role Keaton plays in *The General*. Feinstein says: "In *The General*, the boy is a *schlemiel*." Keaton replies: "In *The General*, I'm an engineer."

In his films, Keaton was very much aware of the generic formulae to which dramatic films at the time conformed. Many of his films parody generic conventions. He was also interested in resisting a collapse of his own style of comedy into what he referred to as "farce comedy." Joan Franklin asks Keaton to characterize "farce comedy" in order to distinguish it from Keaton's style of comedy. Keaton responds with a

wonderful short exposition of this generic form that by contrast illumi-
nates his own comic vision. "Farce comedy," he says, "as a rule is based
on a simple misunderstanding or a mistaken identity. There's always a
couple of characters in that show, and if they come out and say, 'Wait a
minute, this is the case,' all the problems would be solved. And, [there's]
a farce tempo. In all farce comedies, everybody works automatically
faster than they do when they're telling a legitimate story. They take
things bigger. People get hysterical easy."

Of course, there is a lot of fast action in Keaton's films. Yet, even in
those of his films in which a misunderstanding plays a significant part
of the narrative (e.g., *Battling Butler* and *The General*), the Keaton protagonist does not rely on some melodramatic recognition of the actual
situation to resolve the problem. If his exploits are framed within a
dream, the Keaton protagonist sets out to overcome the narrative
predicament he faces. One can even see Keaton's set deadpan countenance as fitting in with the protagonist's nonfarcical sense of agency
and as standing opposed to that conventional tendency to "get hysterical
easy."

Selecting the interviews for this volume involved some difficult
choices. Because of the length of the volume stipulated by the press,
not all of the interviews with Keaton could be included. In making the
selection, I relied upon several criteria. One criterion I used was to
include only full interviews. So I did not include selections from either
Keaton's autobiography (Keaton and Samuels, *My Wonderful Life of
Slapstick*) or from Rudi Blesh's *Keaton*, which is based extensively on
interviews with Keaton. Both volumes are essential reading for understanding Keaton's life and career; however, they are not difficult to find,
at least in libraries.

A top priority was to include major unpublished Keaton interviews.
I found that there were four extensive unpublished Keaton interviews.
First, in chronological order, there is Arthur B. Friedman's 1956 "Turning
Point Interview with Buster Keaton." Friedman had published an
excerpt from the interview, but the full interview archived at UCLA had
never been published. I made a new transcription from the taped
recording. Second, there is Robert and Joan Franklin's 1958 "Interview
with Keaton." Again, I made a new transcription of the interview from
the taped recording. The third interview is Studs Terkel's 1960

"Interview with Buster Keaton." Terkel has published a condensed selection from the interview, but the whole interview archived at the Chicago Historical Society had never been published. I transcribed the full interview. Finally, there is Kevin Brownlow's 1964 interview, "Buster Keaton." Brownlow has published an excerpt from the interview, and the interview served as the basis for his chapter on Keaton in *The Parade's Gone By*; however, the complete interview had never been published.

Another criterion I used was to include the best interviews available, even if they were widely known. So, although the Bishop interview has been reprinted several times, because of its insights about Keaton's films, it deserved a place in the volume. Keaton interviews have appeared in different media, and I thought some nonprint ones should be included. The 1964 Markle interview originally appeared on Canadian television. Some of the television interviews and shows that featured Keaton did not lend themselves well to being presented as a print transcript. One needed to see the image, and for that reason I excluded them.

Whether interviews were publicly accessible was also a consideration. A few of the television interviews (e.g., *The Today Show: Buster Keaton Revisited* [1963]) are available for personal viewing at the Museum of Television and Radio at their locations in Los Angeles and New York. *Buster Keaton Rides Again* (1965), the documentary about Keaton's appearance in *The Railrodder*, contains some very interesting conversation with Keaton. Nevertheless, it is available as a VHS videotape from Kino on Video (www.kino.com/). If an interview were available in an on-line version, I usually opted not to include it. Some of the early interviews from the 1920s are available at the Generally Buster web site, (www.geocities.com/~oldbrit/busterindex.htm). Keaton had an international reputation, and there are several foreign language interviews with Keaton. I chose to include a fairly obscure one, George Sadoul's 1962 "A Dinner with Keaton." It appears in an English translation for the first time. Finally all of Keaton's films from *One Week* to *Steamboat Bill, Jr.*, are available from Kino on Video. Information about the availability of other Keaton films is listed on the International Buster Keaton Society ("The Damfinos") web site, www.busterkeaton.com/.

Many people assisted me in locating hard-to-find Keaton interviews, aided me in obtaining permission to publish them, and opened doors so that I could transcribe the unpublished ones. Deserving special thanks are Kevin Brownlow, Bob Borgen, Eileen Whitfield, Peter Krämer, Charles Wolfe, Joanna Rapf, David Pearson, Larry Shiner, and especially Elizabeth Winston. Bo Berglund, Jean-Pierre Coursodon, and David Bordwell offered sage advice which steered the project around some problems. Archivists at the following institutions were extremely helpful: Jessica Wiederhorn, formerly at the Columbia University Oral History Research Office; Lesley A. Martin at the Chicago Historical Society; Sean Delaney at the British Film Institute; Genie Guerard, Department of Special Collections, UCLA Library; Barbara Hall and Sandra Archer at the Margaret Herrick Library of the Academy of Motion Picture Arts and Sciences; Mickey Wells and Elizabeth Barron at the Macdonald-Kelce Library of the University of Tampa; and, for much generous assistance over many years, the staff at the Library of Congress Film Archive, especially Madeline Matz, Rosemary Haines, and Zoran Sinobad. I would also like to thank Louise Jones, Patricia Tobias, Melissa Talmadge Cox, Darcy Dapra, and Marion Meade. For their patience, good counsel, and timely assistance, I extend a special thank you to my editors: Seetha Srinivasan, Anne Stascavage, and Walter Biggins.

Finally, I wish to acknowledge the financial assistance of a Delo Research Grant from the University of Tampa.

KWS

Notes

1. Marion Meade, *Buster Keaton: Cut to the Chase* (New York: HarperCollins, 1995), pp. 18–20.

2. Peter Krämer, "A Slapstick Comedian at the Crossroads: Buster Keaton, the Theater, and the Movies in 1916/17," *Theatre History Studies* 17 (June 1997): 133–46.

3. For a still image of this grin, see Tom Dardis, *Keaton: The Man Who Wouldn't Lie Down* (New York: Scribner's, 1979), p. 39.

4. Buster Keaton with Charles Samuels, *My Wonderful World of Slapstick* (1960: rpt. New York: Da Capo Press, 1982), p. 142.

CHRONOLOGY

1895	Joseph Frank Keaton is born October 4 in Piqua, Kansas (a small farming community not far from Iola in southeastern Kansas) to Myra and Joseph Hallie Keaton.
1896	Keaton acquires the name of "Buster." Legend has it that Harry Houdini gave him the name, although it was more likely his father.
1900	In October at Bill Dockstader's Wonderland Theatre in Wilmington, Delaware, Keaton joins his father and mother on stage as a salaried member of their vaudeville act, later to be called "The Three Keatons."
1917	February–March: After years as one of the most famous acts in American vaudeville, The Three Keatons break up. Keaton goes to New York and gets a contract to appear in the Shubert brothers' *The Passing Show of 1917* at the Winter Garden theater on Broadway. However, after running into Lou Anger, an old vaudevillian acquaintance, Buster is invited to do a scene with Roscoe "Fatty" Arbuckle who was beginning to make two-reel comedies for Joseph Schenck at the Colony Studio on East Forty-eighth Street. Buster appears in Arbuckle's *The Butcher Boy* and, breaking his contract with the Shuberts, starts working under Arbuckle's direction for the Comique Film Corporation, acting in two-reel comedies. October: Keaton and the rest of the Comique crew move to Long Beach, California, to make their films.
1918	During World War I, Keaton is drafted into the army. He serves in France, mostly entertaining the troops.

1919   In April, Keaton returns to Los Angeles and resumes work with Arbuckle making films. That December Arbuckle receives a contract from Adolph Zukor at Paramount to star in feature-length films. Schenck turns Comique over to Keaton to make and star in two-reel comedies to be released through Metro. Keaton sets up production in the old Chaplin studio in Hollywood, now named the Keaton Studio.

1920   With Eddie Cline as co-director, Keaton shoots but does not release *The High Sign*. That summer Keaton stars in *The Saphead* for Metro. In the fall, Keaton shoots and releases *One Week* to rave reviews. Between 1920 and 1923 he will make nineteen two-reel comedies.

1921   Keaton marries Natalie Talmadge at Joseph Schenck's estate on Long Island, New York. Schenck, who is married to Norma Talmadge, is now his brother-in-law. After releasing eight two-reelers through Metro, Keaton, through Schenck's negotiations, gets a contract to release his remaining eleven comic shorts through First National, beginning with *The Playhouse*. Roscoe Arbuckle is tried on charges of raping and murdering Virginia Rappe in a San Francisco hotel. After three trials, Arbuckle is exonerated, but the scandal effectively ends his career.

1922   To avoid connection with the Arbuckle scandal, Schenck changes the Comique Film Corporation to Buster Keaton Productions.

1923   In the spring, Keaton releases his last two-reeler, *The Love Nest*. That fall he releases through Metro his first comic feature, *Three Ages*, shortly followed by his second, *Our Hospitality*, in which he, his wife Natalie, their infant son, and Keaton's father all appear.

1924   Keaton releases *Sherlock Jr.* in the spring and *The Navigator* in the fall.

1925   *Seven Chances* is the spring release; *Go West* is the fall release.

1926   *Battling Butler* is released. Joseph Schenck becomes president of United Artists. That summer Keaton shoots *The General* in Cottage Grove, Oregon.

1927   *The General* is released through United Artists. *College* is released that fall.

1928   In order to devote all his energies to United Artists, Schenck gives up independently producing Keaton's films and closes the Keaton Studio. He convinces Keaton to sign a contract with MGM to star in comedies that they will produce. Some of his crew from Buster Keaton Productions work with Keaton on the first two MGM comedies. In the spring, the last Buster Keaton Production film, *Steamboat Bill, Jr.*, is released. That fall MGM releases the first Keaton-starring comedy, *The Cameraman.*

1929   *Spite Marriage* is released. It is generally considered to be the last Keaton-shaped film he stars in at MGM.

1930   Keaton stars in his first sound film, *Free and Easy*, followed later that year by *Doughboys.*

1931   Keaton stars in *Parlor, Bedroom and Bath* and *Sidewalks of New York.*

1932   Keaton co-stars with Jimmy Durante in *The Passionate Plumber*, the first of four films they will make together. Keaton's wife, Natalie, divorces him.

1933   In February, Louis B. Mayer fires Keaton from his position at MGM. Keaton has problems with alcohol. Keaton marries Mae Scriven.

1934   Keaton stars in *The Gold Ghost*, the first of what will be sixteen Educational Pictures short comedies made over the next four years.

1936   Mae Scriven divorces Keaton.

1937   Keaton makes *Love Nest on Wheels*, the last of his Educational Pictures short comedies. From 1937 to 1950, Keaton works intermittently for MGM as a gag-writer and occasional director of short films.

1939   Keaton is hired by Columbia Pictures to star in two-reel comedies. From 1939 to 1941, Keaton appears in ten Columbia shorts. His first film is *Pest from the West.*

1940   Keaton marries Eleanor Norris. He will be happily married for the rest of his life.

1947   Keaton performs for a season at the Cirque Médrano in Paris. He is a huge hit and returns off and on for several years.

1949   Keaton plays a supporting role to Judy Garland in MGM's musical, *In the Good Old Summertime*. He writes and directs a sequence of the film. His role in the film puts him back in the public eye, as does James Agee's famous *Life* article about Hollywood silent comedy, "Comedy's Greatest Era." In December, Keaton starts a weekly half-hour television show in Los Angeles, *The Buster Keaton Show*. The success of the show leads to other commercial film and television ventures.

1953   Keaton appears with Charlie Chaplin in Chaplin's *Limelight*.

1954   Raymond Rohauer starts to search out and preserve Keaton's silent films.

1956   Keaton starts making television commercials.

1960   Keaton receives a special Oscar from the Academy of Motion Picture Arts and Sciences.

1964   Keaton appears in *Film*, Samuel Beckett's modernist short film shot in lower Manhattan.

1965   Keaton stars in *The Railrodder* for the Canadian National Railways. That fall he is given a standing ovation at the Venice Film Festival.

1966   On February 1, Keaton dies at his Woodland Hills home of lung cancer.

FILMOGRAPHY

THIS FILMOGRAPHY only lists films that Keaton either directed or directed portions of. The most complete Keaton filmography, which includes his acting and writing credits in both film and television, is Jack Dragga's "Filmography" in Marion Meade's *Buster Keaton: Cut to the Chase* (New York: HarperCollins, 1995), pp. 313–80.

1920
ONE WEEK
Production Company: Comique Film Corporation
Producer: Joseph M. Schenck
Directors: **Buster Keaton** and Eddie Cline
Screenplay: **Buster Keaton** and Eddie Cline
Cinematography: Elgin Lessley
Technical Director: Fred Gabourie
Cast: **Buster Keaton**, Sybil Seely, Joe Roberts
Distributor: Metro Pictures
35 mm, B&W, 2 reels

CONVICT 13
Production Company: Comique Film Corporation
Producer: Joseph M. Schenck
Directors: **Buster Keaton** and Eddie Cline
Screenplay: **Buster Keaton** and Eddie Cline
Cinematography: Elgin Lessley
Technical Director: Fred Gabourie
Cast: **Buster Keaton**, Sybil Seely, Joe Roberts, Joe Keaton, Eddie Cline

Distributor: Metro Pictures
35 mm, B&W, 2 reels

THE SCARECROW
Production Company: Comique Film Corporation
Producer: Joseph M. Schenck
Directors: **Buster Keaton** and Eddie Cline
Screenplay: **Buster Keaton** and Eddie Cline
Cinematography: Elgin Lessley
Technical Director: Fred Gabourie
Cast: **Buster Keaton**, Sybil Seely, Joe Roberts, Joe Keaton, Eddie Cline, Luke (Roscoe Arbuckle's dog)
Distributor: Metro Pictures
35 mm, B&W, 2 reels

NEIGHBORS
Production Company: Comique Film Corporation
Producer: Joseph M. Schenck
Directors: **Buster Keaton** and Eddie Cline
Screenplay: **Buster Keaton** and Eddie Cline
Cinematography: Elgin Lessley
Technical Director: Fred Gabourie
Cast: **Buster Keaton**, Virginia Fox, Joe Roberts, Joe Keaton, Eddie Cline, James Duffy, The Flying Escalantes
Distributor: Metro Pictures
35 mm, B&W, 2 reels

1921
THE HAUNTED HOUSE
Production Company: Comique Film Corporation
Producer: Joseph M. Schenck
Directors: **Buster Keaton** and Eddie Cline
Screenplay: **Buster Keaton** and Eddie Cline
Cinematography: Elgin Lessley
Technical Director: Fred Gabourie
Cast: **Buster Keaton**, Virginia Fox, Joe Roberts, Eddie Cline

Distributor: Metro Pictures
35 mm, B&W, 2 reels

HARD LUCK

Production Company: Comique Film Corporation
Producer: Joseph M. Schenck
Directors: **Buster Keaton** and Eddie Cline
Screenplay: **Buster Keaton** and Eddie Cline
Cinematography: Elgin Lessley
Technical Director: Fred Gabourie
Cast: **Buster Keaton**, Virginia Fox, Joe Roberts, Bull Montana
Distributor: Metro Pictures
35 mm, B&W, 2 reels

THE HIGH SIGN

Production Company: Comique Film Corporation
Producer: Joseph M. Schenck
Directors: **Buster Keaton** and Eddie Cline
Screenplay: **Buster Keaton** and Eddie Cline
Cinematography: Elgin Lessley
Technical Director: Fred Gabourie
Cast: **Buster Keaton**, Bartine Burkett, Al St. John
Distributor: Metro Pictures
35 mm, B&W, 2 reels

THE GOAT

Production Company: Comique Film Corporation
Producer: Joseph M. Schenck
Directors: **Buster Keaton** and Mal St. Clair
Screenplay: **Buster Keaton** and Mal St. Clair
Cinematography: Elgin Lessley
Technical Director: Fred Gabourie
Cast: **Buster Keaton**, Virginia Fox, Joe Roberts, Mal St. Clair, Eddie
Cline, Jean Havez
Distributor: Metro Pictures
35 mm, B&W, 2 reels

THE PLAYHOUSE
Production Company: Comique Film Corporation
Producer: Joseph M. Schenck
Directors: **Buster Keaton** and Eddie Cline
Screenplay: **Buster Keaton** and Eddie Cline
Cinematography: Elgin Lessley
Technical Director: Fred Gabourie
Cast: **Buster Keaton**, Joe Roberts, Virginia Fox
Distributor: First National
35 mm, B&W, 2 reels

THE BOAT
Production Company: Comique Film Corporation
Producer: Joseph M. Schenck
Directors: **Buster Keaton** and Eddie Cline
Screenplay: **Buster Keaton** and Eddie Cline
Cinematography: Elgin Lessley
Technical Director: Fred Gabourie
Cast: **Buster Keaton**, Joe Roberts, Sybil Seely, Eddie Cline
Distributor: First National
35 mm, B&W, 2 reels

1922
THE PALEFACE
Production Company: Comique Film Corporation
Producer: Joseph M. Schenck
Directors: **Buster Keaton** and Eddie Cline
Screenplay: **Buster Keaton** and Eddie Cline
Cinematography: Elgin Lessley
Technical Director: Fred Gabourie
Cast: **Buster Keaton**, Joe Roberts, Virginia Fox
Distributor: First National
35 mm, B&W, 2 reels

COPS
Production Company: Comique Film Corporation
Producer: Joseph M. Schenck

Directors: **Buster Keaton** and Eddie Cline
Screenplay: **Buster Keaton** and Eddie Cline
Cinematography: Elgin Lessley
Technical Director: Fred Gabourie
Cast: **Buster Keaton**, Joe Roberts, Virginia Fox, Eddie Cline
Distributor: First National
35 mm, B&W, 2 reels

MY WIFE'S RELATIONS
Production Company: Comique Film Corporation
Producer: Joseph M. Schenck
Directors: **Buster Keaton** and Eddie Cline
Screenplay: **Buster Keaton** and Eddie Cline
Cinematography: Elgin Lessley
Technical Director: Fred Gabourie
Cast: **Buster Keaton**, Kate Price, Monte Collins, Joe Roberts, Tom
Wilson, Wheezer Dell
Distributor: First National
35 mm, B&W, 2 reels

THE BLACKSMITH
Production Company: Comique Film Corporation
Producer: Joseph M. Schenck
Directors: **Buster Keaton** and Mal St. Clair
Screenplay: **Buster Keaton** and Mal St. Clair
Cinematography: Elgin Lessley
Technical Director: Fred Gabourie
Cast: **Buster Keaton**, Joe Roberts, Virginia Fox
Distributor: First National
35 mm, B&W, 2 reels

THE FROZEN NORTH
Production Company: Buster Keaton Productions
Producer: Joseph M. Schenck
Directors: **Buster Keaton** and Eddie Cline
Screenplay: **Buster Keaton** and Eddie Cline

Cinematography: Elgin Lessley
Technical Director: Fred Gabourie
Cast: **Buster Keaton**, Bonnie Hill, Joe Roberts, Freeman Wood, Eddie
Cline, Sybil Seely, Robert Parker
Distributor: First National
35 mm, B&W, 2 reels

DAYDREAMS
Production Company: Buster Keaton Productions
Producer: Joseph M. Schenck
Directors: **Buster Keaton** and Eddie Cline
Screenplay: **Buster Keaton** and Eddie Cline
Cinematography: Elgin Lessley
Technical Director: Fred Gabourie
Cast: **Buster Keaton**, Renée Adorée, Joe Keaton, Joe Roberts,
Eddie Cline
Distributor: First National
35 mm, B&W, 3 reels

THE ELECTRIC HOUSE
Production Company: Buster Keaton Productions
Producer: Joseph M. Schenck
Directors: **Buster Keaton** and Eddie Cline
Screenplay: **Buster Keaton** and Eddie Cline
Cinematography: Elgin Lessley
Technical Director: Fred Gabourie
Cast: **Buster Keaton**, Virginia Fox, Joe Roberts
Distributor: Associated First National
35 mm, B&W, 2 reels

1923
THE BALLOONATIC
Production Company: Buster Keaton Productions
Producer: Joseph M. Schenck
Directors: **Buster Keaton** and Eddie Cline
Screenplay: **Buster Keaton** and Eddie Cline

Cinematography: Elgin Lessley
Technical Director: Fred Gabourie
Cast: **Buster Keaton**, Phyllis Haver
Distributor: Associated First National
35 mm, B&W, 2 reels

THE LOVE NEST
Production Company: Buster Keaton Productions
Producer: Joseph M. Schenck
Directors: **Buster Keaton** and Eddie Cline
Screenplay: **Buster Keaton** and Eddie Cline
Cinematography: Elgin Lessley
Technical Director: Fred Gabourie
Cast: **Buster Keaton**, Virginia Fox, Joe Roberts
Distributor: Associated First National
35 mm, B&W, 2 reels

THREE AGES
Production Company: Buster Keaton Productions
Producer: Joseph M. Schenck
Directors: **Buster Keaton** and Eddie Cline
Screenplay: Clyde Bruckman, Jean Havez, and Joseph Mitchell
Cinematography: Elgin Lessley and William McGann
Technical Director: Fred Gabourie
Cast: **Buster Keaton**, Margaret Leahy, Wallace Beery, Joe Roberts,
Lillian Lawrence, Oliver Hardy, Horace Morgan, Blanche Payson,
Lionel Belmore
Distributor: Metro Pictures
35 mm, B&W, 6 reels

OUR HOSPITALITY
Production Company: Buster Keaton Productions
Producer: Joseph M. Schenck
Directors: **Buster Keaton** and Jack C. Blystone
Screenplay: Clyde Bruckman, Jean Havez, and Joseph Mitchell
Cinematography: Elgin Lessley and Gordon Jennings

Technical Director: Fred Gabourie
Electrician: Denver Harmon
Costumes: Walter Israel
Cast: **Buster Keaton**, Natalie Talmadge, Joseph Keaton, James Duffy,
Edward Coxen, Jean Dumas, Buster Keaton, Jr., Kitty Bradbury, Joe
Roberts, Leonard Clapham [Tom London], Craig Ward, Ralph Bushman
[Francis X. Bushman], Monte Collins
Distributor: Metro Pictures
35 mm, B&W, 7 reels

1924
SHERLOCK JR.
Production Company: Buster Keaton Productions
Producer: Joseph M. Schenck
Directors: **Buster Keaton** and Roscoe Arbuckle
Screenplay: Clyde Bruckman, Jean Havez, and Joseph Mitchell
Cinematography: Elgin Lessley and Byron Houck
Technical Director: Fred Gabourie
Costumes: Clare West
Cast: **Buster Keaton**, Kathryn McGuire, Ward Crane, Joe Keaton,
Erwin Connelly, Jane Connelly, Ford West, George Davis, Doris Deane,
Ruth Holley, Horace Morgan, John Patrick
Distributor: Metro Pictures
35 mm, B&W, 5 reels

THE NAVIGATOR
Production Company: Buster Keaton Productions
Producer: Joseph M. Schenck
Directors: **Buster Keaton** and Donald Crisp
Screenplay: Clyde Bruckman, Jean Havez, and Joseph Mitchell
Cinematography: Elgin Lessley and Byron Houck
Technical Director: Fred Gabourie
Electrician: Denver Harmon
Cast: **Buster Keaton**, Kathryn McGuire, Frederick Vroom, Clarence
Burton, H. M. Clugston, Noble Johnson
Distributor: Metro-Goldwyn Pictures
35 mm, B&W, 6 reels

1925
SEVEN CHANCES
Production Company: Buster Keaton Productions
Producer: Joseph M. Schenck
Director: **Buster Keaton**
Screenplay: Clyde Bruckman, Jean Havez, and Joseph Mitchell, adapted
from the play by Roi Cooper Megrue
Cinematography: Elgin Lessley and Byron Houck
Technical Director: Fred Gabourie
Electrician: Denver Harmon
Cast: **Buster Keaton**, Ruth Dwyer, T. Roy Barnes, Snitz Edwards, Frankie
Raymond, Jules Cowles, Erwin Connelly, Jean Arthur, Jean Havez,
Rosalind Byrne, Loro Bara, Alma Bramley, Bartine Burkett, Doris Deane,
Hazel Deane, Connie Evans, Eugenia Gilbert, Edna Hammon, Marion
Harlan, Judy King, Rosalind Mooney, Peggy Pearce, Barbara Pierce, Kate
Price, Pauline Toler
Distributor: Metro-Goldwyn Pictures
35 mm, B&W with Technicolor prologue, 6 reels

GO WEST
Production Company: Buster Keaton Productions
Producer: Joseph M. Schenck
Director: **Buster Keaton**, assisted by Lex Neal
Screenplay: Raymond Cannon
Cinematography: Elgin Lessley and Bert Haines
Technical Director: Fred Gabourie
Electrician: Denver Harmon
Cast: **Buster Keaton**, Howard Truesdale, Kathleen Myers, Ray
Thompson, Joe Keaton, Roscoe Arbuckle, Babe London, Brown Eyes
(the cow)
Distributor: Metro-Goldwyn-Mayer
35 mm, B&W, 7 reels

1926
BATTLING BUTLER
Production Company: Buster Keaton Productions

Producer: Joseph M. Schenck
Director: **Buster Keaton**
Screenplay: Paul Gerard Smith, Albert Boasberg, Charles Smith, and
Lex Neal adapted the Broadway play, *Battling Butler*, by Stanley
Brightman, Austin Melford, Philip Brabham, Walter L. Rosemont,
and Douglas Furber
Cinematography: Devereaux Jennings and Bert Haines
Technical Director: Fred Gabourie
Electrician: Ed Levy
Cast: **Buster Keaton**, Snitz Edwards, Sally O'Neil, Walter James,
Bud Fine, Francis McDonald, Mary O'Brien, Tom Wilson,
Eddie Borden
Distributor: Metro-Goldwyn-Mayer
35 mm, B&W, 7 reels

THE GENERAL
Production Company: Buster Keaton Productions
Producer: Joseph M. Schenck
Director: **Buster Keaton**
Screenplay: **Buster Keaton** and Clyde Bruckman, based on William
Pittinger's book, *The Great Locomotive Chase*
Production Manager: Fred Gabourie
Cinematography: Devereaux Jennings and Bert Haines
Technical Director: Frank Barnes
Electrician: Denver Harmon
Wardrobe and Makeup: Bennie Hubel, J. K. Pitcairn, Fred C. Ryle
Cast: **Buster Keaton**, Marion Mack, Charles Smith, Frank Barnes,
Frank Agney, Frederick Vroom, Glen Cavender, Ross McCutcheon,
Charles Philips, Jack Dempster, Red Thompson, Anthony Harvey, Ray
Hanford, Tom Moran, Bud Fine, Jimmie Bryant, Al Hanson, Jim Farley,
Joe Keaton, Mike Donlin, Tom Nawn
Distributor: United Artists
35 mm, B&W, 8 reels

1927
COLLEGE
Production Company: Buster Keaton Productions

Producer: Joseph M. Schenck
Directors: James W. Horne and **Buster Keaton** (uncredited)
Screenplay: Carl Harbaugh and Bryan Foy
Supervisor: Harry Brand
Cinematography: Devereaux Jennings and Bert Haines
Technical Director: Fred Gabourie
Electrician: Jack Lewis
Cast: **Buster Keaton**, Florence Turner, Ann Cornwall, Flora Bramley,
Harold Goodwin, Buddy Mason, Grant Withers, Snitz Edwards, Carl
Harbaugh, Sam Crawford, Lee Barnes
Distributor: United Artists
35 mm, B&W, 6 reels

1928
STEAMBOAT BILL, JR.
Production Company: Buster Keaton Productions
Producer: Joseph M. Schenck
Directors: Charles F. Reisner (Riesner) and **Buster Keaton** (uncredited)
Screenplay: Carl Harbaugh
Supervisor: Harry Brand
Cinematography: Devereaux Jennings and Bert Haines
Technical Director: Fred Gabourie
Electrician: Jack Lewis
Cast: **Buster Keaton**, Marion Byron, Ernest Torrance, Tom Lewis, Tom
McGuire, Louise Keaton
Distributor: United Artists
35 mm, B&W, 7 reels

THE CAMERAMAN
Produced and Distributed: Metro-Goldwyn-Mayer
Producer: Lawrence Weingarten (uncredited)
Directors: Edward M. Sedgwick (significantly shaped by **Buster Keaton**,
uncredited)
Screenplay: Clyde Bruckman and Lew Lipton
Cinematography: Elgin Lessley and Reggie Lanning
Editing: Hugh Wynn and Basil Wrangell

Technical Director: Fred Gabourie
Titles: James Farnham
Costumes: David Cox
Cast: **Buster Keaton**, Marceline Day, Harold Goodwin, Harry
Gribbon, Edward Brophy, William Irving, Vernon Dent, Josephine
(monkey)
35 mm, B&W, 8 reels

1938
LIFE IN SOMETOWN, USA
Produced and Distributed: Metro-Goldwyn-Mayer
Producer: Louis Lewyn
Director: **Buster Keaton**
Screenplay: Carl Dudley, Richard Murphy
Narrator: Carey Wilson
35 mm, B&W, 1 reel

HOLLYWOOD HANDICAP
Produced and Distributed: Metro-Goldwyn-Mayer
Producer: Louis Lewyn
Director: **Buster Keaton**
Screenplay: John Kraft
Cast: The Original Sing Band
35 mm, B&W, 1 reel

STREAMLINED SWING
Produced and Distributed: Metro-Goldwyn-Mayer
Producer: Louis Lewyn
Director: **Buster Keaton**
Screenplay: Marion Mack
Dialogue: John Kraft
Cast: The Original Sing Band
35 mm, B&W, 1 reel

1946
THE EQUESTRIAN QUIZ
Produced and Distributed: Metro-Goldwyn-Mayer

Producer: Pete Smith ("A Pete Smith Specialty")
Director: **Buster Keaton**
35 mm, B&W, 1 reel

1949
IN THE GOOD OLD SUMMERTIME
Produced and Distributed: Metro-Goldwyn-Mayer
Producer: Joe Pasternak
Director: Robert Z. Leonard (**Buster Keaton**, uncredited, directed several
gag sequences.)
Screenplay: Samson Raphaelson, Frances Goodrich, Albert Hackett, Ivan
Tors, and **Buster Keaton**; based on Miklós László's play *Parfumerie*. The
film is a musical remake of Ernst Lubitsch's *The Shop Around the Corner*
(1940) with James Stewart and Margaret Sullavan.
Cinematography: Harry Stadling
Editing: Adrienne Fazan
Cast: Judy Garland, Van Johnson, S. Z. Sakall, Spring Byington,
Buster Keaton (Hickey), Clinton Sundberg, Marcia Van Dyke, Lillian
Bronson, Anna Q. Nilsson, Liza Minnelli (baby)
35 mm, Technicolor, 102 minutes

BUSTER KEATON

INTERVIEWS

"Poor Child!"

ELIZABETH PELTRET/1921

YOUNG AS HE IS, Buster Keaton has seen much of the face of
the earth. He began moving when, at the ripe young age of two weeks,
he was moved from the little town of Pickway, Kansas, where he was
born. And it is a noteworthy thing that, no matter how famous he may
become, he can never go back to that town. He can make millions, but
he can never buy the house in which he was born. No committee of
leading Pickwayan citizens will ever greet him with a brass band and a
parade to proclaim him the town's most famous son; he can never
"go home" to die!

Sad; isn't it? But it must not be supposed that Buster is in any way to
blame for this banishment. No, indeed! In this respect, he was very
much the victim of circumstances outside of his control.

You see, at the time Buster was born, his father and Harry Houdini,
the "Handcuff King," were owners of a medicine show. (No, they were
not chased out of town!) They left Pickway of their own accord. But
about two months after they had started on their way, along came a
lively young cyclone and blew the town off the face of the earth. (It
never was on the map.) And nobody thought it of enough importance
to build it up again.

So Buster became a wanderer. And he did wander too! As soon
as he was old enough to walk, he would go wandering off on

From *Motion Picture Classic*, vol. 12, no.1 (March 1921): 64, 66, 97.

exploring expeditions as soon as the show landed in a town that was new to him.

"I have never gotten lost," he said.

His parents used to say of him that he couldn't get lost any more than he could get killed. In fact, it was his propensity for not getting killed that got him his name of "Buster."

"Up to the time I was six months old, I had the somewhat dignified name of Francis Joseph. And then, one day, I fell down stairs; all the way down; from the top to the landing.

" 'What a buster,' said Harry Houdini, when he found I wasn't hurt. And 'Buster's his name!' said my father; so I've been Buster ever since!"

The little Buster soon became quite the most talked of member of "The Three Keatons." This was after the medicine show days were over and the Keatons and Houdini were giving separate acts in vaudeville.

"But we were often on the same bill," said Buster, "and I used to watch Houdini by the hour to see how he did his tricks. I used to watch him from the flys and from underneath the stage. I used to peak at him from little holes in pieces of scenery, or watch him through keyholes, but I never discovered how he did a single trick!"

Perhaps, this is one reason for the settled look of sadness in Buster's eyes. Be this as it may, he has a settled look of sadness, as though from a secret sorrow. (It must not be supposed that this secret-sorrow expression belongs peculiarly to dramatic actors.) Actually, it belongs to the comedians. Being laughed at is a serious proposition. If a comedian doesn't take his laughs seriously, it naturally follows that he isn't funny. And Buster Keaton is funny, to wit—*One Week, Convict 13, The Scarecrow*, and "The Backyard" [*Neighbors*], all recent comedies in which he has been starred.

It will be remembered that before Joseph Schenck decided to star Buster, that young man appeared with Roscoe Arbuckle in *The Butcher Boy, A Reckless Romeo, [The] Rough House, His Wedding Night, Fatty at Coney Island, A Country Hero, The Bell Boy, Moonshine,* and *Good Night, Nurse!*

At the same time, the child Buster was, perhaps, the most vociferously pitied youngster in the country. This was especially the case in the State of New York, where the Gerry Society repeatedly accused his father of cruelty. And not the Gerry Society only. Managers of theaters, at which The Three Keatons appeared, would be deluged with notes from sympathetic women protesting at the way in which "that poor child" was treated.

"My father used to carry me on the stage and drop me. After explaining to the audience that I liked it, he would pick me up and throw me at a piece of scenery. Sometimes knocking the scenery down with me and sometimes not. He would often throw me as far as thirty feet."

Naturally being arrested in New York grew to be one of the commonest occurrences in his life, but he always got off because he wasn't breaking the law. It seems that the law read that no child should act, walk a tight rope, or do a number of things, but it said nothing about knocking a child down, or throwing him around, so they invariably got off.

"When we were in England, the manager of the theater insisted that I must have been stolen, or adopted, or something. He said that no parents would treat their own child as my father and mother treated me!

"And on another occasion in New York, I had to be carried before the Governor of the State and stripped in order to prove that I had no broken bones! As a matter of fact, I didn't even have any bruises."

He had been thoroughly taught to take his falls.

Keaton lives with his mother and father in a typical California bungalow in the Wilshire district of Los Angeles. He has a brother and sister, both younger than himself, attending high school. It is interesting that, though Buster Keaton has been all of his life in the theatrical profession, he has never been separated from his family.

"Never, that is, except when I was in the service." In 1917, he left the stage for moving pictures, planning to settle down in one city for more than two weeks, for the first time in his life. But his plans were upset, just as were the plans of thousands of other boys, and he marched away to make a tour of Europe with "The In-fan-tree, the Infantree."

"I made something of a record," he said, "a month after I was mustered in at Camp Kearney (near San Diego, California), I was on a ship in New York Harbor leaving for France; quicker than we could have done it for a picture without leaving Los Angeles." He was on the other side until about five months after the signing of the armistice.

"There were days when I had any number of things to laugh at," he said; "there was always something funny for anyone to see who had a sense of humor." And if there wasn't anything funny happening, he would start something himself. For instance:

"Because of my size, I was the last man in the last squad. (He is five feet, six.) When we were marching down French roads there would always be a crowd of kids watching us. I'd stump my toe and fall down . . . make it look like an accident, you know. Then I'd run to catch up with the file and fall down again. After a while, there would be another regiment of kids following us. And then, the rest camps!"

It was not until after the signing of the armistice that he was detailed to a company of entertainers. However, his largest number of escapes from death, occurring in a single day, happened not in France but in Kansas, when he was three years old. After his habit when arriving in a new town, the little Buster went wandering off to see the sights, and stopped to watch a woman washing clothes. She didn't notice that he was trying to find out what made the wringer go 'round, so the next time she gave it a turn, it took his index finger off to the first joint. After his finger was wrapped up, he took a little nap. After he awoke, he felt all right, so he went out again. He had walked about a block, when he saw some nice ripe fruit on a tree. Now he wanted that fruit, but he couldn't possibly reach it, so, imitating the boys he had seen, he picked up a big stone and threw it directly into the air. It didn't hit the fruit. But when it came down again it hit him directly on the head. He was picked up unconscious. That same evening, he was leaning out of a third-story window, trying to see what was going on in the street, when along came a cyclone and blew him completely out of the window. After carrying him a mile, it deposited him very gently on the ground, without a scratch.

"But," he said, "I never went back to that town again."

The Man Who Never Smiles

W. E. MULLIGAN/1921

BUSTER KEATON, advertised throughout the world as the funniest man in pictures, never smiles—in the pictures. Moreover the cashier at his studio in Hollywood asserts positively that the only time he ever sees Buster smile, is once a week—when he draws his pay. He smiled just fifty-two times last year—which is a pretty fair season, if you ask us.

But before the camera not even a Sphinx or a preacher in a dry town could be more sober. You'd think there would be a reason for this. There is. Says Keaton: "Smile and the world smiles with you; weep and you weep alone!" That's fine. But it doesn't say someone else won't smile if you weep. "I don't believe in weeping but people get a lot more enjoyment in watching me on the screen if I don't wear a stand-up-and-starched silly grin throughout the picture. Anyway, I'm too busy being tossed and knocked around to spend much time in smiling."

"Sometimes, when I go to a theatre and see some comedian grinning after he has finished some stunt, it makes me feel the same as when I hear some fellow who admits he's witty, tell a funny story and then get in the first laugh on it. Still, it's being done by some of our very best comedians and I'm not criticizing them for showing their molars whenever they see fit."

Buster is twenty-five now and he started on the stage just nineteen and a half years ago. His father owned a medicine show which he transported from one town to another. Buster Keaton Sr. was an accomplished gymnast and tumbler, and he started his offspring in his footsteps as soon as the little fellow was able to stand.

From *Pantomime*, vol. 1, no. 2 (October 5, 1921): 5.

Buster took naturally to his stage work and soon was far better than any other child gymnast in the country. His father went to England and played in the leading music halls of London. Buster was with him and was the cause of their return to America. It happened that Buster's ability to take punishment without feeling ill effects were [sic] soon discovered, and his father sewed a trunk handle inside his coat. Grabbing this trunk handle, his habit was to pick the youngster up and hurl him against any nearby scenery. Nothing ever suffered but the "drops" and "props." Buster never was even so much as bruised.

It was fine business and they were earning princely incomes when suddenly it became advisable for them to cancel their contracts. It happened that the Londoners considered the act inhumane, and despite the fact that oft repeated examinations of Buster's little body always failed to show any bruises, they still maintained the act was brutal.

Young Man Keaton has always been in comedies, from the time he started with his father until the formation of the Buster Keaton Company. Until 1917 he was on the legitimate stage. In that year he joined forces with Roscoe Arbuckle, the fat man. Roscoe never failed to smile forty times in every scene while Buster never smiled more than once in forty scenes. It made a good combination.

Then Roscoe decided to make only five reel comedies, and Buster came to the conclusion that his place was starring in two-reelers. And it seems that his decision was right.

"The boss says to make one comedy every six weeks, so that's just what I'm doing and I'm here to say that it keeps me busy," says "the world's greatest smileless comedian." "When you remember that often fifteen to twenty-five thousand feet of film are shot to get the two thousand feet that comprise the finished product, it's easier to understand that there's a lot of work connected with each little film—a half hour's entertainment."

How Buster Keaton Got That Way

MARGARET WERNER/1923

SOME PEOPLE ARE BORN with silver spoons in their mouths, others with that Midas touch which turns everything to gold, but all that our fairy godmother came across with was a tin can. We are not by nature bitter or morbid, but wouldn't you think with a nice popular subject like Buster Keaton, we'd be lucky enough to get a big story? But no, Fate was against us.

Buster is a dear, pleasant boy, and I know that if we had had him all to ourself in some secluded nook, the confidences would have flowed like beer at a German picnic. But as it happened—

We were ushered through a mystic maze of offices, past busily pounding typists, who looked up in surprise as we walked into one of those "bossy" executive-looking offices. We smiled at them and said under our breath, "We're not as important as we look, girls. We're fresh from the Underwood ourself."

In a corner of the private sanctum above referred to, a young man of slender build rose politely, and we were shaking the hand of Buster Keaton. Of course, we were holding our breath, waiting to see whether he would smile, and smile he did. For the benefit of those who have heaved the jolly chuckle and bellowed the lusty laugh at the antics of this solemn-faced funmaker, let us assure you that if there are smiles more spontaneous and friendly than Buster's, we'd like to see them.

However, as we were saying, this interview was conducted under difficulties. Here we were, face to face with our victim, with a large man smoking a huge cigar listening attentively to every word, and secretaries flitting in and out, and numerous other distractions. Our spirits were sinking lower and lower, but we stuck manfully to our guns, and began our attack thus:

"Mr. Keaton, tell us something of your career."

Had we asked him to do a nose dive from the window, the poor dear could not have looked more horrified. The blue eyes grew wide as a frightened child's and he looked so imploringly that we were tempted to say:

"There, there, sonny. Mama won't spank."

But he told us that he became a vaudeville performer at the ripe age of five, being one of the Four Keatons, whom thousands of you will remember. Then he went into the movies with Fatty Arbuckle, using the same funny line he had been using on the stage.

"But here's what's really agitating all of us, Mr. Keaton. How can you possibly go through all that clowning and make us all nearly pass out with mirth, and all the while keep your face as straight as a stick. What's the trick?"

"There's no trick to it, really," he replied. "You see, when I was pulling my stuff on the vaudeville stage, it would look terrible for me to grin from ear to ear every time I did something funny. That queers it, you know."

We nodded our complete understanding.

"And so," continued Buster, "I learned at a very early age that I simply was not allowed to grin while working. And what with the habit of years growing on me, it's really no trick at all. So that is how I got this way."

And he handed us some pictures of his young son.

"Don't you think he resembles—er—Norma?" he asked us.

"No sir!" we answered. "This baby has the Keaton expression!"

This time we were rewarded, not by a smile, but by a hearty, delighted laugh.

The large man with the huge cigar handed around [some] cigarettes. We wished he would go away. Wasn't there a ball game this afternoon? But he merely settled back more comfortably, and we tried to forget his presence.

Buster was perched on a bookkeeper's stool, his hair tumbling into his eyes, and his fingers played with a silver locket which he wore on his watch chain (he also had a watch, though).

"What's that, Buster?" we inquired.

He handed us watch, chain, locket and all, and we snapped the locket open to discover another picture of the baby! Great heavens, what will he do when he has three or four? Keep pictures of them in his hatband, we suppose.

"What are you aiming to make of this young hopeful?" we asked. "Is he going to be a comedian, too, or will Shakespeare be more in his line?"

"Neither one, I hope." Buster twisted his feet around the legs of the bookkeeper's stool and regarded the picture fondly. "This kid is going to be his own boss, and whatever profession appeals to him when he grows up, well, that's the profession he's going to ornament. President or plumber, it's what little Buster chooses. That's the way they're bringing them up nowadays. The individuality of the child, and all that. The kid's recovering now from a long siege of work. There were three generations of us in *Hospitality*, which I've just finished—my dad, my son, and myself."

Buster is in New York for the World Series, and as we said good-bye, he told us he was going to dash right uptown to the game. We breezed past the staring typists, and ardently longed for a chance for a real tête-à-tête with the engaging Buster, the result to be called, "Buster Keaton as His Friends Know Him."

Turning Point Interview with Buster Keaton

ARTHUR B. FRIEDMAN / 1956

FRIEDMAN: *This is Art Friedman. I'm speaking to you today from the Los Angeles home of one of the screen's all time greats. He is the recent recipient of the coveted George Eastman House Award and has been known to a loyal and enthusiastic audience for many, many years as the Great Stone Face, Mr. Buster Keaton. Mr. Keaton, it is a great pleasure to welcome you to Turning Point. Before we get on, I would like to tell you that I'm tickled to death to learn with the rest of the millions of people throughout the world that you've made this recent recovery from your rather serious illness, and we welcome you back to the fold.*

KEATON: It kind of scared me a bit.

FRIEDMAN: *I bet it did. Now, Mr. Keaton, now you've been in show business and a performer in show business for as long, I suppose, as you can remember. Can you tell me when you got started?*

KEATON: Well, to start with, I was born with the show, on a one-night stand in Kansas.

FRIEDMAN: *What show was that?*

KEATON: It was called "The Keaton & Houdini—that was Harry Houdini, the handcuff king—Medicine Show Company."

Full interview conducted on January 27, 1956, printed here by permission of Genie Guerard, Manuscripts Division, UCLA Library, Department of Special Collections; and by permission of Madgel Friedman and Melissa Talmadge Cox. About a third of this interview has been revised and published as: Arthur B. Friedman, "Buster Keaton: An Interview," *Film Quarterly*, vol. 19, no. 4 (Summer 1966): 2–5. Copyright © 1966 by the Regents of the University of California.

FRIEDMAN: *But it bore your name as well. Was this your parent?*
KEATON: Yes, my father and mother.

FRIEDMAN: *What kind of an act was it that they had?*
KEATON: Well, he was a comedian and a great high jumper and eccentric dancer—home-talent sort of acrobat.

FRIEDMAN: *And what did your mother do with this act?*
KEATON: Oh, sing and dance, and she played a musical instrument. In fact, she's the first woman in the United States to play a saxophone. They didn't even know what the name of the instrument was then. They called it a French horn or something like that.

FRIEDMAN: *What year was this?*
KEATON: I was born in '95.

FRIEDMAN: *And did they incorporate you in their act very soon?*
KEATON: Well, they had me out in front of an audience just as soon as I could walk, but I became a regular member of the act when I was four years old.

FRIEDMAN: *What were your duties as a regular member of that act?*
KEATON: Well, we just did a rough, knockabout act. I'd just simply get in my father's way all the time and get kicked all over the stage.

FRIEDMAN: *He threw you in the orchestra pit, I understand. Was this a regular part of the . . .*
KEATON: Oh, we've had that accident happen a few times. I fell in more than once.

FRIEDMAN: *And did you travel throughout the country with this act?*
KEATON: Yes, I was lucky. I didn't have to go through any of the small-time vaudeville. By the time I was introduced into the act, my father and mother had advanced to the two-a-day theaters. So, I saw none of the small-time. I played Tony Pastor's theater, when Tony Pastor was alive. First played there when I was five years old.

FRIEDMAN: *With your father and mother?*
KEATON: Yeah. I played the Orpheum circuit when I was six. Played in London when I was thirteen.

FRIEDMAN: *Can you recall what the central idea of the act seemed to have been? Your mother sang and played a musical instrument. What was behind the comedy that your father did?*
KEATON: Well, we did just grotesque gags. That's all.

FRIEDMAN: *They were all in pantomime?*
KEATON: Well, yes. You'd call it pantomime, although my father kept talking all the time. He never said the same thing twice. He just tried to convince the audience that there was only one way to bring up children and that was to make 'em mind. Be gentle and kind to them, but make them mind. By that time I'd knocked both of his feet out from under him with a broom or something—the chase was on again.

FRIEDMAN: *Was there a training period for you? Did your father teach you to take falls?*
KEATON: Nope. It seemed to come natural, being brought up and getting thrown around the stage like that. You just automatically develop. That's all.

FRIEDMAN: *Well, as a child performer, I imagine there were a number of child welfare agencies that were after you or your parents, weren't there?*
KEATON: Oh, every other place we played.

FRIEDMAN: *Oh, how did you manage to stay out of the law?*
KEATON: In Massachusetts, for instance, they thought I was a midget. They took it for granted. But we were arrested many times. But, we always managed to get around the law because the law read: No child under the age of sixteen shall do acrobatics, walk wire, play musical instruments, trapeze—and it named everything—but none of them said you couldn't kick him in the face.

FRIEDMAN: *What did you do about school, if anything? What did your parents do about your schooling?*
KEATON: They carried a tutor with me. He doubled in brass. He was a nursemaid and a teacher at the same time.

FRIEDMAN: *What kind of attention were you able to give to studies under these conditions of performance?*
KEATON: Just mornings.

FRIEDMAN: *Yes. And how about other things kids usually do, about going out with other kids your own age and things like that?*
KEATON: Oh, I managed to round them up in different towns. And we played so often in New York that we lived in an old-fashioned German boarding house on Thirty-eighth Street, and I knew that whole neighborhood. So, I was in ball teams and everything else. And I joined the YMCA and got onto basketball teams and everything else that there was.

FRIEDMAN: *Well, being a kid working in a vaudeville act, did you have any trouble with other kids who didn't like that idea? Did they ever think you were apart from them?*
KEATON: Oh, no, no. I never had trouble that way.

FRIEDMAN: *How long were you with your parents in this act?*
KEATON: Continued until I was twenty-one in 1917.

FRIEDMAN: *Of course, that was during the heart of the vaudeville in this country.*
KEATON: That's right. See, I saw the great days of vaudeville. I got in just in time to see vaudeville go from the ten, twenty, and thirty-cent admission fees to the two dollar. And, in fact, The Three Keatons, that's what we were called, we held Hammerstein's Theater record for playing it the most times. You were only supposed to play there about once a year, and if they liked you, you got to play there twice a year. We used to average four to six times a year.

FRIEDMAN: *What about your brother and sister?*
KEATON: Oh, we put them in the act too as fast as they grew up, but when they got to be around seven and eight years old, we finally put them in a school in our . . . . We had a summer home in Muskegon, Michigan, and we put them in school there.

FRIEDMAN: *Well, then you must have been developing in your own process of maturing?*
KEATON: Oh sure. I became my own gag man.

FRIEDMAN: *Well, how did that come about? What was the process there?*
KEATON: Well, just . . . that's a natural thing to do, and you're always trying to invent new things, new ways to get a laugh, odd pieces of business and things like that. So, my training was perfect for me to go into pictures.

FRIEDMAN: *Were you considering some way of distinguishing yourself from other comedians who were also knocking about vaudeville at the time?*
KEATON: Never gave that a thought of trying to be different than anybody else. You just simply worked your natural way. I developed the "Stone Face" thing quite naturally. I just happened to be, even as a small kid, I happened to be the type of comic that couldn't laugh at his own material. I soon learned at an awful early age that when I laughed the audience didn't. So, by the time I got into pictures, that was a natural way of working.

FRIEDMAN: *Where did this name for you come from, this "Great Stone Face"?*
KEATON: From pictures, because I had made three of my own pictures when I started to get the nickname of "Stone Face," so we went in the projecting room at the studio and ran our first three pictures to see if I'd smiled in them.

FRIEDMAN: *To check yourself.*
KEATON: Yeah, and, sure enough, I hadn't. I just naturally don't work that way.

FRIEDMAN: *What about this name, "Buster"? Where did that come from?*
KEATON: I got it from Harry Houdini [in a] hotel lobby, and I was six months old, and I fell down a flight of stairs, and he says, "What a buster." And I never lost the name.

FRIEDMAN: *When you started in film, did you start with Mack Sennett?*
KEATON: No. I started with Roscoe Arbuckle, who was being produced by Joe Schenck, independent producer. Joe Schenck had two other companies: There was Norma Talmadge and Constance Talmadge.
And Arbuckle signed with him and left Sennett. While on his first picture—before he made it—he met me in New York and asked me if I'd ever been in a picture, and I told him, "No, I've never even been in a studio." And he says, "Well, come on down and play a scene with me and see how you like it." So, in his first picture for Schenck, I worked in it. Well, instead of just playing a scene, I went all the way through it. And at the time, I was under contract to the Shuberts. I was to go in *The Passing Show of 1917.* I got one load of that motion picture business and went back to my agent and said, "I want to get out of this Winter Garden." "Go ahead," he said, "I'll just tear up the contract." I said, "Well, what's Shubert got to say about that?" He said, "We'll tell him afterwards." [laughter]

FRIEDMAN: *Well, what was it about making a film, all of a sudden, that appealed to you so much?*
KEATON: The mechanics of it. The way of working—fascinating. One of the first things I did was tear a motion picture camera practically to pieces, and found out [about] the lenses and the splicing of film and how to get it on the projector.

FRIEDMAN: *This appealed to you?*
KEATON: Oh, this fascinated me because later on I did my . . . I cut all my own pictures, and besides I directed most of them. I was with Arbuckle a year, then I was in the army a year, and then I made my first picture in 1919—of my own—and I never stopped after that.

FRIEDMAN: *Where did your story material come from?*
KEATON: You have your own little scenario staff, and the ideal staff, working with somebody like me, would be three men.

FRIEDMAN: *What did they do?*

KEATON: Just the scenario department. We all sat down for our ideas, and if somebody gets one, why we all set out to work on it and see how—what opportunities—and the main thing with laying out a story is, it's easy to get a start, the finish is always the tough thing. So, the minute somebody had an idea—we said what is it going to lead to? We don't go to the middle of the story; we jump right to the finish. So the finish—this would be the natural finish—says now does that give us any opportunities for gags? Make it exciting, fast action sometimes, and a couple of outstanding gags. We've got to be able to place those naturally, 'cause one of the worst mistakes you could make in those pictures was dragging in a gag by the heels. A misplaced gag, even though it's good, it's wrong to do.

FRIEDMAN: *So, you'd sit down with your team and decide on a basic idea . . .*

KEATON: Basic idea, and when we got that finish and knew what we were heading for, then we went back and wrote the middle.

FRIEDMAN: *Well, what about a shooting script, did you really work from a script? Did the script . . .*

KEATON: Never saw a script.

FRIEDMAN: *Script usually came after the show was . . .*

KEATON: We never had a script; we never did have one.

FRIEDMAN: *And you'd go out and shoot this and let the cameras grind and see what they could pick up. Is that the idea?*

KEATON: Well, we didn't need a script. I knew in my mind what we were going to do, because with our way of working, there was always the unexpected happening. Well, any time something unexpected happened and we liked it, we were liable to spend days shooting in and around that.

FRIEDMAN: *'Cause your vaudeville training, I suppose, let you take advantage of that?*

KEATON: Sure. We had the most ad lib act in the world. We never did it twice alike in our lives.

FRIEDMAN: *Your father and mother didn't follow you into films or come*
with you?
KEATON: Oh, after I got established here, I sent for them, and then
I made my father work in a lot of them.

FRIEDMAN: *How, in your opinion, did the pictures differ in the silent days*
in terms of basic comedy styles and demands on comedy from what happened
to film when the talkies came in?
KEATON: We didn't pay any attention to it. We simply laid out our
picture first . . . sound, talking pictures, but we still stuck to our . . .

FRIEDMAN: *Basic premise.*
KEATON: . . . basic idea of making motion pictures. In other words,
where dialogue came natural we used it, but we didn't depend on jokes
or puns, trying to make darn sure we didn't get long dialogue scenes.
We'd do anything in the world to break them up. The only time we
ever had to resort to them, of course, was in plot. You start the first part
of your picture laying out the plot. Well, you're stuck using a lot of dialogue to get it set. But we used to tighten that up as sharp as we could
so we wouldn't waste much time on it.

FRIEDMAN: *Well, what were the conditions like in the studios at the time*
that you were working?
KEATON: Well, they were a lot different than making a motion
picture now. For instance, you see I was an independent outfit
working in my own studio. My cameraman, my technical man, the
entire staff, they're under salary fifty-two weeks a year, because I went
for years—when I got into making feature-length pictures—only making two a year, one for spring release and one for fall release. Well, it
actually didn't make any difference to us when I put the camera up.
We owned our own camera. We weren't renting it. We had all our own
equipment. So, it was a common thing, even after the picture was finished, I'm in the projection room looking at rough-cut sequences put
together, and says, "That one is mistimed. Let's do that one over tomorrow. Get those people back." So that cost nothing. Well, today, if you
did that in a motion picture, you'd wreck the company. They have to

shoot to that shooting schedule and a script all laid out on paper and everything else. And an unexpected scene comes up, and says, "Oh, let's carry this one further. Let's go off . . ." That's going to put us back a couple days behind shooting schedule. So you run into that problem. Well, an independent outfit like I worked then, today could still work the way I did.

FRIEDMAN: *Do you feel that there was more spontaneity in the films that were done years ago than in the films done today?*
KEATON: Oh, yes. Yes, on account of this.

FRIEDMAN: *Do you think that this is a necessary element to comedy?*
KEATON: It is very important. I'll show you exactly what you are talking about. It's worse today than it was in the silent days because you've got so many technical things such as all your sound equipment. But a director today will rehearse people into a scene until he has got it mechanically perfect and the way he wants it. But in doing it, the scene has become mechanical, your people have. They're just walking through it now like a parrot. So we used to say even in the silent days, if we have to rehearse a scene very many times, one of the worst problems you've got on your hands is to unrehearse it.

FRIEDMAN: *It gets stale on you.*
KEATON: You get stale on it. So, to make it look spontaneous and throw the pep into it so everything is unexpected and you don't anticipate so much. It was a very important thing with us. So, for that reason we used to just practically slowly walk through scenes and just talk it over and then shoot that first actual take, because invariably that'd be the scene you'd take, even though you did it three or four times afterwards. The first take was generally the one to use.

FRIEDMAN: *Of course, it would occur to me in terms of the spontaneity we are talking about now that there was another condition that existed years ago that is no longer here and that is that there was a vast and tremendous training ground such as you went through in vaudeville.*
KEATON: Well, I was lucky.

FRIEDMAN: *And, people were able to get the basic idea of a scene and to take advantage of whatever came up, but chances are comedians aren't brought up that way anymore.*

KEATON: No. You don't have that training. The minute something goes wrong, everybody stops cold. Well, that's when we used to keep cranking.

FRIEDMAN: *Can you remember any particular things that worked well for you in motion pictures that were an accident?*

KEATON: Yeah. For instance, I went to jump across an alleyway on top of a tall building. We built the sets over the Third Street tunnel—or the Broadway tunnel—looking right down over Los Angeles. Now, by getting your cameras up on a high parallel and shooting past our set in the foreground with the street below, it looked like we were up in the air about twelve, fourteen stories high. And we actually had a net stretched from one wall to the other underneath the camera line so in case you missed any trick that you were doing—one of those high, dizzy things—you had a net to fall into, although it was about a thirty-five-foot drop.

FRIEDMAN: *And you didn't use doubles?*

KEATON: No. So, my scene was that with the cops chasing me, that I came to this thing and I took advantage of the lid of a skylight and laid it over the edge of the roof to use as a springboard. I backed up, hit it, and tried to make it to the other side which was probably about eighteen feet, something like that. Well, I misjudged the spring of that board and I didn't make it. I hit flat up against that other set and fell to the net, but I hit hard enough that it jammed my knees a little bit, and hips and elbows, 'cause I hit flush, flat—and I had to go home and stay in bed for about three days.

And, of course, at the same time, me and the scenario department were a little sick because we can't make that leap. That throws the whole chase sequence, that routine, right out the window. So the boys the next day went into the projecting room and saw the scene anyhow, 'cause they had it printed to look at it. Well, they got a thrill out of it, so they came back and told me about it. "It's a miss." Says, "Well, if it looks that good let's see if we can pick it up this way. The best thing to do is to put an awning on a window, just a little small awning, just enough to break my fall." 'Cause on the screen, you could see that I fell about, oh I guess about sixteen feet, something like that. I must have passed two stories. So, now you go in and drop into something just to slow me up, to break my fall, and I can swing from that onto a rainspout and when I get ahold of it, it breaks and lets me sway, sways me out away from the building hanging onto it. And for a finish, it collapses enough that it hinges and throws me down through a window a couple of floors below.

Well, when we got back and checked up on what this chase was about—the chase was this: I was getting away from policemen, and we used the old Hollywood Station on Hollywood, which was right next door to the fire department. Well, when this pipe broke and threw me through the window, we went in there and built the sleeping quarters of the fire department with a sliding pole in the background. So I came through their window on my back, slid across the floor, and I lit up against the sliding pole and dropped to the bottom on the slide. I bounced from that to set on the rear of one of the trucks and as I hit the rear the truck pulled out, so I had to grab on for dear life, but I'm on my way to a fire—but the fire was in the police department. So we went back and shot the scene where I accidentally, not knowing it, had set fire to the police department before the cops started to chase me. Well, it ended up . . . it was the biggest laughing sequence in the picture.

FRIEDMAN: *And this was partly because of this accident that you had?*
KEATON: . . . because I missed it in the original trick.

FRIEDMAN: *That's wonderful. That's wonderful.*
KEATON: Then I had another one that was actually a godsend. I had a bad picture, and we knew it, too. And there was nothing we could seem to do about it.

FRIEDMAN: *What picture was it?*
KEATON: It was called *Seven Chances*, and I had a short sequence in there where I was running away from a batch of women. Man had advertised for a bride. Didn't say what age or anything else, just a bride wanted at the church by three o'clock, or something like that, and

these women, all shapes and forms, showed up with home-made bridal outfits on, lace curtains, gingham table cloths for veils, and this chase was on. And I led them off into open country and was coming down the side of the hill, and there were some boulder rocks on that hill, and I hit one accidentally, sliding down that hill on my feet most of the time. And I jarred this one rock loose, and it actually hit two other rocks, and I looked behind me in the scene and here come three boulder rocks about the size of bowling-alley balls coming at me, bouncing down the hill with me, and I actually had to scram to get away from them.

FRIEDMAN: *And the cameras were grinding on you?*
KEATON: Oh, sure. Well, this was only the one scene of that in the picture but at the preview—the second preview—when this was in there, the audience sat up in their seats and they were ready. I says, "Oh, oh, that's all we need." We went back, and I think for a finish we built fifteen hundred rocks, starting from grapefruit-size up to one was eight-foot in diameter, and we went out on the ridge route and spotted one of those big barren mountains with these rocks and then I went up there and got started. At least I was working with paper maché, although some of them . . . for instance, that big one weighed four hundred pounds. By the time you built the framework, it weighs something, but you could get hit with them all right. Well, I got into the middle of the rock chase, and it saved the picture for me, and that was an accident. It hadn't been framed. It was an out-and-out accident.

FRIEDMAN: *Mr. Keaton, I imagine that among the many films on which you worked and in which you had a hand in the story,* The Navigator *probably ranks among the top of these, doesn't it for you?*
KEATON: Yes. It's one of my pets.

FRIEDMAN: *Will you tell me how this* [The Navigator] *came into being and what remains about this to give you such a wonderful feeling about that film?*
KEATON: Well, sitting around the studio with the scenario outfit between pictures and we're all groping for an idea, and we happen to hit a rut and nobody could think of anything that looked worthwhile. About that time, Frank Lloyd was making a picture for Metro, which was right across the street from our studio, called *The Sea Beast*

[*The Sea Hawk*]. I had a great technical man and they borrowed him from me and sent him up to 'Frisco to see if he could find old four-masted schooner hulls.

FRIEDMAN: *Frank Lloyd hired this man from you?*
KEATON: Yes. They sent him up, all up to Seattle and 'Frisco and Portland—all around there.

FRIEDMAN: *What was his name? Who was this man?*
KEATON: "Gabe" Gabourie. And while he was up there looking for these four-masted schooners, the ones he could find and those that could be repaired enough to use—'cause Frank had to have four or five in a fleet or something like that for that picture—he found this ocean liner up there that they were going to salvage. It was called the *Buford*. It only had one time it was ever in the newspapers, I guess. It was the boat that brought from Russia that last princess over to this country, smuggled her out. And we found out that you could have the boat for twenty-five thousand dollars.

FRIEDMAN: *Buy it?*
KEATON: We could buy it! Now, it's an ocean liner about five hundred feet long, a passenger ship.

FRIEDMAN: *What year was this?*
KEATON: This was '23. So the minute we heard of that, we set out to see what we could do with it. Well, we got our start. Our start was a pip. Now this is that same construction. We got the start and jumped to the finish. Well, our start was that if I take a couple of very rich people who establish a beautiful home in San Francisco, up on the hill, with all kinds of servants to wait on you—that was me. I was a young fellow, a bachelor, very young at that time. And the girl was the same thing. Her father was a ship owner, a wealthy ship owner, and she had servants to wait on her. So you know they'd been raised with that silver spoon in their mouths from the time they were born.

Take those two characters . . . my opening gag in the thing was that I came down and got into my automobile in front of my house with a chauffeur and a footman, and the car just drove across the street to her house, and I got out and called on the girl. I just went in there and said, "Will you marry me?" And she said, "No." I came back with my head down and the footman opened the car door for me and I said, "No, I think the walk will do me good," so I walked across the street. The plot was that I had already sent down for tickets to go on a honeymoon, and my butler advised Honolulu. So, I said, "Get me two tickets for Honolulu." So when I got home, he handed me my tickets.

FRIEDMAN: *But you had nobody to go with you.*
KEATON: Yeah, so I tear up one ticket. I put the other one in my pocket and I says, "What time does it sail?" He says, "Nine o'clock." I says, "In the morning?" He says, "Yeah." I says, "It's too early, so I'll go aboard tonight." All right. Now we went to the night shot, and we showed the night watchman coming out with his punch clock. And I was supposed to go to pier 2, and we see this watchman come up to punch at this pier. He slid the gate over on 12, but the gate hid the 1.

FRIEDMAN: *And the 2 was still showing.*
KEATON: And I see it from the car and decide that's the ship. And I go out there to get on this ship. Oh—and here's your plot—we went to a bunch of men in a building overlooking the bay of San Francisco and looking down at the boat at the pier. [One of them] says, "That boat has just been bought by our enemies, this country that we're on the verge of going to war against. That ship will carry ammunition and supplies. It's up to us to see that she doesn't get there." He says, "Tonight, we'll go down there, we'll overcome the night watchman, or anybody else that gets in our way, throw her ropes off or cut them off and set that boat adrift. The wind and tide will do the rest. It's a cinch to go up against those rocks on the other side of the Golden Gate, and it's a doomed ship." That's the plot.

So, I come down, and I get on this boat. Now, there's nobody to meet me. There's no lights. It's a dead ship. There's no water, no nothing running. But I finally find my stateroom, and when I get inside I have to light matches to see what I'm doing. But I put myself to bed.

About this time, these foreign agents arrive and overpower the watchman, put him in a little room, one of the pier cabins or sheds. And they go out to set this boat free. And they no more complete their job—they ignore the gang plank that goes onto the ship—but you could see that the ship is going away from the pier and that gang plank is just siding. When the girl and her father, all dressed to go to a dinner party someplace, and she brings the car to a stop—she's driving a coupe—and he says, "I had to have you drive me down past the Navigator because I left some papers in the pilot house that I want, and I'll only be a few minutes." He comes down onto this pier, and he runs into these agents. Well, they grab him, but before they can put a hand-kerchief in his mouth, he yells "HELP." She hears it in the car. Well, they drag him into this little shed to bind him up. She doesn't know that but passes on down and goes over the gang plank onto the ship. And, she no more gets onto the ship when the ship is far enough away from the dock now that the gang plank falls. So, she's on the ship.

FRIEDMAN: *And this is the way you got your characters together.*
KEATON: And it fades out. Now, your story is that you've got . . . she has never been in a kitchen in her life. Now, you put her in a ship's gal-ley where it takes two people to lift a frying pan; the coffee pot holds ten gallons; the soup tureen holds twenty.

FRIEDMAN: *And this was the day before cans.*
KEATON: No cans, and two people to pick up a spoon. You see the trouble we got her in. And a jack-of-all-trades is something that I have never heard of, so I'm not very handy around the place, either. Well, there's your start. Then we knew the finish. The finish was that I finally drifted on to a South Sea Island and met a batch of head hunters and cannibals and had to fight them off. We figured how to do that. Then that rounded that out. Then we went back to work on the middle.

FRIEDMAN: *Wasn't there a great storm scene in there as well? Was there a storm scene?*
KEATON: No. There was no storm.

FRIEDMAN: *Not in* The Navigator?
KEATON: Oh, that was a picture I made—in a two-reeler about 1921—called *The Boat.* Well, I'll tell you how you might remember this one. I built this family cruiser. It was about a thirty-five footer, and I had it

on the launching cradle down at Balboa—and the wife and the two little kids to pull the blocks out from under it and spring it loose as soon as she christened it. I stood on the nose of the boat, the proud owner and captain, and she christened the boat. They pulled the blocks out, and the boat slid down into the ocean and never stopped. It went right to the bottom. The last the audience saw of me, my hat was floating.

FRIEDMAN: *I can see how you can appreciate what happened with* The Navigator. *What do you suppose there was about this film that brings it so close to you as against some of the other films that you worked on? How did this come across?*
KEATON: Well, it was so unusual. It lent itself to gags that you'd never think of.

FRIEDMAN: *And it fit you pretty good.*
KEATON: Oh, sure.

FRIEDMAN: *Was there another film that you've made similar to* The Navigator *that holds the same kind of feel for you?*
KEATON: Nope. Never have.

FRIEDMAN: The Navigator . . .
KEATON: An out-and-out novelty—such a screwy story, starting with using an ocean liner, for the love of Mike. There is a scene in there where I am trying to row it. I launched one of the life boats and tried to tow it.

FRIEDMAN: *Well, you've had a long and wonderful, varied career in both vaudeville and motion pictures. You've done some work quite recently—in recent years—in television. Tell me, how do you feel about the work you do in television compared with the fun and good times you had making your films?*
KEATON: I love television. It gives you new life, but I only like television to work to an audience, live.

FRIEDMAN: *You don't like the film work with them?*
KEATON: No. The film thing is all right as long as I'm working to an audience. I haven't been successful making pictures for television. I got to work to that audience, 'cause it is a different type of work altogether. You work different.

FRIEDMAN: *You didn't have an audience for your films in your past years, though, that you made motion pictures?*
KEATON: No. That's a different technique altogether. You work different.

FRIEDMAN: *But you feel you need that audience for television?*
KEATON: But when you can only do a thing once, and it had better be right that time. If it's not, you make the best of it. Well, that's what I liked, the live audience, because we're so used to having things go wrong, and I don't mind that at all. I go ahead and do it the best that I can regardless. And the audience knows it is not supposed to work that way either, see. I guess I get the best laughs when things go wrong in TV.

FRIEDMAN: *What was the straight dramatic role that you've done?*
KEATON: I did one of the Doug Fairbanks, Jr., Rheingold shows.

FRIEDMAN: *On television?*
KEATON: In England, there. I'd been playing at the Cirque Royal in Belgium, and I went over there and spent a week with him and made one of those shows. Well, that was straight drama, not one snicker, not one laugh of any kind in the half-hour show.

FRIEDMAN: *Now, you haven't been quite so active in motion pictures as you used to be for some time. And then you did this magnificent bit with Charlie Chaplin in his . . .*
KEATON: *Limelight.*

FRIEDMAN: Limelight. *Now how did it feel to get back into that kind of . . . ?*
KEATON: Oh, old home week. And then I just did *Around the World in Eighty Days.* That was fun, being out on location. The location was in Colorado. I haven't been on location in something like twenty years.

FRIEDMAN: *And you've just recently, in November it was, went back East with other film notables to receive your George Eastman House award.*
KEATON: That's right. Oh, they treated us marvelous there. From this end there was Mary Pickford, Ronald Coleman, Harold Lloyd, and from

New York came Dick Barthelmess and Mae Marsh and Lillian Gish. The others that were . . .

FRIEDMAN: *Norma Talmadge, was she one?*
KEATON: Norma Talmadge was too sick at the time to go. And the other one, Gloria Swanson, was making a picture in Italy at the time, so she couldn't make it either.

FRIEDMAN: *How does this award differ from some of the other awards that are around at various fan magazines?*
KEATON: Well, all of those awards [are for those who] did the best thing this past year. Well, the Eastman award is for all time.

FRIEDMAN: *Your award reads from 1915 to 1925, is that right?*
KEATON: Yes. They just wanted to get just ahead of sound pictures coming in. Well, they missed that of course by about three years, but that's all right. And they only voted the awards to people still alive.

FRIEDMAN: *Well, Mr. Keaton, let me ask you this: What have been some of the happiest moments that you can recall in terms of your career?*
KEATON: Oh, I guess, when I first was convinced that I was in pictures to stay and from then on until I stopped making them, I guess.

FRIEDMAN: *You were just happy all the time you were . . . ?*
KEATON: Oh, yes. Nothing bothered us.

FRIEDMAN: *Was there any particular instant that occurred that changed the direction in which you were going or gave you a particular boost that you might look back on as your turning point in your career?*
KEATON: No. I don't remember any one.

FRIEDMAN: *Of course, that would be unusual since you were born into the trade and stayed with it all of your life.*
KEATON: We were practically headliners in high-class vaudeville. So, if I hadn't gone into pictures with Arbuckle and Joe Schenck, it was just a matter of time and I would have gone in anyhow.

FRIEDMAN: *Have you had any children?*
KEATON: I have two boys. I'm a grandfather, let's see, last counting it was five. I think I've got one more coming next month. And they call on me, and they wreck the joint.

FRIEDMAN: *Well, are your grandchildren as adept at tumbling as you were at the same age?*
KEATON: Well, all kids seem to be.

FRIEDMAN: *Do you see any future for them in the theater as you had yours cut out for you?*
KEATON: Oh, no.

FRIEDMAN: *Not at all. What about your own children, your boys? Have they ever had an inclination towards the . . . ?*
KEATON: No. No desire at all. They never had any desire to go in front of the camera.

FRIEDMAN: *Well, then you are at the end of your line as far as your family is concerned in the entertainment field. Is there any advice, for example, that you could give youngsters today who think that they'd like to get into the entertainment world in terms of . . . ?*
KEATON: I don't know of anything. It comes natural, it seems. It seems like every kid in the world sometimes has an opportunity to get up in front of a batch of people. And some sing; some just talk; some get into school plays and things like that. Once they get bit, and they generally get bit when they have been encouraged. In other words, there is a possible show of talent some place, and it's recognized, and they go ahead and develop, and if nothing else stops it, well they end up trying.

FRIEDMAN: *Do you think that this is a basic talent that a person is born with, or do you think that it is a matter of training that he can get?*
KEATON: No. I think that any good actor is practically born.

FRIEDMAN: *You got it or you haven't.*
KEATON: I believe it. I recall my first years on the stage as training. Well, you wouldn't really call it training. You'd call it experience—and

practical experience too, always in front of an audience. Well, that's a great help.

FRIEDMAN: *And this kind of opportunity just really isn't around anymore.*
KEATON: Oh, I don't know. Of course, your old-time variety shows, your minstrel shows, and your local stock companies used to put on a weekly drama. You don't have those anymore. But, now you have night-clubs and, well, television and things like that. So, it's a different back-ground. It's not as good as it used to be, but your scope's not as wide. So, if a guy today thinks he's going to be a comedian, the first thing he does is to try to think up a lot of funny jokes, to get up and talk. The training for the type of things that we did, we just don't have them anymore, no place to try them out.

FRIEDMAN: *Is there anything that you've done in your past during your career, looking back on now, that you wished you'd done another way?*
KEATON: Oh, sure. Any time that you'd done a bad picture, you say, "Oh, I wish I hadn't have done that one, wish I could tear that one up."

FRIEDMAN: *Your record doesn't show many bad pictures, I'm sure. Mr. Keaton, I want to thank you very much for giving us the time today to hold this interview with you and to go back over some of your pleasant mem-ories. And I'm sure that I'd be joined by millions of people who've loved you and watched you for many, many years on the screen and wish you good health for many, many more years to come.*
KEATON: Thank you very much.

FRIEDMAN: *Thank you, Mr. Keaton.*

"Anything Can Happen—and Generally Did": Buster Keaton on His Silent-Film Career

GEORGE C. PRATT / 1958

The name of Buster Keaton (1895–1966) appears as co-director or director on almost every film he made from 1920 through 1929, when his final silent, Spite Marriage, *was released. In spite of his activity in the sound period and stints on TV, Keaton's reputation as a great figure in the world of film is based on his earlier work. The following interview was conducted in Los Angeles in 1958.*

BK: Well, I was born with a show—with a tent show, in fact. It was a one-night stand in Kansas, a little town called Piqua. And the show left my mother and me there for two weeks and then she rejoined the show. So I was born really with the show.

. . . My father and mother with their act got into vaudeville and got to New York, and of course they had a makeup on me as soon as I could walk. My father had slap shoes on me, misfit clothes, even a bald-headed Irish wig on me. But by the time I was four years old, I was a regular member of the act, getting a salary. . . . [We were billed as] "The Three Keatons."

From *Image*, vol. 17, no. 4 (1974): 19–29; reprinted in *"Image" on the Art and Evolution of the Film: Photographs and Articles from the Magazine of the International Museum of Photography,* ed. Marshall Deutelbaum (New York: Dover, 1979), pp. 195–204. Reprinted by permission of George Eastman House, Rochester, New York.

. . . The "Buster"? I got that [name] for falling down a flight of stairs when I was six months old, and I lit at the bottom of my father's partner in the show. And he says, "That's a buster!" And the old man says, "That's a good name for 'im." So that's the name I got. My father's partner was Harry Houdini . . . the Handcuff King.

. . . [The dead pan] was a natural. As I grew up on the stage, the experience taught me that I was the type of comedian that if I laughed at what I did, the audience didn't. Well, by the time I went into pictures when I was twenty-one, working with a straight face, a sober face, was *mechanical* with me.

. . . In the spring of 1917 vaudeville wasn't quite as good as it used to be, and I went to our agent and told him I wanted to get out and [he] said, "All right. Send your folks to your summer home in Muskegon, Michigan, and I'll put you at the Shuberts." So they signed me at the Winter Garden for *The Passing Show of 1917*. I had about ten days to wait for rehearsal to start when I met Roscoe ["Fatty"] Arbuckle on the street on Broadway and he says, "Have you ever been in a motion picture?" And I said, "I've never been in a studio." He says, "Well, I'm just startin' here for Joe Schenck. I've left [Mack] Sennett . . . and . . . [Schenck's] puttin' me up here to make pictures in the Norma Talmadge studio. He says, "Come on down and play a scene with me and see how you like it. I'm startin' tomorrow morning."

I went down and did a scene in the picture [*The Butcher Boy* (1917)] and as long as I had a few days to spare, he carried me all the way through the picture. Then he talked to me like a Dutch uncle. He says, "See if you can get out of the Winter Garden. Stick with me." . . . So that was it . . . .

. . . [There was] no script. We simply talked over what we were goin' to do and we got our ideas, and went to work. Arbuckle was his own director and I'd only been with him probably about three pictures when I was his assistant director. In other words, I was sittin' alongside the camera when he was doin' the scene. And he taught me the cutting room also because he was his own cutter. . . . We made about six pictures in New York and then moved . . . to the [West] Coast because we were too crippled and too handicapped in the East trying to do exteriors. [In] those type of pictures, at least 75 percent of all our pictures would be exteriors.

PRATT: *Did you learn much about timing from Arbuckle?*
KEATON: No, I had that *long* before I came into pictures. Because I did the same type of work on the stage—The Three Keatons was a rough knockabout act. . . . [Arbuckle] would turn you loose. Because he didn't care who got the laughs in his pictures. He wanted 'em in there.

. . . The Arbuckle pictures were Paramount release [1917–19], and as soon as Joe Schenck sold Arbuckle to Paramount—I mean his contracts— . . . [Schenck] turned the troupe over to me and set me out makin' pictures of my own. He got me the old Chaplin studio so it became the Keaton Studio. And I was right next to the old Metro. Well Marcus Loew wanted our pictures immediately, so before I made one he signed us. And even before I made one of my two-reelers he put me in a big featured picture that was [based on] a famous show in New York called *The New Henrietta* . . . [where] it starred William H. Crane and Douglas Fairbanks—this was before Fairbanks went into pictures. [Schenck] even sent out the New York stage director, Winchell Smith [to supervise the film]. (John Golden was the owner of the show.) So they put me in the Fairbanks part for this big feature. This was before I ever put on misfit clothes and started makin' my own. The character was called "Bertie the Lamb," and his father is a Wall Street multi-millionaire. So I had to dress with the best clothes that the tailors could fit me to for the makin' of that picture—a little bit unusual for me. *The Saphead* [1920] was the name of it.

Then, following that, I made my first series of [my own] two-reelers and I made eight for 'em. On the ninth picture I broke a leg on a studio-built escalator and that laid me up for six months. . . . It was called *The Electric House* [1922–23] {1921} and we shelved everything I had shot on it and then later on . . . I remade the picture.

. . . We always had a scenario department and I found that the ideal size was three men to work with you. They were Jean Havez, Clyde Bruckman, and a Joe Mitchell. . . . I had off and on Bob [Robert E.] Sherwood (he wrote a story for me and I didn't do it—we couldn't get a finish to it). . . .

. . . I started makin' features in '22 and I didn't leave my studio until '28 to go to MGM, but I did my regular two pictures a year—there was a spring and a fall release. None of those pictures—that's *Our Hospitality*, *The Navigator*, *The General*—all of 'em—there was never a script on any one of those pictures. . . . And our detail work in things like *Hospitality* and *The General*, period pictures, had to be correct. We did our own research right up there in the scenario room. We were very particular about details, costumes and backgrounds, props and things like that. And never a script. Because when we had what we knew was a story, and had the material and opportunities to get our high spots, we'd bring in our cameraman, our technical man who builds our sets, the head electrician and the prop man—those boys are on weekly salary with us—we didn't just hire 'em by the picture, they were right there. And we go through what we had in mind on things. They make notes. They know what's going to be built. The prop man knows the props he's got to have and the stuff to be built. The electrician knows what he needs in the way of lights and stuff like that. By the time that we're ready to shoot, there's no use havin' it on paper because they all know it anyhow.

And with us, we may lay out a routine in a nice set that we've built for this and we start out in this thing and we find out we're not getting any place. The material is not working out the way we thought it would. . . . [We knew that because] we could feel it. Not only looking at our own rushes, we could feel it also. Now, in a broom closet or somethin' like that, we're liable to find a very good routine. So we shift right then and there. We just devote our time on that and the thunder with that big set. We didn't care about [big] production. We didn't give a darn about that. So—if we were workin' by the script, you see, that would throw the whole thing right out the window. Well that would happen to us with the first and second day of shootin'. . . .

We didn't shoot by no schedule at all. We didn't know when we started whether we was goin' to have the camera up five weeks or ten weeks. And it didn't make any difference. We owned our own camera. We're not paying rent on anything. All our people are on weekly salary anyhow. . . . We've just got two pictures a year to make and that's all there is to it.

I'll show you what happens to you. Up until I'll say twenty years ago, if I phoned out to the Production Department at MGM and say, "I want an insert of a man's hand coming in and picking up a book off of a desk." Now that's not a big lighting job. That's not a big set job. It's nothing. That cost me twenty years ago exactly $8,000. So today, twenty years later, that same scene would cost almost $12,000. Where it didn't cost us [in the early 1920s] only the price of the film we bought, which is $2.68—somethin' like that. That was the difference. So if I don't work to schedule at MGM, I wreck the studio, according to their system. Which of course is the—

Another thing that hurt is that we lose all chance of spontaneity—ad libbing, in other words. Because half of our scenes, for God's sakes, we only just talked over. We didn't actually get out there and rehearse 'em. We just walk through it and talk about it. We crank that first rehearsal. Because anything can happen—and generally did. And we got our best sequences that way. . . . We used the rehearsal scenes instead of the second take.

Today, and especially since sound came in (they were pretty strict before on rehearsing scenes until the director thought they were perfect before he'd crank), with us, we used to say one of the hardest things in the world to do in pictures is to *un*rehearse a scene. In other words, you get so mechanical that nothing seems to flow in a natural way. Cues are picked up too sharp and people's actions are just mechanical. Well now to get that feeling out of it is unrehearse the scene, and we generally did that by going out and playing a coupla innings of baseball or some-thin'. Come back in and someone'd say, "Now what did I do then?" I'd say, "I don't know. Do what you think best and then go ahead and shoot." That's unrehearsing a scene. Coffee break or somethin'. . . .

One Week [1920], my first two-reeler, was a *very* big laughing picture, and the biggest one I ever made was called *Hard Luck* [1921]. . . . Eddie Cline co-directed most of the two-reelers with me . . . [and Elgin Lessley was the cameraman.] In fact everybody in our staff—that went for the assistant prop man, the assistant director, the cameraman, they were all gag men—you couldn't stop that. . . .

Well [in making *The Playhouse* (1921)], we just set out to kid Thomas H. Ince. Ince started takin' himself very seriously and his pictures come out saying, "Thomas H. Ince presents Dorothy Dalton in *Fur Trapping on the Canadian Border*. Written by Thomas H. Ince. Directed by Thomas H. Ince. Supervised by Thomas H. Ince, and this is a Thomas H. Ince Production." Well, we started the picture with that, saying "This is a Keaton Picture. Keaton Presents Keaton. Supervised by Keaton." (Laughs). . . .

I was the cameraman. I was the electrician—everything that there was to be, and then I set out to be the only one in the picture. And I did a minstrel first part. I was nine times on the screen. I was the whole orchestra. Nine exposures. Then I put different makeups on and I was four different sets of characters in the boxes. And for a finish, I was the whole audience. . . . We set an all-time record with the nine exposures. . . . This exposure thing is *very* tedious [to do, however].

But the mechanical things for a picture like *The Boat* [1921] would hold you up longer. Well, for instance [in that], I built a family cruiser in the basement of my house and had to knock out the end of the house to get the boat out of it. Then when I got it on the landing cradle and launched it, she went straight to the bottom. Well, it took us three days to get that launching because we kept running into bugs. She simply would not go straight down to the bottom. . . . But this past year when they did *The Buster Keaton Story* at Paramount [1957], and they wanted that scene with Donald O'Connor playin' me, I could get all the bugs out of it for 'em before they built it. So they got the scene in one morning—the first take.

. . . [In *One Week*] my uncle gave me the portable house and my aunt gave me the lot to build it on, as a wedding present. Only my former rival for the girl's hand changed the numbers on the crates so when I put the house up it was the darndest looking thing you ever saw. And then for a finish, I found out I'd built it on the wrong lot.

. . . I remember we had trouble one summer. Standard Lab had all our negatives and handled all our film work from the studio. And durin' the heat of one of our severest summers, the cooling system went out and all of those negatives just fell apart. The emulsion ran right off of 'em with that heat, see. So we lost pretty near all of our negatives. So the only thing that would be in existence [now] would be what prints were out and hadn't been run to death and all chewed up. . . .

. . . After eight pictures with Metro, I released eleven First Nationals [two-reelers]. Then I came back to Metro to do features.

. . . Well, that's what put us into feature-length pictures because an exhibitor, if he got one of a [short] Chaplin, a Lloyd or one of mine, he would bill it above the feature picture he had. And of course we never got any big stars on the bill with us. We never got any Bill Harts, Mary Pickfords, Gloria Swansons, or Fairbanks or anybody. We got the darndest stars you ever heard of. Well, your natural rentals in those days—for instance if he paid $300 rent for a two-reeler for the week, he would be paying $900 for the feature. Well, long as the exhibitor was featuring us anyway, we weren't gettin' the best of the program by doin' it. We stopped makin' two-reelers—and went into features.

. . . I wasn't impressed with motion pictures until Sennett hit his stride with the Keystone Cops and then I saw *The Birth of a Nation* [1915]. From then on I was sold. I was sold from then on. I was a picture fan. Then of course the next picture that caught my eye was Sennett's [feature-length comedy] *Tillie's Punctured Romance* [1914].

. . . [Griffith's *Intolerance* (1916) was] terrific. . . . It's a beautiful production. That was somethin' to watch then. You weren't used to seein' big spectaculars like that.

. . . [In *Three Ages* (1923)] we used Wallace Beery as a villain. And what I did was just tell a single story of two fellows calling on a girl, and the mother likes one suitor and the father likes the other one. And in fighting over the girl and different situations we could get into, and finally winning her. But I told the same story in three ages. I told it is the Stone Age, Roman Age, and Modern. In other words, I just show us calling on the girl, the two of us, gettin' sore at each other because we were in each other's way. Then I went from the Stone Age to the Roman Age, did the same exact scene with the same people, only the setting was different and the costumes. And the same thing in the Modern Age. So every situation we just repeated in the three different ages. That was the picture.

. . . It was all right because as far as story construction goes it didn't mean much to the audience, but there was enough laughs to hold it up.

. . . The second picture was really a big seller, called *Our Hospitality* [1923] and there I used a story of a feud in the South, and placed the period in . . . [1831] to take advantage of the first railroad train that had been built. That's when they just took the stagecoaches and put flanged wheels on 'em. And they had those silly lookin' engines—one called the Stephenson "Rocket" and [one called] the "De Witt Clinton." And they're naturally narrow-gauge, and they weren't so fussy about layin' railroad track [then]—if it was a little unlevel, they just ignored it. They laid it over fallen trees, over rocks (laughs). So I got quite a few laughs ridin' that railroad.

But when [in the picture] I got down South to claim my father's estate, I ran into the family who had run us out of the state in the first place. And the old man of the outfit wouldn't let his sons or anybody shoot me while I was a guest in the house 'cause the girl had invited me for dinner. Well, I'd overheard it and found out. As long as I stayed in the house I was safe. But I had a good story to tell and it rounded out swell and it was a big seller for me.

. . . The next picture was *Sherlock Jr.* [1924]. . . . I did a lot of trick photography work in that thing. . . . [About that gag where I dive right through the middle of a person] No, I just did this recently on Ed Sullivan's "Toast of the Town." I put it in the Donald O'Connor film, see. And they sent me East to plug the picture, so naturally Sullivan had me there. And we had this set built, and he says, "It's marvelous what the trick department with the cameras can do." And I said, "I want to show you how to do this camera trick." So I did it in front of his [TV] audience. Of course, it is no camera trick. You do it in full view of the audience and on a full-lit stage. There's no lighting effects, no mirrors or anything. And it's really a great trick and it shocks an audience. And after the show was over, Sullivan sent for me. And I went up to his dressin'-room and he says, "So I can sleep tonight—how'd you do it?" I wouldn't tell 'im.

PRATT: *Now, tell me about* The Navigator *[1924]. That's your favorite film?*
KEATON: Yeah. We were workin' on a story, the scenario department, and we didn't have a good idea yet—all fishin' around for somethin'. And I had just lent my technical man to Metro, to Frank Lloyd. He wanted to do *The Sea Hawk* and that called for about five fourteenth-century sailing vessels. So he was up and down the Pacific Coast lookin' for those hulls that they could build up into those pirate ships. . . . But he had just gotten back in town, and he says, "While I was in 'Frisco, I ran into an ocean liner—five hundred feet long—a passenger ship. And they're just about to sell it for junk." Says, "You can have it for $25,000 and do anything you want with it." Says, "Her name's the *Buford*. She was very much in the press at one time because I believe she brought the duchess—or something—of Russia out the night before that slaughter took place over there, with the czar of Russia and his family. So they sneaked her out of Russia over to the United States."

Well, we went to work right then and there and says, "Now, what could we do with an ocean liner?" Says, "Well, we can make a dead ship out of it. No lights aboard. No water running. Just afloat." How could we get it afloat? Well, we set out to figure out how to do that and to write a story around it. Only to get a boy and a girl alone, and adrift in the Pacific Ocean. And we plant the characters so that the audience knows that she never saw a kitchen in her life, doesn't know how to boil a cup of tea. I am the son of a very wealthy man in San Francisco, so I've been waited on all my life with valets, chauffeurs, and private tutors and everything else. So *I* don't know what I'm doin'. And set those two characters adrift in the Pacific Ocean on a dead ship. Well, that's *The Navigator*. And it worked out beautifully.

. . . The opening gag in that picture with me is one of the most stolen gags that was ever done on the screen. I think I knew at one time of twenty-seven times it had been done by other companies. With us, the gag was more to establish the fact that I was so helpless, that I went to call on the girl, and I came down and got in my car with a chauffeur *and* a footman. The footman wrapped a blanket around my knees—a big open Pierce-Arrow Phaeton—and drove across the street. That's all. I got out to call on the girl. I asked the girl if she'd marry me and she said, "No," and I come back down [to the car]. The guy opened the door in the car for me, and I said, "No, I think the walk will do me good." So I walked across the street with the car followin' me, makin' a U-turn.

PRATT: *How about the underwater sequence? Did you have any trouble with that?*
KEATON: *Terrible* problems with that. Well, we says, we'll try and build a camera box and shoot some place off the shores of Catalina. That's good clear water. But when we got over there we found out that time of year there was a milky substance in that water that you *couldn't* see very good in. Says, "Well, the next thing is we rent the tank down at Riverside." And of course the tank isn't deep enough for us. So we'll build it up another ten feet. Because I've got to have the rear end of an ocean liner in it—the propeller and the rudder. Because in the picture we drift ashore on a cannibal island in the Pacific and spring a leak in the stuffing box. Well, it can only be fixed from the outside. And . . .

[she sends] me down in a deep-sea diving outfit . . . [while she pumps air to me].

Well, we thought that would work out fine because we know the clear water we're goin' to get down there. But the base of the swimming pool is built to only hold seven or eight feet of water. Wouldn't take eighteen. The bottom just went out from under it. The weight of the water pushed the bottom out. So we wrecked that pool. Had to build them a new swimmin' pool. It's the Municipal Pool down there, for God's sakes.

So then we moved to Lake Tahoe. So I was *one month* up there shooting that sequence. One of the worst problems in Tahoe was the water so clear you could really see, but so cold that I could only stay down about thirty minutes at a time. [That was] as along as I could stay down. It'd go right through ya. . . .

PRATT: *Did you ever use the preview system much in your own films, Buster?*
KEATON: Always. . . . Well, we used to sneak a picture out of town. One of our main reasons for takin' it out of town was that so none of the carpenters or extra people or anybody connected with studios would be in that audience. Because if we had an outstanding sequence or cute gags or good gags or anything like that, these people would sell it to other studios. Sometimes they'd sell it and sometimes just to get in good with somebody, says, "Here'd be a good gag for you."

And we had that happen to us a few times. So our previews—we'd take 'em out to Los Angeles, Long Beach, San Bernardino, Santa Barbara, Riverside, Santa Ana—places like that. And we don't tell the audience they're lookin' at a preview. See, we want a cold reaction. We'd send the print down there to the exhibitor, and he's goin' to have two shows that night, he runs the picture twice. And he advertises—a Keaton picture, that's all. So we're in there to get . . . a normal reaction. Well, we have never made a picture—I know I never did, and I know [Harold] Lloyd never did, and I'm sure Chaplin never did—that we didn't go back and set the camera up again. Because we helped the high spots, and redid the bad ones, and cut footage out, and get scenes that would connect things up for us. We always put a makeup on and set the camera back up after that first preview.

And generally after the second one, also. . . .

. . . [We used the preview system from my] first picture. Arbuckle, in those days, it didn't make much difference to him. They says, "This is it," and that was it. But when it started gettin' a little more serious—we took advantage of the preview. But our system was not lettin' the audience know so that the audience wouldn't yes us. The minute you got in one of the major studios—oh, I fought my head off at MGM when I went there—and find out that they ballyhoo it. So that you got the audience in there, the minute it says, "MGM Presents," the audience applauds. And different characters come on the screen, they applauded 'em. They applauded the director's name, they went out of their way to laugh at things that the normal audience didn't laugh at. They yessed the b'j—the life—right out of ya. (Laughs) Well, that hurt me. I didn't want that at all. I couldn't stop 'em. Well, that's because workin' at a major studio, all companies are assigned to a producer. Well, the producer wants to make sure that the high brass of the studio sees a good picture even at the first preview.

PRATT: *Did you ever cut a major gag clear out of a picture?*
KEATON: Oh yes. Because it didn't fit.

PRATT: *Do you remember, did that happen in the case of* The Navigator?
KEATON: It did. I had a beautiful gag in *The Navigator*. I'm down tryin' to fix the stuffin' box of that ocean liner, and here's a school of fish goin' past and there was a big jewfish tryin' to get through the school of fish, and he couldn't make it. So I reached down there and pulled a starfish off of a rock, and let it grab my breastplate and I stepped in the middle of the school of fish and brought 'em to a stop and then turned like a traffic cop and brought the big fish through. And when he went through, then I turned and brought the traffic on its way again. And the gag folded right up [went smoothly] like a million bucks. It was perfect. And it was a son-of-a-gun to do. It took us three days to get the gag. We had somethin' like twelve hundred rubber fish, all around ten inches long, and they had to be solid rubber so they wouldn't float and hang 'em all with violin string, catgut. And a piece of apparatus built by the Llewellyn Iron Company, and sink four telegraph poles under water up there to operate this apparatus overhead, to control the school of fish. But the gag photographed perfect. And we previewed this picture,

and not one giggle did it get. We didn't trust that preview. Says, "We'll keep it in for a second [preview]. Somethin's wrong." We kept it in for a second. And the same thing. It finally dawned on us—I had gone down there to fix that stuffing box. The girl and I both are at the mercy of cannibals off of a cannibal island. I had no license in the world to go help a fish go through a school of fish. I quit what I went down to do.

. . . [People were worried about that situation.] And also get mad at me for doin' it. Anything else could happen to me. That was all right. Like a lobster getting' on my pants. And I used his claws for a clipper, for a pair of pliers. A swordfish tryin' to interfere with me. That was all right. Now, to prove the gag, I put the gag in our "Coming Attraction" runner. We used to call 'em runners. The theater would say: "Coming Next Week." And they'd just show you flashes of a picture that was goin' to come. I put the gag in it, and it was an out-and-out belly laugh. [That's because it was out of context.] No story. . . .

. . . [*Seven Chances* (1925)] was not a good story for me. That was bought by someone and sold to Joe Schenck without us knowin' it. As a rule Schenck never knew when I was shootin' or what I was shootin'. He just went to the preview. But somebody sold him this show that was done by Belasco a few years before. . . . And he buys this thing for me and it's no good for me at all. . . . And the only thing that saved me was that I accidentally dislodged a coupla rocks in the chase scene and they chased me down the side of a hill. Well, when we saw that at the preview, and the audience sat up in their seats—they expected somethin'—for the first time in the picture—we built fifteen hundred different shape size rocks and took 'em out on the ridge route and completed a sequence. It's the only thing that saved the picture.

. . . [We shot *Go West* (1925)] about sixty miles out of Kingman, Arizona. We were really out in open country . . . four cameramen (that's [including] the assistants), electrician—generally takes about three men with him (because we took a generator, which takes a couple of men), technical man—takes a couple of dozen carpenters, a prop man must take about four extra helpers with him. . . . Then we house 'em up there, see—we take tents and everything else and a portable kitchen.

. . . Well, I had one bad disappointment in that thing. I thought I had a funny sequence when I had my cattle—I turned 'em loose—and I actually turned 'em loose here in Los Angeles in the Santa Fe depot in the freight yards, and brought 'em up Seventh Street to Broadway (no—up to Spring Street). And we put cowboys off on every side street to stop people in automobiles from comin' into it. And then put our own cars with people in there. And I brought three hundred head of steers up that street. I'd hate to ask permission to do that today. But then I thought that by goin' in a store, and I saw a costume place, and I saw a devil's suit (this was red)—well, bulls and steers don't like red, they'll chase it. 'Course I was tryin' to lead 'em towards the slaughter house. I put that suit on and I thought I'd get a funny chase sequence, and have the cows get a little too close to me, and get scared. Then really put on speed tryin' to get away from 'em. But I couldn't do it with steers—steers wouldn't chase me. I actually ran and had cowboys pushin' 'em as fast as they could go, and I fell down in front of 'em and let 'em get within about ten feet of me before I got to my feet. But as I moved, they stopped, too. They piled up on each other. They didn't mind a stampede at all. But they wouldn't come near me. Well, that kind of hurt when you think that's going to be your big finish chase sequence. We had to trick it from all angles. . . . Some parts I like, but as a picture, in general, I didn't care for it.

. . . *Battling Butler* [1926] I liked. It was a good picture. I told the original story that was taken from the stage show except that I had to add my own finish. I couldn't have done the finish that was in the show . . . [where] he just finds out in the dressing room up at Madison Square Garden that he don't have to fight the champion and he promises the girl he'll never fight again. And of course the girl don't know but what he did fight.

But we knew better than to do that to a motion-picture audience. We couldn't promise 'em for seven reels that I was goin' to fight in the ring and then not fight. We knew that we had to fight. So we staged a fight in the dressing room with the guy who just won the title in the ring—by having bad blood between the fighter and myself. And it worked out swell.

[Then *The General* (1926–27)]—Clyde Bruckman [the co-director] run into this book called *The Great Locomotive Chase*, a situation that happened in the Civil War, and it was a pip. Says, "Well, it's awful heavy for us to attempt, because when we got that much plot and story to tell, it means we're goin' to have a lot of film with no laughs in it. But we won't worry too much about it if we can get the plot all told [laid out] in that first reel, and our characters—believable characters—all planted, and then go ahead and let it roll. And every other situation is more dramatic than it is funny." Well, that was the finished picture, and—it held an audience. They were interested in it—from start to finish—and there was enough laughter to satisfy.

I tell you one thing I was kind of proud of myself for. I made that picture in '26. Thirty years later, Walt Disney did it [as *The Great Locomotive Chase* (1956)], and I guarantee you we had a better picture.

... It was shot up around Cottage Grove, Oregon. Because not only the scenery was perfect for it, but all the narrow-gauge railroads from those lumber camps [were there]. And so much of the equipment. Because we bought engines up there and with very little work remodeled 'em into Civil War engines. Then we built a passenger train and a freight train on their flat cars. They had the rolling stock for us. So we just built box cars and passenger coaches and all the track in the world we wanted to use was already laid for us. And it looked aged, which we wanted, and badly—you know—they don't bother keepin' it looking good, they don't care what grows around it. . . . I wanted it that way.

PRATT: *Did the actual locomotive "The General" appear in that?*
KEATON: Oh no, no. We reproduced that. Because that original locomotive they'd have never let that one out of the depot in Chattanooga. . . . I believe they moved it to Atlanta, Georgia. Because the run of "The General" was from Atlanta to Chattanooga—that's where this chase took place.

PRATT: *How did the [mounted] cannon sequence develop?*
KEATON: We found that. It's an actual gun of the Civil War. The first railroad gun. And we duplicated that cannon. It almost looks like a prop we invented. That's the only thing that kind of scared us. When it comes to using it. They said, "Everybody's going to say, 'Oh, they invented the prop just to get that gag.'" But it's an actual reproduction of a railroad gun built in the Civil War. . . . We found it in more than one book.

PRATT: *Were there more people involved in the making of that film than in any of your others?*
KEATON: Well, when it come to do the battle scenes, I hired the National Guard of Oregon. Got five hundred men there. And we

managed to locate about 125 horses. Then in getting the equipment up from Los Angeles, we had to have a lot of it made. We had to have artillery pieces and army saddles and stuff like that and uniforms for both gray and blue. . . . [I housed the men] for a week in tourist cars given to us by the Union Pacific on a siding. We put up a big tent for a mess hall. And put 'em in blue uniforms and bring 'em goin' from right to left, and take 'em out, put 'em in gray uniforms, bring 'em from left to right (laughs). And fought the war.

PRATT: *There was some criticism at the time, and I'll tell you who was the man who mentioned it—and that was your friend Robert E. Sherwood*—who was a little upset by the fact that you showed men being killed in a* comedy.
KEATON: Well, he was a little sensitive about that. Because you've had to kill people in comedies. You've done that for years. But as a rule, if we could help it, we didn't.

I liked *College* [1927]. . . . [In that] I tried to be an athlete when I was an honor student in high school and of course I flunked everything then. Until I got into a jam. They made me coxswain of the boat in order to make an athlete out of me. Oh—one of my best gags in it was I was at the Coliseum doing a warm-up with all the other athletes, see. No people in the grandstand. . . .

[This was followed by *Steamboat Bill, Jr.* (1928) which Keaton liked "very much," and for which the climax was altered to accommodate a cyclone instead of a flood.]

[Then:] *The Cameraman* [1928] is one of my pet pictures. It's the simplest story that you can find, which was always a great thing for us if we could find it. I was a tintype cameraman down at Battery Park, New York. Ten cents a picture.

. . . I saw the Hearst Weekly [newsreel] man and a script girl with him [at a parade] that I got one look at and fell hook, line, and sinker. Well, immediately, I went down and sold my tintype thing to a second-hand dealer and bought a second-hand motion-picture camera. And of course I got one of the oldest models there was—a Pathé. And I went to the Hearst offices . . . and they got one look at me and my equipment and says, "no." (Laughs intermittently here.) The girl saw me make the attempt and she

---

*Then editor of the old humor magazine, *Life*, and its motion picture critic.

says, "There's only one way you can do anything. You gotta go out and photograph somethin' of interest. And if they see it and they can use the film you shoot, they'll buy it from you. And if you can do that more than once then they'll put you on as a member of the—" Well, I set out to be a newsreel cameraman. And of course I had my problems.

PRATT: *There's one unfortunate gap in our print. Apparently the negative had deteriorated. It's the part where you go out for the first day and everything goes wrong. There's just a little bit of that left. . . .*
KEATON: That's a shame because some of the biggest gags are there.

PRATT: *Tell me about what was in there.*
KEATON: Well, the No. 1 was I think I saw a lot of people around a Park Avenue hotel and I got there and they say, "It's the admiral that's coming out!" So I busted through the crowd and I photographed the admiral going right from the main door into his limousine. Only the mistake I made was, I photographed the doorman. That was my first error. Then I got over to the Hudson River and got a shot of a battle-ship, and then a parade on Fifth Avenue, and I double-exposed it by accident. So I had the battleship comin' down Fifth Avenue and the parade comin' down the Hudson River. I went to a launching of some millionaire's new yacht, one of the Vanderbilts, and I made a mistake and set my camera up on part of the cradle that launched the boat. So I was launched with the boat. In a finish I photographed a disappearing gun—one of those great big things that they had come up and shoot. While I'm photographing one, I didn't know it, but I was right up against another one that nearly took the seat of my pants off (laughs).
    . . . [Later in the film] I got mixed up in that Tong War down there and because they saw me photographin' they came at me. I didn't seem to have any choice but to just leave my camera and dive out the win-dow into a fire escape and get away from 'em. And then go ahead and round out the story. We previewed it and we thought the last reel was a good reel . . . and the last reel just died the death of a dog. It dawned on us what that was. I deserted that camera. So I had to go back and remake that—even with the trouble of tryin' to get away from those wild Chinamen in the Tong War. I still kept my camera. Then it was all right (laughs). It was O.K.

An Interview with Buster Keaton

CHRISTOPHER BISHOP/1958

CB: *Our readers would be very interested to know how you got into motion pictures.*

BK: Well, I was born with a show. My parents were already in vaudeville. When I was four years old I became a regular. When I was twenty-one we decided to try another branch of show business and told our representative to see what he could do and he immediately got me signed to the Winter Garden in New York, which was the Shuberts' Theater for *The Passing Show of 1917.*

CB: *This was an annual show?*

BK: Yes, it always started in the summer and generally ran for, oh, about six months in New York and a year and a half on the road. The Winter Garden was Al Jolson's home, and the show I was supposed to go in would have starred the Howard Brothers. But anyhow, they signed me for that show and I was walking down Broadway—down along Eighth or some place—and I met an old vaudevillian, and he was with Roscoe (Fatty) Arbuckle and he told me that he took his make-up off for awhile and was going to try running a motion picture company for Joe Schenck who was producing pictures with Norma Talmadge and Constance Talmadge at the Colony Studio on Forty-eighth Street in New York, and that he had just signed Arbuckle from Sennett. And Roscoe asked me if I had ever been in a motion picture, and I said no, I hadn't even been in a studio. And he said, well come on down to the studio Monday and do a scene with me or two and see how you like it.

From *Film Quarterly*, vol. 12, no. 1 (Fall 1958): 15–22.

I said, well rehearsals don't start for another week or so, so I'll be down.
I went down there and I worked in it. The first time I ever walked in
front of a motion picture camera—that scene is in the finished motion
picture and instead of doing just a bit he carried me all the way
through it.

CB: *This was* The Butcher Boy?
BK: Yes. *The Butcher Boy.* So I was very interested in it—the mechanics
of it. I wanted to know how the picture got together through the
cutting room, and the mechanics of the camera, which fascinated me
the most.

CB: *What part did you play?*
BK: Oh in those two-reelers, they didn't bother to give you any character or name or anything, things just started happening.

CB: *Where was the studio at that time?*
BK: Forty-eighth Street between Second and Third Avenues in
New York.

CB: *They were shooting this in a studio—not on location?*
BK: Yes, but we did in good weather sneak out and shoot exteriors.
Well we stayed there and shot pictures until October—I went in in
May—and altogether I think we made six pictures there—in the East.
Then Arbuckle persuaded Joe Schenck that the East was no place for our
type of motion picture—we needed too many exteriors and changes of
scenery, while in New York in that neighborhood you were kind of
helpless.

CB: *How many were there in the Arbuckle company at that time?*
BK: Oh, there'd be a standard troupe. Your cast were always your leading lady, your villain, and you always carried a handful of bit people—
they were cops or whatever you wanted them to be—you certainly had
two to three in the scenario department helping you lay out pictures,
you had a cutter, you had a cameraman—two cameramen. It's just done
on a bigger scale today, that's all.

CB: *Did all these films star Arbuckle?*
BK: At that time, yes. I was just one of his feature players. I stayed
with him until the spring of '18 when I went into the army, into the
infantry, the 40th Infantry Division. I was in France seven months.
I was released the following May 1919, and went back and made just
two more pictures with Arbuckle when Joe Schenck sold Arbuckle to
Paramount, and then turned Arbuckle's company over to me and got
me a studio of my own in Hollywood called The Keaton Studio. Then I
started there on my own.

CB: *I understand you made a feature in 1920 called* The Saphead.
BK: Yes, that's right. It was before I made one of my own two-reelers.
Loew's Incorporated bought the Metro studio and its exchanges, and
one of the first Broadway shows that they bought to make a special
feature was called *The Henrietta*, and it starred Douglas Fairbanks.

CB: *That was his first film, wasn't it?*
BK: He took the character but he didn't tell the story of "Henrietta."
He took the character called "Bertie." I made that special feature for
Metro. This was quite a while before it ever became Metro-Goldwyn-
Mayer, because when I made my two-reelers then I released through
Metro. I did, for two years, make shorts, and then I went into features
in '22, in *Three Ages*. Wally Beery was the villain in it. It told a simple
story laid in the Stone Age; same thing happened in the Roman Age
and then in the Modern Age. Every sequence of the script was repeated,
one after the other—just doing the same thing, only doing it three different ways.

CB: *Which of the two-reeler shorts was your favorite?*
BK: A picture called *Hard Luck*. It was the biggest laughing two-reeler I
ever made, but I had two other pets. One was called *The Boat*, where I
had a wife and two small boys and I built a family cruiser in the cellar
of my house and had to knock the end of the house out to get the boat
out, and when I launched the boat it sunk.

CB: *Of the features, which is your favorite?*
BK: I have two—*The Navigator* and *The General*.

CB: *How do you rate* Sherlock Jr. *now?*

BK: I like *Sherlock*. It was a good picture for me. It was the trickiest of all the pictures I ever made because there were so many camera tricks and illusions. We spent an awful lot of time getting those scenes.

CB: *How did you ever do the scene on the motorcycle? Is that a camera trick, or were you actually—*

BK: No, there's no camera trick there.

CB: *There is one shot where you can see the motorcycle from a distance and see that it isn't attached to anything. How did you manage to learn to do that?*

BK: I'd just go out and learn to handle a motorcycle on the handlebars. It wasn't easy to keep a balance. I got some nice spills though, from that thing.

CB: *How did the scripts for these features evolve?*

BK: Well, now we will go back to our type of pictures. Now when I say "our type" you've got three people who were making them at that time: Chaplin, Harold Lloyd, and myself. Until I left my own studio and went to MGM—where it was a different proposition—we never had a script.

CB: *You never had any kind of a shooting script?*

BK: We never had a script. We didn't work by one. We just got to talking about a story and laying out all the material that we could think of, and then got it all put together—everybody connected with our company knew what we were going to shoot, anyway, and we didn't have a schedule.

CB: *How long did it take you to shoot a feature in the mid-twenties?*

BK: We averaged about eight weeks of shooting.

CB: *And how much did a feature cost?*

BK: Our pictures cost, on average, about 20 or 30 percent more than the average feature—dramatic feature.

CB: *How much would that be as of about 1925?*
BK: Oh, I'd be spending around $210,000 to $220,000 a feature. At the same time Harold Lloyd would go higher—he would probably be going closer to $300,000. And Chaplin—you had no way of telling at all because he was liable to quit in the middle of a picture and go to Europe, take a trip, start and get lazy and only turn out about one picture every two years, so I never knew what his costs would run.

CB: *About the dream sequence in* Sherlock Jr., *was this something that you thought of on the spur of the moment, or something that had been planned out ahead?*
BK: No, it was planned out ahead because we had to build a set for that one.

CB: *How was that done—did you have an actual screen beforehand on which the characters were appearing?*
BK: No. We built what looked like a motion picture screen and actually built a stage into that frame but lit it in such a way that it looked like a motion picture being projected on a screen. But it was real actors and the lighting effect gave us the illusion, so I could go out of semi-darkness into that well-lit screen right from the front row of the theater right into the picture. Then when it came to the scene changing on me when I got up there, that was a case of timing and on every one of those things we would measure the distance to the fraction of an inch from the camera to where I was standing, also with a surveying outfit to get the exact height and angle so that there wouldn't be a fraction of an inch missing on me, and then we changed the setting to what we wanted it to be and I got back into that same spot and it overlapped the action to get the effect of the scene changing.

CB: *The illusion is perfect.*
BK: I know it was. I've seen it with many an audience.

CB: *Speaking of Chaplin and Lloyd and your other contemporaries, I wonder if you would care to express an opinion of their work as fellow comedians, or tell us which among the other comedians were your favorites?*
BK: Well, my favorites—I guess Chaplin, of course, was number one. But I liked Harry Langdon very much, and I liked an old one called

Lloyd Hamilton. I liked W. C. Fields. Those were my pets, and then probably Lloyd.

CB: *Lloyd actually made the most films, didn't he?*
BK: Yes, he did. He turned out quite a list. He was doing the same as I was, he'd make a spring release and a fall release—two pictures a year.

CB: *How did you pick up the acrobatic skills that turn up in such films as* Sherlock Jr.*?*
BK: Well, I was just a harebrained kid that was raised backstage. He tries everything as he grows up. If there is a wire-walker this week, well he tries walking a wire when nobody's looking. If there's a juggler, he tries to juggle—he tries to do acrobatics—there's nothing he don't try. He tries to be a ventriloquist—he tries to be a juggling fool, a magician— Harry Houdini. I tried to get out of handcuffs and strait jackets.

CB: *Do you look at your early films—have you seen them recently?*
BK: Every now and then I see one. Somebody else gets them; I don't have any prints of them anymore.

CB: *How did you feel about the coming of sound?*
BK: It didn't bother me at all.

CB: *You felt that you could function just as well in sound?*
BK: Why sure. The only thing we did in laying out our material was to deliberately look for action laughs, not dialogue laughs. That has always been my fight with the brass. There were all these writers, and all these writers could think about was funny sayings and puns. I'd try to fight these down.

CB: *How do you feel about the comedians who have come up since sound? Do you have any favorites among people like the Marx Brothers, Fields, and Red Skelton?*
BK: Skelton I like very much. Lou Costello I like very much.

CB: *Did you like the Marx Brothers' films?*
BK: Some of them—when they didn't get too ridiculous.

CB: *Well, there you've got a good many verbal gags and sometimes—*

BK: That's Groucho.

CB: *The gags didn't develop as they did in the silent comedies and as they certainly did in your films—where you get one gag and you keep thinking it is going to end, but it turns into something else.*

BK: Oh, yes, we deliberately tried to keep something rolling.

CB: *Have you seen any of the work of Jacques Tati, the French pantomimist?*

BK: I've seen very little of it, only what's been on television.

CB: *How do you feel about him?*

BK: Well, he's—I don't know what you'd call him. He is just out to be artistic.

CB: *Well, of course I bring him up because he is the one person recently who has made a conscious effort to make comedies almost entirely without dialogue. I wonder how you feel about making a sound comedy—whether they are silent comedies with music and sound effects added.*

BK: I wouldn't want to do that today. I still would look at it just the same as I looked at it when television first got a good hold and they put me out to doing half-hour shows. Well, I said, here's what I'm going to do. We go ahead and talk—put all the dialogue in the first fifteen minutes—let 'em try for little laughs as we go—but for the second fifteen minutes deliberately go for places that just don't call for dialogue. In other words, we don't go out of our way to avoid them, but it is just a natural thing that two people busy building something—there's no reason to talk, you just go ahead and build. Well, that's the type of material I looked for.

CB: *If you were making a feature at this time, what sort of film would it be?*

BK: I'd go back to my old format—that's the way I made 'em before. But I have no intentions of doing it. I just don't think it is worthwhile anymore. I think in making a program picture today you're just asking for trouble. You can't get your money back. You've got to make an

Around the World in Eighty Days, The King and I, you've got to get into one of those big things in order to get your money back. I'm anxious to see the day when television and the motion picture industry marry and set out a system, because it can't continue the way it is. I see only one solution to it. There should be paid television, and they could keep the costs so low that the poorest man in the world could have a television; they can keep the entertainment that low priced. And in that way you'd make pictures exactly the way you used to make them before television—I mean you'd think nothing of spending a million and a half for a program picture.

CB: *What kind of a future do you think screen comedy has—what would you expect a really good screen comedy of the future would be like?*
BK: There won't be any change. Everything seems to travel in cycles—it always did. Some fellow comes along like Jerry Lewis who gets all his laughs talking fast, screaming and making faces and things like that—and he is sure top box office for a while; I don't know but what he is still up there. Then along about this time when our back is turned, someone like W. C. Fields will come along—the funny character type of comic—and he'll be the rage—and you'll find nine more like him working. Then along will come another type and he'll be the rage for the next five or six years, and everybody will try to work like him.

CB: *Did you have imitators yourself?*
BK: Oh, yes.

CB: *Which was the most popular of your features?*
BK: My biggest money-maker was *The Navigator.* And next to that was *The General.*

CB: *How did* Sherlock Jr. *stand up?*
BK: *Hospitality* outgrossed it, *Battling Butler* outgrossed it, *College* outgrossed it, *Steamboat Bill* outgrossed it. And then at MGM both *The Cameraman* and *Spite Marriage* outgrossed it. It was all right, it was a money-maker, but it wasn't one of the big ones. Maybe it was because at the time it was released the audience didn't pay so much attention to the trick stunts that were in the picture.

CB: *Was there any single film, perhaps one of the shorts, that you think did the most for your reputation?*

BK: Perhaps the first short I made, called *One Week.*

CB: *What decided you to go into feature films, instead of continuing with the shorts?*

BK: Well, because the exhibitor would buy two pictures—he'd buy a feature-length picture and a short, and he would advertise one of my shorts, or Lloyd's, or Chaplin's above the feature he bought, and of course the feature he bought with us was always a second-rater. We didn't get William S. Hart, Mary Pickford, or Douglas Fairbanks on the same bill with us. We had the second- and third-rate stars on the bill with us. Well, for instance if the theater, a first-run theater here in Los Angeles was paying us $500 a week rental for our short, he was probably paying only $500 for the feature.

CB: *So it was mainly a financial decision?*

BK: As long as they were going to advertise us above it anyhow—we're the drawing card, we might as well get into the feature field and instead of getting $500 for the picture we take $1,500. It makes a difference.

CB: *Do you feel that there is anyone that you learned most from in your early days—perhaps your father?*

BK: Arbuckle. From the stage it was my father.

CB: *He was quite an acrobat himself?*

BK: Not exactly an acrobat, just a—he was a very funny man.

CB: *He appeared in some of your films?*

BK: Yes, I used him. He was the girl's father in *Sherlock Jr.*

CB: *And then you feel that you learned most from Arbuckle later?*

BK: Picture technique I learned from Arbuckle. But not from an audience standpoint—I learned that for myself and from my father, 'cause I had all that experience. See by the time I'm twenty-one years old I'm a vet.

CB: *Was it your father who persuaded you never to smile?*
BK: No. Nobody did that. I just simply worked that way, because I learned as a kid growing up with an audience that I just had to be that type of comedian—if I laughed at what I did, the audience didn't.

CB: *So you stopped laughing?*
BK: Sure. The more serious I turned the bigger laugh I could get. So at the time I went into pictures, that was automatic—I didn't even know I was doing it.

CB: *Have you ever smiled on the screen?*
BK: I did it for somebody once—just to prove a point—that an audience wouldn't like it—and they didn't. We actually went in the projecting room when I started to get a reputation from film magazines and critics of being a frozen face, blank pan. We ran our first few pictures to see if I had smiled—I was unconscious of it and didn't know it. I hadn't, so everything was fine.

CB: *When you worked with Arbuckle in the shorts, was your screen character essentially what it was in the later features?*
BK: I worked the same way. I always stayed the same way.

CB: *Do you feel that American or European audiences appreciated your films more?*
BK: I did a bigger business in Europe than I did in the United States. I was a box-office draw in the darndest country in the world.

CB: *Which was that?*
BK: Russia. I was a bigger box-office attraction than Chaplin in Russia. And it was the one country we couldn't get any money out of.

CB: *You mean you never got any money out of Russia?*
BK: No. The limit was $5,000. That went for Doug Fairbanks, Mary Pickford, Chaplin—anybody—$5,000 was the most you could get. The reason for this is that they bought from the Berlin Exchange. They rented a picture just to play one week in Moscow, and while it was there they made a dupe negative and made as many prints as they wanted, and they sent them all over the country. They paid you $5,000 for that one week.

CB: *How about the total gross on an average silent feature of yours?*
BK: We'd average between a million and a half and two million.

CB: *Were you much aware of what the critics were saying about you during the twenties? Did you pay much attention to them?*
BK: I hadn't because I'd been reading house notices since I was born, and was used to that. This critic likes you and this one don't, so that's that. I've had some good friends. One of the best critics I think I had was when Bob Sherwood was editor of *Life*. He was always on my side. I could do no wrong for him. The majority thought that I was going to develop good. The biggest mistake I made in my career was leaving my own studio and going to MGM. Chaplin warned me, so did Lloyd—but Joe Schenck talked me into it. And it wasn't that they didn't try, but those types of pictures and those little independent companies working—you could do better. There was an old-fashioned expression that explains the whole thing—too many cooks. When they turned me loose at MGM, they gave me the entire scenario department—there must have been three hundred—all the brass turned gag men for me— and just too much help. And I guess it's silly to say, but it is a fact, they warp your judgment in the role you're working.

CB: *On the features that you made independently, you usually co-directed these—*
BK: Yes. And the majority of them I did alone.

CB: *On the co-direction, did this mean that you were directing the scenes in which you yourself didn't appear, or—*
BK: When I did appear.

CB: The Navigator *is co-directed with Donald Crisp?*
BK: Yes, that's right.

CB: *How did the responsibility for the direction break down in a case like that?*
BK: Well, when we first laid out the story of *The Navigator* ahead, a few dramatic scenes at the start of it were legitimate and not done in a comedy way, and I had mobs stuffed in there, such as the cannibal

island we got onto, and things like that—you get a good dramatic director to take care of those sequences in the picture. We won't worry about the comedy part of it, we take care of that. We do that. The only one mistake we made there, and that was Donald Crisp—he was strictly from the D. W. Griffith school, a topnotch dramatic man—he had just made one of the best pictures for Paramount that year called *The Goose Woman*. But when he joined us, he turned into a gag man. He wasn't interested in the dramatic scenes, he was only interested in the comedy scenes with me. Well, that we didn't want. But we did manage to pull through the picture all right.

CB: *When did you start cutting your own films?*
BK: When I started to shoot my own pictures. I had learned to cut from Arbuckle.

CB: *He did his own cutting, also?*
BK: Yes.

CB: *Some of your films have more melodramatic situations than, say, the Chaplin films—you get into very dangerous situations and then get out of them. Was this something that you were particularly working on?*
BK: Our best format for our type of pictures was to start out with the normal situation, maybe some little trouble—not enough to handicap us for getting little laughs—and introducing our characters if we wanted to, getting into situations and out of them, but when we got down to around about that fourth or fifth reel, we would get into something serious and start getting laughs. And then get out of that situation and end up getting our biggest laughs in that last reel. That was always the perfect format for this type of picture.

CB: *How did you conceive of the screen character you usually played?*
BK: That's not easy. In laying out *The Navigator* for instance, we're going to end by putting two people adrift on an ocean liner and it's a dead ship—there are no lights on it, no water, nobody to wait on them. Well, all right. Now you go back to your first part to establish your character. Well if I was a laborer or a poor guy, or something like that—it would be no hardship for me to be on that ocean liner. But if I started

out with a Rolls Royce, a chauffeur, a footman, a valet, and a couple of
cooks and everything else to wait on me—and the same thing with the
girl—in other words, the audience knows we were born rich, and never
had to lift a finger to do anything. Now you turn those two people
adrift on a dead ship, they're helpless. The same thing as going into the
army in making *Doughboys*. We start in the office with a very rich character, well dressed and everything else. Now when you give me an army
outfit that I was too small for—everything was big that they gave me
in the army—I'm a misfit, and come to living in the barracks and eating in
the mess hall, that was a hardship to me. But if I'd have been a bum in the
first place, it would have been an improvement. Well, then you lay out
your character according to the situations you're going to get into.

CB: *Of course this is very different from Chaplin's character.*
BK: Well, he starts and stays a bum at all times. He was handicapped
there. He was always a bum.

CB: *He was always a bum and Harold Lloyd was usually the country boy.*
BK: Who went to the big city to make good.

CB: *There is a consistent character in all your films who, for instance,
seems to be quite helpless with machinery.*
BK: Well, as a rule—I'll take two different comics. You took Harold
Lloyd off of the farm and you put him into the Ford Motor plant in
Detroit. He would be afraid to touch anything, unless he was forced to
by one of the foremen or something. With me, I would be just as scared
of it, but I would take it for granted that I ought to know what I'm
doing and to set out immediately to try and do it. And of course I'd
gum it up—that's what would happen to me, because I don't know
what I'm doing but I'd make the attempt.

CB: *Could you tell of some of your experiences in stunting for the films?
I understand you broke your neck at one point.*
BK: They found a fracture—years later—I didn't even know it. I was
doing a scene in *Sherlock*. I was running along the top of a freight train,
and I grabbed the rope of a water tower to get on the other train, and of
course all my full weight pulls on the rope and of course I pull the
spout down and it drenches me with the water. Well, when you're up

on top of a freight car you're up there twelve feet high and that water spout is a ten inch pipe. I didn't know how strong that water pressure was. Well, it just tore my grip loose as if I had no grip at all and dropped me the minute it hit me. And I lit on my back, with my head right across the rail—the rail right on my neck. It was a pretty hard fall, and that water pushed me down. I'm pretty sure that's when I did it.

CB: *All of the comedians of that time did their own stunts, didn't they?*
BK: Yes.

CB: *Did you ever use a double?*
BK: Only for special things—such as one of a pole vault into a second-story window. That's in *College*. I went and got Lee Barnes from USC—he was the Olympic champion. When it comes to pole vaulting into a window—I mean, you've got to get somebody who knows what they're doing. But you know the cop that falls off the motorcycle—that was me.

CB: *Oh, that was you, too—your assistant?*
BK: Well, I doubled him because he couldn't fall off the motorcycle, so I took my assistant prop man, Ernie Rossetti [Orsatti], and put my clothes on him to be on the handlebars and I put Gillette's things on on the back seat and of course fell off. I doubled him. There's a pretty good beating in *Steamboat Bill*—working in front of those wind machines is tough. We had six of those machines and they were those big Liberty motor babies. One of them—in the course of a shot of running a truck full of paper boxes—about the size of shoe boxes—between me and the camera, that wind just emptied all the shoe boxes off onto me—just for one shot. We took a truck past there once and that one machine blew it off the bank, and it rolled into the Sacramento River. That's how powerful those wind machines are.

Interview with Buster Keaton

ROBERT FRANKLIN AND
JOAN FRANKLIN / 1958

KEATON: My mother's father, named Cutler, had a medicine show, and my mother was part of it.

R. FRANKLIN: *Do you want to start by saying, "This is Buster Keaton talking"?*

KEATON: This is Buster Keaton talking. The man just asked me the history of my mother and father. My mother was playing in this show—could play piano, bass fiddle, and a cornet—from the time she was around twelve years old. So when she grew up she played old maid parts in shows. She was liable to play anything, from *[From] Rags to Riches* to *Way Down East*.

My father came from an Indiana family on the outskirts of Terre Haute, called Dogwalk. He first heard about the gold rush in California, so he rode freight cars and bummed his way out to get into that. Not much luck. He got back home. About that time, Oklahoma opened up the Cherokee Strip, so he went into that, and he got himself 160 acres near Perry, Oklahoma. The man going alongside of him—they became great friends at the time—was Will Rogers. Couple of years later, they opened up Oklahoma proper, and he went back into that one—another land rush. This time he headed for Perry itself and got two city lots. On the first one, on the Cherokee Strip, he left home with $8, and on the

Interview with Buster Keaton, November 1958, re-transcribed for the Oral History Research Collection, Columbia University, by Kevin W. Sweeney, 2004. Printed by permission of Oral History Research Collection, Columbia University.

border, before he entered the Cherokee Strip, he bought $1 worth of bacon and beans and $7 worth of ammunition, because you had to stay up day and night to protect your claim stake. If they'd catch you sleeping, they'd just knock you in the head, take your name off it, and put their own up.

R. FRANKLIN: *This was the day of the "Sooners"?*
KEATON: Yes. Well, he established this second one from the Oklahoma rush, waiting in line to clear his claim, when this medicine show of Cutler's came through. He goes in and sees the show and falls for the soubrette, who is now seventeen. Soon as he gets his claim filed, he joins the show as a stagehand and works his way into playing bits in the show, and it was just automatically a natural thing for him. He was a natural dancer, a great pair of legs to do eccentric work and high kicking, and a natural clown. He was with the show about six months; he and my mother were married. I was born on a one-night stand in Kansas, in a little town called Piqua. They left my mother there for two weeks, and then she rejoined the show with me, and I've never seen the town since.

R. FRANKLIN: *Isn't that funny.*
KEATON: My father now has left her father's show, so the show I was born with was called "The Harry Houdini and Keaton Medicine Show Company." That's the great Harry Houdini, the handcuff king.

R. FRANKLIN: *That's when he started out.*
KEATON: Yeah. And he gave me the name of "Buster." I was six months old, in a little hotel we were living at in some town. I crawled out of the room, crawled to the head of the stairs, and fell down the full flight of stairs. When I lit at the bottom and they saw that I wasn't hurt badly—I was all right—he said, "It sure was a *buster*," and the old man said, "That's a good name for him." I never lost the name. So that's their background and their start.

R. FRANKLIN: *Did you ever get East with the act subsequently, when you were The Three Keatons?*
KEATON: Yes. Before I was a year old, they'd quit medicine shows and started into the smallest of the small-time vaudeville, trying to work

their way up, and had some very tough times. Of course, they had makeups on me and were walking me out just as soon as I could walk in front of an audience. By the time I was four years old, I was a regular member of the act, wearing grotesque clothes with a bald-headed wig and Irish beard on, and slapshoes. It started when a manager in Wilmington, Delaware, said, "Keep him in the act, and I'll raise your salary $10 a week." That's what started me.

R. FRANKLIN: *Was there any truth to the story that Sarah Bernhardt said, "How can you do this to this poor boy?" They were throwing you around madly or something. Or is that just . . .*

KEATON: No. It wasn't Sarah Bernhardt. Well, everybody said that. From the time I was around seven or eight years old, we were the roughest knockabout act that ever was in the history of the theater, not only in the United States but all of Europe as well. We used to get arrested every other week—the old man would get arrested, see. The Gerry Society is here in New York State. Well, the first crack out of the box here, the Keith office raised my age two years, because the original law said that no child under five could even look at the audience, let alone do anything. So they said I was seven. And the law read that he can't do acrobatics, he can't walk a wire, he can't juggle—a lot of those things—but there was nothing said in the law that you can't kick him in the face or throw him through a piece of scenery. So, on that technicality, we were allowed to work, although we'd get called into court every other week, see.

Once they took me to the mayor of New York City, into his private office, with the city physicians here in New York, and they stripped me to examine me for broken bones and bruises. Finding none, the mayor gave me permission to work. The next time it happened, the following year, they sent me to Albany, to the governor of the state. Then in his office, same thing: state physicians examined me, and they gave me permission to work in New York State.

R. FRANKLIN: *Up till about nineteen . . .*
KEATON: Massachusetts thought I was a midget.

R. FRANKLIN: *Going up till 1910 or 1912 when The Three Keatons become what is known as a "headline act" . . .*

KEATON: Well, we were one of the standard big laughing acts of vaudeville, what you'd call, like, a second headliner. We seldom head-lined, because you always had Lillian Russell, Nazimova, Weber and Fields—so many. We were generally at the bottom of the bill.

R. FRANKLIN: *Let's see, that's when Al Jolson was starting, too, at about that time.*
KEATON: Jolson came later.

R. FRANKLIN: *Did he?*
KEATON: Yes. I'm ahead of Jolson by about fifteen years. Jolson came out of minstrels into vaudeville, from vaudeville into the Winter Garden.

R. FRANKLIN: *Now, you came to New York and more or less settled down around . . .*
KEATON: My first appearance in New York would be 1900, at Tony Pastor's Theatre.

R. FRANKLIN: *Can you recall anything about that?*
KEATON: Yes, sir. I can remember Tony Pastor.

R. FRANKLIN: *Can you talk about that for a bit?*
KEATON: Well there's not much to talk about. That was supposed to be *the* theater of the United States at the time—on Fourteenth Street that was, near Third Avenue. And, of course, right up the block was the Academy of Music, and then the "Keith's Four" Theatre, the Fourteenth Street Theatre. That was the . . .

R. FRANKLIN: *You were about six then?*
KEATON: Five years old.

R. FRANKLIN: *Now, you can't remember too much about it.*
KEATON: Well, I played there about three times for Pastor, and he died around 1902.[1] Then, of course, the theater went into burlesque after that, and dropped out.

---

[1] Tony Pastor died August 26, 1908. See Anthony Slide, *The Encyclopedia of Vaudeville* (Westport, CT: Greenwood Press, 1994), p. 390.

R. FRANKLIN: *Went down hill. It was about 1915 that you more or less set-tled around New York, would you say, just before you went with* The Passing Show, *or were you still with . . . was it still* The Three Keatons?
KEATON: Oh yes.

R. FRANKLIN: *. . . until this* Passing Show *came up in 1917, would you say?*
KEATON: Yeah. Well, we'd had trouble with the United Booking Office, and it forced us to go with Pantages, which was three shows a day. We tried it for a few weeks, and we couldn't stand it. We'd get bruised or sprain something. You couldn't heal up. That odd show just seemed to cripple you.

R. FRANKLIN: *You had been doing two.*
KEATON: Yes. So we quit. I sent the folks home to our summer home in Muskegon, Michigan, and I came down to New York to see what I could do. The first thing they did was slap me into the Shuberts, to go into the Winter Garden. So Arbuckle, who had met me on the street, said: "Have you ever been in pictures?"
    "Nope."
    "Come on down and do a bit with me before rehearsals start."
    "All right."
    I went down there and not only did the bit but stayed and worked through his whole picture, for about a week, and by that time, I went up to our agent and said, "I want to stay in pictures. I don't want to go in no *Passing Show.*"
    He said, "All right, we'll tear up the contract."
    "What'll the Shuberts say about that?"
    He said, "They can't say nothing. We'll just tear up the contract."
[Laughter]

R. FRANKLIN: *Now, had you paid any attention to the films in 1915 and 1916? Had you watched Chaplin? What were your feelings?*
KEATON: Oh yeah. I saw *The Birth of a Nation* three times, *Tillie's Punctured Romance* four times.

R. FRANKLIN: *You felt that that was something you might like to do, then?*
KEATON: Yes.

R. FRANKLIN: *What did you think of Chaplin in those days?*
KEATON: I was in love with him, same as everybody else.

R. FRANKLIN: *Who were . . . other comedians? I think Flora Finch and Larry Semon, then?*
KEATON: No.

R. FRANKLIN: *John Bunny?*
KEATON: John Bunny and Mr. and Mrs. Sidney Drew.

R. FRANKLIN: *At Vitagraph.*
KEATON: Yeah, a little domestic. . . .

R. FRANKLIN: *Was that company called the Arbuckle Company or the Talmadge Company? It was the Colony Studio, actually. That was the technical name.*
KEATON: Yeah, well the Talmadge Company was their own company, and the Arbuckle Company was called the Arbuckle Company.

R. FRANKLIN: *I see, each one . . . all working for Schenck.*
KEATON: That's right.

R. FRANKLIN: *Technically speaking, was your first film* The Butcher Boy?
KEATON: *The Butcher Boy*, with Arbuckle.

R. FRANKLIN: *Now, can you remember anything about making that film in New York?*
KEATON: The one thing that I just told you about, the first time I ever walked in front of a camera was the scene when I came in to buy a bucketful of molasses. They've made me do that half a dozen times on television, since.

R. FRANKLIN: *Are you going to do it this week?*
KEATON: No.

R. FRANKLIN: *How did you get along with Fatty Arbuckle?*
KEATON: Well, the first thing I did in the studio was to want to tear that camera to pieces. I had to know how that film got into the cutting-room,

what you did to it in there, how you projected it, how you finally got the picture together, and how you made things match. The technical part of pictures is what interested me. Material was the last thing in the world I thought about.

R. FRANKLIN: *Projection technique.*
KEATON: You only had to turn me loose on the set, and I'd have material in two minutes, because I'd been doing it all my life.

R. FRANKLIN: *That's right. That was no novelty and this was. Your work with Arbuckle, did you have any feelings about him, any recollections about Fatty Arbuckle?*
KEATON: He was one of the greatest friends I ever had. I was only with Arbuckle about three pictures when I became his assistant director. It wasn't a case where he came up and said: "From now on, you're assistant director." You fell into those jobs. He never referred to me as the assistant director, but I was the guy who sat alongside of the camera and watched scenes that he was in. I ended up just practically co-directing with him because he was considered one of the best comedy directors in pictures at the time.

R. FRANKLIN: *We've recorded a great deal on him. Even Adolph Zukor says that "it wasn't I who did this. It was the public."*
KEATON: That's right. They made him. The complaints were so piling up—every state in the union had a half a dozen boards—and it created a censorship problem. The first thing they did was to go down to Washington—all the brass of the picture industry went down there—and got the best man they could get out of Washington, D.C., which was William H. Hays, to make him head of the censorship of the motion picture industry. That was to offset and stop local censorship boards, because if they hadn't stopped them, the censorship rules in Kansas would have eliminated things from a picture that Massachusetts didn't worry about, and vice versa. By the time you tried to please all the censorship boards, you couldn't have made a motion picture. It would've been impossible.

R. FRANKLIN: *Do you think Fatty Arbuckle was wronged?*
KEATON: Certainly he was wronged. He was no more guilty of that than I was.

R. FRANKLIN: *He was a scapegoat.*

KEATON: My God, it was marvelous. Everybody had their pictures in the paper for days and days and weeks, and it was headline news. W. R. Hearst told Joe Schenck in front of me: "This is hard to believe, but we sold more papers on the Arbuckle trial than we did on the sinking of the *Lusitania.*"

R. FRANKLIN: *Now, after* The Butcher Boy, *can you recall any of the other films that you made? That was just prior to you going into . . .*

KEATON: Now let's see, *The Rough House, His Wedding Night, Coney Island.*

R. FRANKLIN: *Was that done at Coney Island, perhaps?*

KEATON: Yes. We used Coney Island for the location.

R. FRANKLIN: *Can you remember anything about making that there, then?*

KEATON: Yes. I remember making it very well—nothing to write about. We just went down there, went on the concessions at Luna Park, and got in trouble—that was all there was to that.

R. FRANKLIN: *Now, in the army, did you do any entertaining, or were you just in there as one of the doughboys?*

KEATON: I was in at Camp Kearney, California, and in the infantry. I was in France about four months when the war ended. Our division did a lot, same as the other divisions. Headquarters troop sent out to find what talents you've got throughout the division, assembled them all at headquarters, put them under the command of a chaplain, gave them a regimental band to travel with them in trucks, and tried to produce a show—just to entertain the different places around your section—while we're all waiting for boats to go home. There was no money donated, no scenery, no props, no nothing. And a division in the first World War ran around thirty-eight thousand men, almost double to what it was in the second one. So out of that they managed to find around twenty-two men that could sing or dance or do something. We organized a minstrel show. Oh, we'd probably play about three camps a week and always get back to our own base, see.

R. FRANKLIN: *Were you doing any knock-about then?*
KEATON: Oh, I did a couple of screwy things in the show, yes.

R. FRANKLIN: *Now, when you got out of the army, did you come back to New York?*
KEATON: They took me off the boat for having trouble with my ears and sent me to the hospital in Baltimore, the big one. Then they sent me to Michigan to be discharged.

R. FRANKLIN: *From there you went to California or New York?*
KEATON: Right back to California and back to work. While I was in the army, they had moved the Arbuckle Company out of New York, back to California.

R. FRANKLIN: *When you got to California, what happened then?*
KEATON: I made two pictures with Arbuckle. Paramount had just bought the famous Broadway show called *The Round Up,* and they wanted Arbuckle to play the sheriff in it—which is a straight part, not a comedy. They made the deal with Schenck. Also, they would like to keep Arbuckle to make features with him, and use big stories like *Brewster's Millions* and things like that. So Schenck sold Arbuckle's contract to Zukor, and immediately turned Arbuckle's Company over to me and went and bought Chaplin's old studio in Hollywood and named it "The Keaton Studio."

R. FRANKLIN: *Oh, that was the studio. I couldn't find out anything about that. So, it was the old Chaplin studio?*
KEATON: Yes, before Charlie built his one that he's had for all these years.

R. FRANKLIN: *Were any other films made there or just Keaton films?*
KEATON: Just the Keaton films. A couple of times we just rented space to some friends of ours to come in and shoot.

R. FRANKLIN: *You were one of the owners of the Keaton Studio?*
KEATON: I had 25 percent of that company. Now, this was a very poor outfit, this Arbuckle Company that I fell heir to. These were my

stockholders: Joe Schenck was president; and his brother, Nicholas Schenck, vice-president; David Bernstein, secretary-treasurer—he was also secretary-treasurer of Loew's, Inc.; Marcus Loew; "Doc" Giannini, the original president of the Bank of Italy which later became the Bank of America; Irving Berlin . . .

R. FRANKLIN: Music, *Irving Berlin?*
KEATON: Yes. Those were my stockholders.

R. FRANKLIN: *That was quite an illustrious board. Now, was it about at that time that you made this film that Loew's called—based on this* Henrietta *thing—and I think it was called,* The Saphead?
KEATON: Yes. When they first made the deal to take my pictures, which would have been two-reelers, Loew had now bought the Metro studios in Hollywood. They bought a show from John Golden called *The [New] Henrietta.* It was done twice on Broadway. Revived—it was done in the gay nineties first. The second show starred William H. Crane and Douglas Fairbanks.

R. FRANKLIN: *That was one of his first . . .*
KEATON: One of his great Broadway hits. This is before he went into pictures.

R. FRANKLIN: *That's right. That was his first film, wasn't it?*
KEATON: And the character in the show was called "Bertie the Lamb." His father was a Wall Street tycoon or something, and he was the "Bear of Wall Street," and they called his son, "Bertie the Lamb." So in one of Fairbanks's second or third pictures—something like that—he used that character, but he didn't use the original show. He just used the character.

R. FRANKLIN: *Do you have any recollections of Doug Fairbanks, Sr., at that time?*
KEATON: Oh yes. I knew him from the stage before either one of us ever saw a studio.

R. FRANKLIN: *Oh really. I think his real name was Prescott?* [2]
KEATON: Oh nobody paid any attention to it. I've forgotten what it was.

R. FRANKLIN: *He's from Colorado originally.*
KEATON: John Golden comes out to Hollywood, and he's up at Doug's house for dinner and says: "Metro's going to make *The [New] Henrietta,* and William H. Crane's going to play his own part."

He says, "Who's going to play my part?"
Says, "We don't know."
And Fairbanks says, "I know who to get."
"Who?"
He says, "Keaton." He says, "Well, after all, Keaton's never had anything on but misfit clothes and slap shoes all his life." And he says, "You dress him up and he'll play Bertie the Lamb for you." So I did.

R. FRANKLIN: *I think right after that you went on to do something with Beery called* The Three Ages?
KEATON: I made two-reelers for two years. Then I went into features.

R. FRANKLIN: *The Keaton Company?*
KEATON: Yes, the Keaton Company, then we went into features, and once we started into features, why it was the set routine of making two pictures a year, a spring release and a fall release.

R. FRANKLIN: *Now the Keaton two-reelers, I think a lot of those have been lost somehow.*
KEATON: Oh, yes. You can't find them all. They've tried.

---

[2] Douglas Fairbanks, Sr.'s father was H. Charles Ulman. Born in Denver, Colorado, on May 23, 1883, Fairbanks at his birth was Douglas Elton Thomas Ulman. The father deserted the family when Douglas was five years old, and the mother, divorcing her deserted husband, assumed the name of her first husband, Fairbanks. Douglas Fairbanks, Sr., used the character of "Bertie" in his first film, *The Lamb* (1915). See John C. Tibbetts and James M. Welsh, *His Majesty the American: The Films of Douglas Fairbanks, Sr.* (New York: A. S. Barnes, 1977), pp. 13, 210, and 220.

R. FRANKLIN: *Could you say anything about what you tried to do in those two-reelers, since I don't even have any reference to the titles. What you were trying to convey, because this is when . . . ?*

KEATON: You didn't stick to any format. We just got ideas. Get an idea that once you started on it would lend itself to gags and natural trouble of any kind. So, no format, just anything.

JOAN FRANKLIN: *Have any kind of a script?*

KEATON: I'll answer this one for you in a second. We started making features; let's see, in '22.

R. FRANKLIN: *That would be* Hard Luck, *I guess.*

KEATON: No. *Hard Luck* was a two-reeler. *Three Ages* was the first feature. Then I made *Our Hospitality*, then one called *Sherlock Jr.*, and then *The Navigator.* Two pictures a year, and I stayed there till '28 doing that before we shifted over to the Metro-Goldwyn studio. At no time in The Keaton Studio did we ever have a script.

R. FRANKLIN: *For the two-reelers or features?*

KEATON: No, never for the two-reelers or the features.

R. FRANKLIN: *Could you re-create for us the atmosphere in making these films without a script?*

KEATON: Well, when myself and the three writers had decided on a plot—we always looked for the story first—and the minute somebody came up with a good start, we always jumped the middle. We never paid any attention to that. We jumped to the finish. If a man gets into this situation, how does he get out of it? As soon as we found out how to get out of it, then we went back and worked on the middle. We always figured the middle would take care of itself.

Well, by the time we got something all laid out and were talking about it, the head technical man that builds your sets and also gets your locations for you, the head cameraman, the head electrician, the prop man, the wardrobe man—those fellows are on weekly salaries, they're right there in the studio anytime we wanted 'em—they know about as much about what we are going to do as we do. So we'd say,

"All right, Gabe, we'll need a set," and we'd take a piece of paper and a pencil and just draw, saying, "put it on that angle, so I can get around out of there quick and get back through there."

He'd say, "All right, we'll fix that and that and that."

"All right. Where do you think we ought to go?"

"Well, Kernville is a good location for this."

"Start in Scene One?"

"Yes."

"Well then, we'll start on location. I'll have the sets here in case of bad weather."

Well, everybody knew what you wanted, so there was no problem there. You didn't have to have it written down. Now the thing happens to us when we start into production, here we put up this nice living-room set, and right off of it is a broom closet. Well, he made this a very good-looking set because we were going to do a pretty long routine in this thing—it calls for a lot of action. We'd get in there and start to shoot, and find out that it ain't working right. We were going out of our way to make things happen; it's not good, but I found out I got in trouble in the darn broom closet. Well, right then and there I'm liable to spend three days in that broom closet and only half a day in this living room that we've filled with forty-five or fifty extra people.

Well, when a big studio today has got their schedules laid out, and those people are called and everything, you go in there and shoot regardless.

R. FRANKLIN: *No improvising.*
KEATON: No. Why, we'd change every other minute. We never knew what we were running into. When we ran into something, we stuck with it.

R. FRANKLIN: *Isn't that what made it great comedy?*
KEATON: Sure. That's a great handicap today.

R. FRANKLIN: *No flexibility at all.*
KEATON: No, and the minute you're not flexible that way, the desire to originate and ad-lib, as they call it, is gone. You've lost that. You're too damn mechanical.

R. FRANKLIN: *What can you recall about the cameras that you used then?*
KEATON: The first cameras we used were the Bell and Howell cameras, and they were hand-cranked.

R. FRANKLIN: *Were you using hand-cranked then?*
KEATON: Yes. We didn't start putting motors onto the cameras until about '24.

R. FRANKLIN: *Had you gotten to the point where you could actually run a camera then?*
KEATON: Oh, I've cranked a camera on a scene. The reason I did that is because I'd be on a location someplace, and I'd run out of actors to do bits. So I'd put makeup on the cameraman and send him in to do the bit, and I'd crank the camera.

R. FRANKLIN: *Did you start cutting at that time?*
KEATON: Yeah. I always cut my own pictures.

R. FRANKLIN: *Oh, did you?*
KEATON: Oh yes, from the time I started making them.

R. FRANKLIN: *You just developed that skill yourself, too.*
KEATON: Oh yeah, sure. I just watched Arbuckle do it, and that's all there was to it.

R. FRANKLIN: *Arbuckle did his?*
KEATON: Oh yes, he cut his own pictures.

R. FRANKLIN: *This is another skill I guess that's died out.*
KEATON: Yeah. We've lost that because soundtracks kind of have made that almost mechanical. We used to study frames of pictures, for the love of Mike.

R. FRANKLIN: *Study each frame as a cell. Now, after* The Three Ages— *wait, I guess before you did* The Three Ages—*you did one called* Hard Luck, *which is supposed to be one of the greatest comedies ever made. Will you talk about* Hard Luck?

KEATON: There's only one way you might remember that picture. There was something like four outstanding, what we called, "belly laughs." Now, what we called a belly laugh, today they call just a substantial hearty laugh. They call that a belly laugh; we didn't—that was just a laugh.

R. FRANKLIN: *What you mean is for someone to fall out of a seat.*
KEATON: I mean a rock-the . . . I mean that the theater didn't forget for a while. That picture, a two-reeler, had about four of those in it. The last one was one of the most talked-of gags that's ever been done in the picture business.

I got out by a country club, in an open-air swimming pool, and there was a very high diving platform there for some professionals. So just to show off in front of the girls lounging around the pool, I climbed up to the top of it, and posed, and did a beautiful swan dive off the top of that thing. And I missed the pool! I made a hole in the ground, disappeared; people came up and looked down in the hole, shrugged their shoulders, and the scene faded out. It faded in to a title that said, "Years Later," and faded back in: the swimming pool now was empty; it was cracked, nobody around, the place deserted. And I came up out of the hole with a Chinese wife and two kids, and pointed up to the high thing and said, "I dove off there, and that's what happened."

That was the fade-out of the picture, and that audience would be laughing getting into their cars out in the parking lots. It was so darned ridiculous that there was no way to time the laugh, because if the audience stayed in there and watched the feature picture coming on, they'd still be laughing at the middle of the next reel of the feature.

R. FRANKLIN: *Cutting must have had a great deal to do with it, conveying this after you went into the hole.*
KEATON: All the timing—all timing.

R. FRANKLIN: *Then the thing must have been sustained, and how long?*
KEATON: It was short. It might seem a long time on the screen, but actually, probably from one scene to the other, including the subtitle, it would probably have been about twenty feet.

R. FRANKLIN: *I was going to say twenty-five seconds at best probably for the whole. . . .*
KEATON: Something like that.

R. FRANKLIN: *I've heard of that but never seen it. Are there any prints of that still around?*
KEATON: I haven't seen one. No. I've tried to locate one.

R. FRANKLIN: *Now, after* Hard Luck, *of course, you did* The Three Ages, *and then I guess you went on to* The Navigator *and* The General.
KEATON: *The Navigator* was the fourth picture I made, and *The General* would have been about the tenth, or something like that, about three or four years later.

R. FRANKLIN: *I've lost my chronology. Could you talk about* The Navigator *which is again supposed to be one of your . . . ?*
KEATON: Well, *The Navigator* was so unusual a plot, because we're not doing Keystone comedy now. Once we started into features, we had to stop doing impossible gags and ridiculous situations. We had to make an audience believe our story.

R. FRANKLIN: *You think that's what killed the two-reelers eventually, that they just began to get so preposterous and ridiculous?*
KEATON: Yes.

R. FRANKLIN: *. . . that Sennett never grew up and tried to evolve what you were doing in the early twenties?*
KEATON: Well, no. If Sennett could have continued to make pictures the way he did for a while, he would have been making them for a great many years longer than he did. But the minute you take Ford Sterling, Arbuckle, Charlie Chaplin, Mabel Normand, and Marie Dressler away from Sennett, you don't replace those people. I know Sennett didn't. He couldn't find them.

R. FRANKLIN: *Could we talk about the comedians of that time and your impressions of them? Let's take Charlie Chaplin first, and then we'll get back on the film, because I think this was the great Sennett era. So I want to go into your feelings about Charlie Chaplin, Harry Langdon, Ben Turpin, Laurel and Hardy, and so forth. So, just a few words about, let's say, Chaplin. Have you thought about yourself in terms of these various people, what you thought they were trying to do and what you were trying to do?*

KEATON: No. I never gave that much of a thought, because, I don't know, being raised in the theater, you know the different types of comics, and those that can work together, the contrasts, the Weber and Fields. Chaplin and I could have made a picture together, and not conflicted at all.

R. FRANKLIN: *But you did, at the end.*
KEATON: For a finish, I worked with him in *Limelight.*

R. FRANKLIN: *That's right, which was one of your greatest roles. You are probably one of the few comedians that could have an audience laughing and crying at the same time.*
KEATON: When you get two characters that are two different personalities and the audience knows they think in different channels, that's the idea of it.

R. FRANKLIN: *You do think in different channels.*
KEATON: I know. Yeah. I mean, but the audience thinks that. We automatically think in the same channel, but my way of doing it and Chaplin's way are two different ways, and that's where the trouble starts, which is where you get your fun.

R. FRANKLIN: *Were you friendly with Chaplin socially?*
KEATON: Oh yes.

R. FRANKLIN: *You regarded him as a great craftsman, comedian? Actually, your backgrounds were quite similar, he with his parents in England and you here.*
KEATON: That's right.

R. FRANKLIN: *But there was always a great deal of affection between you.*
KEATON: Yeah. We spoke the same language. I've changed gags with Chaplin—given him gags that didn't fit me.

R. FRANKLIN: *Could you define his comedy in any way, what you thought he was trying to do, as you saw it?*
KEATON: Well, no. W. C. Fields worked very much like Chaplin—a dignified bum. That's about the only way you could classify him.

R. FRANKLIN: *I think that's a good classification.*
KEATON: A dignified bum.

R. FRANKLIN: *How about Harry Langdon?*
KEATON: Langdon was about five years old at all times.

R. FRANKLIN: *He really was emotional off the screen?*
KEATON: I mean on the screen, his character on the screen. Harry Langdon was always about five or six years old. He did everything like a kid that age would do it. Langdon and W. C. Fields were the two greatest film comedians, next to Chaplin, and a runner-up in there would be Lloyd Hamilton.

R. FRANKLIN: *He had the cap.*
KEATON: Yeah. The little cap. I'll tell you who works very much like him today is Jackie Gleason.

R. FRANKLIN: *You really regarded Harry Langdon as a genuinely funny person?*
KEATON: Yes. One of your greats.

R. FRANKLIN: *The thing has been said about him by people who admired him greatly—he was not one of my favorites—that he began to take himself seriously.*
KEATON: When he did that, his pictures went to pieces.

R. FRANKLIN: *Could you talk about that? This is the only thing that anybody has ever said. How did he take himself seriously? What do you think a comedian like that . . . ?*
KEATON: I don't know whatever got him off on the wrong foot. He started in to feature-length pictures, and his first two were swell. They were good pictures. Then, for some silly reason, he picked out *An American Tragedy* to do a satire on; he thought he'd get a funny picture

out of it and the situation, sticking right to the story of the original. In the original, of course, the boy has been going with this little country girl for a long time, and her folks have taken it for granted they're going to marry. So the talk of the community is that it's just a matter of time till they have the wedding. And he meets a city girl who's got money and who falls for him. To get rid of the country girl, he gets her out in a rowboat and drowns her. Now, where Langdon thought he was going to have an audience rooting for him, or laughing, at him taking a girl out to drown her! Now, the minute the comic had the idea of drowning somebody, he's killed himself and his picture. Even the thought, whether he goes through with it or not. Once he's thought of the idea, he's a dead character to a motion picture audience. That didn't dawn on him. Now, if he was so in love with the dog-gone story and wanted to do it, if he'd reversed it, he might have got some fun out of it—if the girl was the one who took him out and tried to drown him, it might have worked into a funny story.

R. FRANKLIN: *Do you think off the screen he was an intelligent, sensitive person or not very mature emotionally?*
KEATON: Oh no, he was normal.

R. FRANKLIN: *Then there was somebody else—and we don't have a word on him—Ben Turpin. Do you have any feelings about him?*
KEATON: Oh, Ben Turpin was just out-and-out a freak and a funny-looking character. Ben seldom did anything funny. You know what I mean? You asked Ben just to come in here and just clean up the room and make it tidy—he wouldn't get laughs doing it. But you give it to W. C. Fields or Harry Langdon, tell them, "Clean up this room and make it look nice," and you're going to get a few laughs. Ben didn't do things funny. He was just a funny-looking guy. One of the best laughs I ever saw him get was in a Sennett picture. To introduce him, Sennett said: "Rodney St. Clair, a man's man," and Ben Turpin entered.[3] That's as big a laugh as I ever heard him get, and he didn't do a darned thing. It was just Ben Turpin with those crossed eyes, "a man's man."

---

[3] Playing Rodney St. Clair in *A Harem Knight* (1926), Ben Turpin parodied Erich von Stroheim's role as Count Karamzin in von Stroheim's *Foolish Wives* (1922).

R. FRANKLIN: *I think that takes care of that. Then, Laurel and Hardy?*
KEATON: Oh well, Stan Laurel is one of your great comedians.

R. FRANKLIN: *Anything about what they did that you . . . ?*
KEATON: Well, their slow way of working was always delightful.

R. FRANKLIN: *You admired them greatly, then?*
KEATON: Always.

R. FRANKLIN: *Are there any so-called comedians of that time that you didn't think were very funny, that you thought I'd missed, that you want to say anything about?*
KEATON: I had some pets from the stage.

R. FRANKLIN: *Please mention those.*
KEATON: Bert Williams is one of my favorite comedians, and Marceline I think is the greatest clown I ever saw.[4] Roger Imhof was the greatest character Irish comedian I ever saw.

R. FRANKLIN: *That was* Imhof, Corinne, and . . .
KEATON: Imhof, Conn, & Corinne.[5]

R. FRANKLIN: *Great act.*
KEATON: Joe Welch was a great Jewish comedian.[6] A tramp—Joe Jackson.

---

[4] Bert Williams (1874–1922) was a black comedian and pantomimist, one of the universally acknowledged greatest performers on the vaudeville stage (Slide, pp. 556–59); Marceline Orbes (1872–1927) was a star clown at New York's Hippodrome in the 1910s (Slide, p. 240).

[5] Roger Imhof (1875–1958), together with his wife Marcelle Coreene, and Hugh Conn, formed a popular comic vaudeville troop, *Imhof, Conn, & Corinne* (Slide, 259, and Joe Laurie, Jr., *Vaudeville: From the Honky-Tonks to the Palace* [New York: Henry Holt, 1953], p. 22).

[6] Joe Welch (1869–1918) was a very popular Jewish-character vaudevillian (Slide, p. 543).

R. FRANKLIN: *. . . and his bicycle.*[7]

KEATON: . . . and his bicycle. For an eccentric little comedian, a guy by the name of Willard Simms. He was known as "the paper hanger."[8] A very funny man.

R. FRANKLIN: *Some of the greatest of them never got into films.*

KEATON: No. In films, you lost the characters, for some reason. Well, of course, with Roger Imhof, unless you heard his voice and his dialect, he was lost in the silent motion pictures, and so was your Jewish comedian, Ben Welch.[9]

R. FRANKLIN: *Could we talk about* The Navigator *and* The General, *and what you were trying to convey in those films?*

KEATON: There was nothing to convey. We just had a story to tell. That was all. We just got the situation. It was because Frank Lloyd was about to make a picture called *The Sea Hawk,* and he had to have a batch of fourteenth- or fifteenth-century sailboats. So we were between pictures, and I lent him my technical man, Gabe Gabourie. So, Gabe went up to Seattle, Vancouver, back down to Portland, 'Frisco, looking for hulls, to buy. Then of course they'd rebuild the superstructure. He ran across this concern in 'Frisco with this boat called the *Buford.* The only historical thing she did was to get that one duchess or princess out of Russia just before they caved in on the czar's family. It smuggled her out to this country. And they were about to scrap it, sell it to an old iron place up there for $25,000. Now, she was an ocean liner five hundred feet long. So he came down and said, "We could get that boat, we could tow her out into the Pacific Ocean and set fire to her if we wanted, or blow it up; we could do anything we want."

So I said, "All right, let's make a deal with the scrapping outfit. We'll put a skeleton crew on the boat, sail her down here to Los Angeles . . ."

---

[7] Joe Jackson (1875–1942) was known in vaudeville for his comic bicycle-riding act (Slide, p. 265).

[8] Willard Simms's very popular wallpaper-hanging act was called "Flinder's Flats" (Laurie, p. 51).

[9] With the coming of sound, Imhof appeared in many films, including John Ford's *Young Mr. Lincoln* (1939) and *The Grapes of Wrath* (1940) (Slide, p. 259); Ben Welch (?–1926), the brother of Joe Welch, was also a well-known, Jewish-character, vaudeville comedian (Slide, 542–43).

R. FRANKLIN: *It still had its engines?*

KEATON: Yes. ". . . and we'll use her till we're through with it and turn it back to them." Now we set out to write a story.

R. FRANKLIN: *What did you buy it for?*

KEATON: Twenty-five thousand dollars, but that paid for a skeleton crew and for sailing it down to Los Angeles and back to Frisco.

R. FRANKLIN: *That's why it had that eerie quality, that everything had been stripped from it.*

KEATON: Sure. We painted her too, see, to make her look better. We moved our generators and lighting equipment on, and put cooks and assistants on there, and we lived on that boat for a month, and shot all around it. We could take it anyplace and drop anchor, or have her out at open sea, or anything we wanted to do. And the story, [from] a writer with me by the name of Jean Havez, was a natural. [The story] established me as the son of a wealthy family in San Francisco. They had a private valet, chauffeur, and footman for the car. The girl across the street—her father who was a boat owner, very wealthy—she'd been waited on all her life, too. They're both on Nob Hill. My first gag in the picture was that I saw a wedding outfit go past, dragging tin cans, and wearing a sign on the back, "Just Married," and people blowing horns and things, and I said, "It's time I got married. I think I'll settle down."

Settle down—I hadn't been out yet, see. I didn't even light my own cigarette. The guy lit that for me, too.

R. FRANKLIN: *That was wonderful.*

KEATON: I said, "Get James and the car out. I'll get married. Get me two tickets. Where's a good place to go on one's honeymoon?"

He said, "Honolulu's very popular."

"All right, get me two tickets for Honolulu."

This is before I've asked the girl. So I come down and get in the car. The footman opened the door and put me in the back seat, put a robe over my knees, got in the front seat with the driver, and they . . .

When we did *The Navigator*, I said: "Now look, we're going to this cannibal island, and in the first part I want foreign agents that don't want that boat to fall into their enemy's hands."

[Someone said:] "Why don't you get a dramatic director over here?" He said: "Why don't you get Donald Crisp? He just did a great picture for Paramount called, *The Goose Woman*."

I said, "All right. Call him up and see if he wants it." [I told Crisp:] "Don't worry about the comedy part of it; we know what we are doing there."

[Crisp said,] "Swell. Fine. It'll be an experience. Great."

Well, that camera wasn't up one day but that he absolutely ignored . . . he wasn't interested in any dramatic scenes. He'd sloughed those off; he'd okay anything. He was only interested in the scenes I did. He just got interested in the comedy part of it, and he was only interested in me and the gags, which was the reverse-English of what we wanted. Nothing to do about it; we carried him through the picture. After he left, I actually re-shot some of the dramatic scenes.

R. FRANKLIN: *Really?*
KEATON: Yes.

R. FRANKLIN: *You were on this wonderful bit when you were going aboard . . .*

JOAN FRANKLIN: *. . . getting into the car [to go to] the girl's house.*
KEATON: I went across the street in the car, to call on the girl. I went in, and her butler took my hat and the flowers that I brought. I walked right in there and said, "Will you marry me?"

She said, "No."

I turned around, and before he could put it up in the cloak closet, I got my hat and came back out. The footman jumped out to open the door, and I said, "No, I think the walk will do me good." They looked at me as if I was crazy. I walked across the street, and they followed me, circling in the car. When I got back home, my valet came running in with the two tickets for Honolulu. I said, "When does the boat sail?" He said, "Nine o'clock in the morning." I said, "That's too early. I'll go aboard tonight." "Very well, sir," And I tore up one of the tickets.

Comes night, and I start for that boat. The girl is all dressed to go out with her father. He said, "Drive past the dock, I've got some papers I've got to get off of *The Navigator*. I've just sold it."

We immediately went to this foreign outfit, looking down through their window. They said, "There she lays. If this boat has just now been sold to Argentina"—or Panama, somebody down there—"that boat will carry some ammunition and supplies, and even eventually may become a troop ship. It's up to us to see that she doesn't leave the Bay of 'Frisco. So we'll go down to the docks tonight, before the new crew goes aboard. We can overpower the night watchman, cut her hawsers. The wind is always blowing towards the open sea or towards the other side of the bay. She'll go adrift and end up piled up on the rocks and she's worthless. Very simple thing to do."

I come down to the docks. The watchman came past to punch a clock on the other side, the outside, and they brought the gate over—it was Pier 12—and the gate covered "1" so only "2" stood out, and that's the pier I was looking for, 2. So I go on in. I even take my own grips with me. I won't even let the valet come with me. I go on down there; I go aboard the ship. I can't find any lights; there's nobody to help me. I finally find the stateroom and go in there, and end up lighting a candle in it to put myself to bed.

About this time, the foreign agents arrive, overpower the night watchman, go in there with an axe, and cut the big hawsers, ropes. Now, as they're overpowering the watchman, the girl and her father arrive, and the old man comes down. Well, the minute this strange man came down, they jumped him too. But as they jumped him, he yelled "Help," enough for the girl to hear it. They dragged him into the little dock house and muzzled him and tied him up. She doesn't know that. She runs right for the boat. She goes on there, and she starts right for the wheelhouse, where she knows her father was going. So while she's on the inside, going up the stairs to get there, the agents come down and cut the ropes, and that boat drifts away from the pier.

R. FRANKLIN: *That was the actual boat drifting?*

KEATON: Oh sure, 'cause the gangplank fell off the side of the boat, off the pier, just as she arrived at it. She's in an evening gown. There's the boat, pulls away with her. The only thing that goes wrong is the wind changes and takes that boat out of the Golden Gate to open sea.

The following morning, she's just hunched up in a corner, sick. I wake up, ring for service—no bells are working. It's a dead ship; there's nothing going . . . I came down to the dining room, tried to get waited on; nobody waited on me.

R. FRANKLIN: *Is that the beautiful scene with the big pot where you do the eggs?*
KEATON: Later. Sure, because I went back in the galley—there are no cooks; there's nobody. I started to roam the decks. I'm on this deck roaming; she's on that one roaming.

R. FRANKLIN: *That is the most beautiful thing, and you keep . . . you never . . .*
KEATON: Yeah. Well, for a finish, I threw a cigarette down from the upper deck, and it lit on the open deck down there, and she saw the lit cigarette and knew there was somebody on board, and then she started running. I heard her voice, and started running. Well, we just kept missing each other, because we keep going up and down the stairs. The camera can see us doing it, but we can't find each other.

R. FRANKLIN: *It was superb timing.*
KEATON: We finally met. Of course, your situation is that you've got two people on a dead ocean liner, adrift on the Pacific Ocean, out of sight of land. Neither one has ever been in a kitchen in their lives. She wouldn't know how to make a cup of tea; he's worse. You couldn't get two more helpless people. That's all you set out to do, to survive. That was *The Navigator.*

R. FRANKLIN: *How did that end?*
KEATON: We drifted off of a cannibal island, and drifted onto it stern first, so we sprang a leak in the stuffing box. We could hear the water rushing, and we went down and saw it. She says: "Try and stop it." Well, trying to stop that from the inside was impossible, and that I could tell, and I said, "That would have to be stuffed from the outside." She sees a deep-sea diving outfit and says, "All right, you fix it." So I didn't have any choice but to put that on and go down and try to fix it while she pumped air to me. And we're right off a cannibal island. Anything would be better than falling into the hands of the cannibals. So, of course, you know how that rounds out.

R. FRANKLIN: *Now. Here's a point I would like to talk about. Much of the charm and edge of your comedy lies in the subtle leverages of expression that you work against—your nominal dead pan. Do you have any thoughts on this? What you do with these expressions, with your face, and control in these comedy situations? Do you realize what you are doing?*

KEATON: Oh sure. In my early experiences, as a kid growing up in front of an audience, I had learned at an early age that I happened to be the type of comedian that couldn't laugh at anything he was doing. I also learned that the more seriously I took everything, and how serious life was in general, the better laughs I got. So by the time I went into pictures, working with a straight face was absolutely automatic with me, and mechanical. I didn't set out to do it for motion pictures. I'd worked that way already for years on the stage. To make sure, when I started getting the reputation of being called "Frozen Face" and "Blank Pan," we went into the projecting room and ran our first two pictures to see if I'd smiled. We didn't know whether I had or not. I hadn't.

R. FRANKLIN: *You didn't even realize it.*

KEATON: No. We didn't realize it.

R. FRANKLIN: *You had to look at it. Now, here's another interesting point, that Buster Keaton "was the only major comedian who kept sentiment almost entirely out of his work. . . ." How do you feel about that? It goes on, and "brought pure physical comedy to its greatest heights."* [10]

KEATON: Well that we did, the physical work . . .

R. FRANKLIN: *Now, this was written by James Agee, who was one of the greatest students, who has since passed away, but was one of the greatest students of comedy and regarded you as either the number one or the number two comedian in the world, and this is what he said about you, that you were "the only major comedian who kept sentiment almost entirely out of [your] work and . . . brought pure physical comedy to its greatest heights."*

---

[10] James Agee, "Comedy's Greatest Era," *Life*, vol. 27, no. 10 (September 5, 1949), p. 85; reprinted in *Agee on Film: Reviews and Comments* (Boston: Beacon Press, 1958), p. 16.

KEATON: Well, in our early successes, we had to get sympathy to make any story stand up. But the one thing that I made sure—that I didn't ask for it. If the audience wanted to feel sorry for me, that was up to them. I didn't ask for it in action.

R. FRANKLIN: *I think Chaplin does this.*

KEATON: He has done that. I've seen him do it, get sorry for himself. The only time I did it was . . . I did it more in a burlesque way, because it was one of the early two-reelers—this *Hard Luck* we were talking about. I started out in that picture—because I was down in spirit and heart and everything—to do away with myself. So I set out to commit suicide. There were about six gags in there that were pips. Number One is I got a rope and got out on a sawed off log, which put me three or four feet above the ground, and I could throw a rope up over the limb of this tree, tied myself off to it, bid "Goodbye" to the world, stepped off the stump, but the limb I'd tied off to was so limber that it just let me go down to the ground, with just a light strain on the rope. I ended up lying flat on my back on the ground, trying to get up. Of course, it didn't work. By that time, somebody over there says, "Hey. Will you catch that dog or cat or something?" and I got up to run, forgetting I was tied off, and nearly killed myself. I got that rope off my neck in a hurry then.

Then, the next thing I did was go to Westlake Park and dove off the bridge. I didn't know there was only two feet of water there. I nearly broke my neck with that dive. I mean not actually, but that was the gag.

R. FRANKLIN: *Is that the sort of thing about bringing "pure physical comedy to its greatest heights"?*

KEATON: Yes.

R. FRANKLIN: *Now, here's another point. "Beneath . . . [Buster Keaton's] lack of emotion . . . uninsistently . . . giving a disturbing tension and grandeur to the foolishness, for those who sensed it, there was . . . [with] his comedy a freezing whisper not of pathos but of melancholia."*[II]

[II] Agee, p. 16.

JOAN FRANKLIN: *Sad clown?*

R. FRANKLIN: *A sad clown quality, and he goes on to talk about* The General *and what you achieved which is regarded as one of the greatest bits of comedy ever done . . . a kind of Matthew Brady quality. Can you think of any melancholy—I can't myself—this melancholy quality?*

KEATON: I used to daydream an awful lot; I've done that so often in pictures. I could get carried away and visualize all the fairylands in the world.

R. FRANKLIN: *Did you personally feel this, or was this purely your screen role? Because you did it in* Sherlock Jr., *of course. This was probably the . . .*

KEATON: Dream sequences.

R. FRANKLIN: *The cold degree of melancholy . . . Did you think of yourself in any way as a melancholy person?*

KEATON: I guess it just came as my natural way of working.

R. FRANKLIN: *Off screen, were you inclined to be sad?*

KEATON: For instance, did you ever see a picture called *The Cameraman?* Marceline Day was the leading girl in it. I got myself into the news weekly business because I saw her in it. I went and got me a motion picture camera and tried to be a newsreel cameraman. I finally got a date with her, and it was raining in New York cats and dogs. I managed to get her to her house, and she kissed me on the cheek, good-night. Well, I just went right off on Cloud One. I just started down the street, and it was raining. I was drowned, and "Eddie" [Harry] Gribbon was a cop, and he had on his raincoat, the rain cover to his hat, boots and all. He just walked along with me for half a block looking at me while I just stared into space, peaceful. He finally sat me down, and he examined my eyes, tried reflexes on my knees to see if that would work. Nobody in their right mind could possibly be walking down the street in this rain the way I was.

R. FRANKLIN: *No rain coat.*

KEATON: No nothing.

R. FRANKLIN: *This was said about that: "[Keaton] could create utter and hilarious disorder by the subtlest change of expression, the flicker of an eyelid, the beginnings of a frown."* [12] *Could we talk a little bit about* Sherlock Jr.?

KEATON: I think the reason we started off on that story is because I had one of the best cameramen in the picture business, Elgin Lessley. He originally was with Sennett. We laid out a few of these tricks; some of these tricks I knew from the stage. I seldom did camera tricks. I tried to do the real illusion. I have done an awful lot of camera tricks too, as far as that goes. But I laid out some of those gags. And the technical man that builds the sets, I showed him how I have to get them built for the things I had to do. When I got that batch of stuff together, he said, "You can't do it and tell a legitimate story, because there are illusions, and some of them are clown gags, some Houdini, some Shing-Ling-Fu. It's got to come in a dream. To get what we are after, you've got to be a projectionist in a projecting room in a little local small-town motion picture theater, and go to sleep, after you've got the picture started."

R. FRANKLIN: *This was a motor-driven projector?*
KEATON: Yes. "Once you fall asleep, you visualize yourself as one of the important characters in the picture you're showing. You go down out of that projection room, go right down, walk up on the screen and become a part of it. Now you tell your whole story." And all I had to round out was that I was in trouble at the start of the picture with my girl's father. He thought I stole his watch. Well, on the screen I became the world's greatest detective, to solve this mystery. Of course, while I'm asleep the girl finds out that I didn't steal it, and she's the one who woke me up at the finish. But on the screen I was a sun-of-a-gun, the world's greatest detective. No matter how they tried to surround me and kill me or get me, I got out of it.

R. FRANKLIN: *That particular film about two years ago, you couldn't get into the Museum of Modern Art when they showed that one. It was superbly received.*
KEATON: When they sent me East to plug *The Buster Keaton Story* for Donald O'Connor and Paramount, they had reached back and taken

---

[12] Christopher Bishop, "The Great Stone Face," *Film Quarterly* 12, 1 (Fall 1958), p. 10.

out some of the gags that weren't too darn expensive to do, because some of the ones they wanted would have broke Paramount to have duplicated them today. They picked up that one gag especially, of where I dive through that woman. So when they shipped me here, I said, "I going on Sullivan's show with that gag, because the world, including the motion picture people, take it for granted that that's a camera trick, and it's not."

So, in front of Sullivan's audience, with a full-lit stage—full-lit—no mirrors, no wires, no nothing, I did it in front of them. And if you don't think the effect was good! And it was done clean. After the show ended, Sullivan sent for me, and I come up, and he said, "So I can sleep tonight, how'd you do that?" He's standing right there on top of it and can't figure it out. It's a beautiful trick. Well, it's in *Sherlock Jr.*, and that picture was made in '23. That's thirty-five years ago!

R. FRANKLIN: *Now, we'll move along to sound. This has been said about you: "But his dark dead voice, though it was in keeping with the visual character, tore his intensely silent style to bits and destroyed the illusion within which he worked."* [13] *I disagree violently with that, but I think your opinions are what matter.*

KEATON: We found this out—we found this out from our own pictures—that sound didn't bother us at all. There was only one thing I wanted at all times, and insisted on: that you go ahead and talk in the most natural way in your situations. Don't give me puns. Don't give me jokes. No wisecracks. Give that to Abbott and Costello; give that to the Marx Brothers.

R. FRANKLIN: *Situation comedians.*

KEATON: Yes. Because as soon as our plot is set and everything is going smoothly, I'm always going to find places in my story where dialogue is not called for. There can be two or three people in a room working at jobs—well, they work at them without talking. That's the way I want it. So you get those stretches in your picture of six, seven, eight, nine minutes where there isn't a word of dialogue. When in those, we get

---

[13] Agee, p. 17.

our old routines, and when it's natural to talk, you talk. You don't avoid it. But you lay out your material that way—that doesn't call for a dialogue.

R. FRANKLIN: *But from 1927 when* The Jazz Singer *was done until 1931 when you did that musical for Metro, you didn't do any sound films. Was there a reason for that?*
KEATON: No. Let's see, in '28 I made *The Cameraman*; in '29 I made *Spite Marriage*. That was the last of the silents. In the start of the season of 1930 was our first sound picture. Then I made six more for MGM in the next three years.

R. FRANKLIN: *The Durante things.*
KEATON: Yes.

R. FRANKLIN: *How did you feel about sound yourself?*
KEATON: But in every picture, it got tougher. Like I said before, too many cooks. Everybody at Metro-Goldwyn-Mayer was in my gag department, including Irving Thalberg. They'd laugh their heads off at dialogue written by all your new writers. They were joke-happy. They didn't look for action; they were looking for funny things to say. You just keep fighting that, see.

Then, of course, when you give me a Jimmy Durante—they just brought him in there to play a part in a picture with me. Well, Durante just can't keep quiet. He's going to talk no matter what-in-the-thunder happens. You can't direct him any other way.

R. FRANKLIN: *He not only talked, he practically knocked you out of the room.*
KEATON: Oh sure. He really . . .

R. FRANKLIN: *There was the vicious rumor—don't go into this if you don't want to—but it was said that Jimmy Durante was brought out there to replace you and to . . .*
KEATON: Louis B. Mayer liked him very much. That could have been the case. I don't know.

R. FRANKLIN: *It was personal animosity on somebody's* . . .

KEATON: But I know for a finish, they were picking stories and material without consulting me, and I couldn't argue them out of it. They'd say, "This is funny," and I'd say, "I don't think so." They'd say, "This'll be good." I'd say, "It stinks." It didn't make any difference; we did it anyhow. I'd only argue about so far, and then let it go. And I knew better. The last two pictures I made at MGM, I knew before the camera was put up for the first scene that it was practically impossible to get a good motion picture out of them.

R. FRANKLIN: *What were those two?*

KEATON: *Sidewalks of New York* and . . .

R. FRANKLIN: *That was that patrol wagon thing, and* . . .

KEATON: Oh, I forgot. Everything happened, and it was no good.

R. FRANKLIN: *Weren't you a millionaire or something?*

KEATON: Yeah.

R. FRANKLIN: *Oh brother!*

KEATON: Absolutely impossible.

R. FRANKLIN: *Yeah. You seemed to be unhappy when you were* . . . *Of course, we just saw it on* . . .

KEATON: Another bad one was *What! No Beer?*

R. FRANKLIN: *That wasn't as bad as* . . .

KEATON: Oh, the other one was impossible.

R. FRANKLIN: What! No Beer? *wasn't too bad. You did that with Henry Armetta and* . . .

KEATON: Jimmy Durante.

R. FRANKLIN: *And Durante and so forth. I thought you didn't come off too badly in that.*

KEATON: We got criticized also for trying to do a farce. We did *Parlor, Bedroom and Bath*, and we had Charlotte Greenwood. But, that's an out-and-out farce story. Well, I shouldn't have been put into anything that was a farce, because I don't work that way. Life is too serious to do farce comedy.

JOAN FRANKLIN: *I was going to ask you, if you would mention the fine line between farce and the work that you did.*

KEATON: Farce comedy as a rule is based on a simple misunderstanding or a mistaken identity. There's always a couple of characters in that show, and if they come out and say, "Wait a minute, this is the case," all the problems would be solved. And, [there's] a farce tempo. In all farce comedies, everybody works automatically faster than they do when they're telling a legitimate story. They take things bigger. People get hysterical easy.

R. FRANKLIN: *There's a frenetic quality. Do you think that something was beginning to happen? First of all, I don't think that your comedy could ever be called slapstick comedy?*

KEATON: It was in the two-reelers.

R. FRANKLIN: *It was then, yes. But do you think something began to happen to comedy then?*

KEATON: No, you see, the minute we got into features, where an audience had to believe the story we were telling, we had to stop pie-throwing. There was never a pie thrown in any of our pictures once we started into features. No impossible gags were done.

R. FRANKLIN: *But do you think comedy in general . . . because by that time Harry Langdon was getting finished. He did the last thing with Al Jolson. Ben Turpin was about . . .*

KEATON: Sennett was through.

R. FRANKLIN: *And Sennett was through. Do you think this was a natural waning? That they then began to move into the more sophisticated comedies, which you did subsequently in stocks with* Three Men on a Horse *and that sort of thing. Do you think that something began to evolve itself then, so that comedy was on the wane?*

KEATON: No, except that the minute sound came in, it was everybody talking their heads off and going for dialogue laughs. All your writers did the same thing. Once that started, it took years to ever get anybody even to touch that type of material again.

R. FRANKLIN: *Not until Abbott and Costello came along in their own . . . and this was a poor imitation of it at best. And the Marx Brothers did their one thing a year.*
KEATON: Yeah, but the Marx Brothers—most of their laughs are dialogue laughs.

R. FRANKLIN: *But then comedy really hit the road in the middle thirties. That was about the end of it.*
KEATON: I tried every so often. You've got people now—Red Skelton could have worked in the silent pictures just as well as he does in the sound. But he was trained, and his first success and first love is radio, which is jokes. So today it's almost impossible to get Red to do a sequence without talking.

R. FRANKLIN: *His training was not unlike yours, either.*
KEATON: No, but he could do it.

R. FRANKLIN: *He got farther and farther away from it.*
KEATON: He just got further and further away.

R. FRANKLIN: *What do you think happened in your own career then? This was supposed to be the . . . the decline of the great Buster Keaton or the great decline.*
KEATON: Oh, everything happened. I got to the stage where I didn't give a darn whether school kept or not, and then I started drinking too much. When I found out that they could write stories and material better than I could anyway, what was the use of my fighting with them? It only takes about two bad pictures in a row to put the skids under you.

R. FRANKLIN: *Actually this happened to every other comedian too. Harold Lloyd says the same thing. It happened to Chaplin in his own way. So, apparently you were all in the same boat.*
KEATON: Well, Chaplin was just lazy. He could have made pictures for a long time. What was his last picture? Oh I don't mean that thing; I mean going back a few years.

R. FRANKLIN: Limelight *was the last thing he . . .*
KEATON: *Modern Times* was after *The Gold Rush.*

R. FRANKLIN: *He did* City Lights, *and then* The [Great] Dictator.
KEATON: Following *The [Great] Dictator* was when he got good and
lazy. By the time he'd decide on a subject and make it, it was three
years later or something like that. And of course, the ones that got
the greatest break in the world—and I don't think anybody ever
explained it to them—because if you go back and look at that first
Abbott and Costello picture of that army thing, you'll find a very bad
motion picture. But at the time they came out with that, there were
no Harold Lloyd pictures being made, there were no Chaplin pictures
being made, there were no Keaton pictures being made—and hadn't
been made for a couple of years or three years or something like that.
There was no opposition. And they were such a relief to the picture-
going public, to see those two screwballs. But if they'd come out with
that same picture about five years sooner, you would never have
heard of it.

R. FRANKLIN: *Now, what happened in your own work between '35 and
'40? What were you doing then?*
KEATON: Oh, I tried making a picture in Mexico, found that was
impossible. I tried making one in France, one in England.

R. FRANKLIN: *Which one did you do in England?*
KEATON: I did one called *In a Little Spanish Town* [*An Old Spanish
Custom*]. I did one in France. Oh, it was a bad picture. It was
impossible to make those types of pictures there. I couldn't do it in
Mexico, although I had a funny story for Mexico. But getting them
done right . . .

R. FRANKLIN: *Then they were dubbed.*
KEATON: Oh, I was speaking Spanish. I spoke French, too. I even did
one for Metro-Goldwyn in German; I did *Parlor, Bedroom and Bath* in
German. All I did was memorize a sentence at a time, see. Then cut,
and back to me, and I'd memorized another speech in German. I did it
in French and Spanish.

R. FRANKLIN: *You didn't care for any of them.*

KEATON: Oh, it was all right. It was awfully hard work, because by the time I satisfied the Spanish dialogue supervisor, I'd then get the French cast, and by the time I get to the German, he'd say: "Oh, I understood him very well, only he's speaking with a French-Spanish accent."

I couldn't have done the work I did and been a heavy drinker. That didn't happen to me until I started getting in trouble. I had trouble at home at the same time as I had trouble at the studio.

R. FRANKLIN: *But they had it going back to the twenties . . .*

KEATON: Oh, no.

R. FRANKLIN: *. . . because of the film* [The Buster Keaton Story], *though.*

KEATON: Oh, I know it. They had to do that, the way they constructed the story.

JOAN FRANKLIN: *I'm sure you had to be in training all the time.*

KEATON: I couldn't have done what I did on the screen . . .

R. FRANKLIN: *Through the war, did you get into the theater then? Were you doing stock then? Or, were you still making these films?*

KEATON: Oh, I came East twice. I did the *straw hat* things. I did a show called *The Gorilla*, then I did *Three Men on a Horse*.

R. FRANKLIN: *In New York, or were you still living in California?*

KEATON: Yes.

R. FRANKLIN: *You just came East?*

KEATON: Yes . . . bring your car with you and play that nine or ten weeks, whatever it is. It wasn't bad; it was fun. A year ago last summer, I did *Merton of the Movies* for ten weeks.

R. FRANKLIN: *Where'd you do that?*

KEATON: Oh, Spring Lake, in Jersey, and Hyde Park, Binghamton, Chicago.

R. FRANKLIN: *A circular.*
KEATON: Yeah. I ended up doing two weeks of it at Hartford, and then Hollywood.

R. FRANKLIN: *Your last motion picture work was the Chaplin?*
KEATON: I've only been in two pictures in the last ten years, and that's Chaplin's *Limelight* and *Around the World in Eighty Days.*

R. FRANKLIN: *And in Around the World in Eighty Days you were . . . ?*
KEATON: A railroad conductor in it.

R. FRANKLIN: *That's right. You came through on the western scene.*
KEATON: Yeah. They were going to fight a duel with guns on the train, and I said, "Be sure you hit, and don't hit my woodwork."

R. FRANKLIN: *That's right. You just came and went in that.*
KEATON: Everybody did. I must have been on the screen at least a minute and a half, and I was three weeks in Colorado on location to do it.

R. FRANKLIN: *Really, because I know that Ronald Colman went like that.*
KEATON: That's right.

R. FRANKLIN: *Now, could we take the rest of the time and talk about something that is very dear to all of our hearts? That is, there is no comedy, despite the fact that Hal Wallace says there is and a couple of other Hollywood wheels. We don't think that there is any comedy—either great, small, or indifferent—other than this Jerry Lewis person. Now would you talk about what you think has happened to it now, comedy in general and so forth?*
KEATON: Well, so dog-gone many things. For the last few years—and it still is—their conception of making that type of picture is so foreign to the way we used to think. I was called up to come out and play "play doctor" to three Skelton pictures, besides being in on the start of a couple of his, and working on them. Skelton remade three of my pictures that Metro gave him to do. In every case, in those three remakes, the second picture didn't compare to the original for laughs or entertainment. Now, all for one reason: the writers there today and the producers

insisted on improving the originals. So, all three pictures died of improvement.

R. FRANKLIN: *Just for the sake of making changes.*
KEATON: Yeah. They'd say, "We'll improve that," and in improving it, story construction went out the window, so did character. There were badly done gags, misplaced gags. They made a picture with Skelton— and were going to try to get it as near to *The General* as they could— called *A Southern Yankee*. They started that off with a battle scene, cavalry plowing over the hill towards the camera, guns going, flags waving—heavy music, very heavy music.

R. FRANKLIN: *They load all of these things—everything.*
KEATON: Everything. The minute that picture started, it came on with the fanfare and the flash. From the time the Lion roared on the screen (this is an MGM picture), the blast was on. Now, we would go out of our way to see how quiet we could start a motion picture. In other words, I wanted an audience to sit back in their seats at the start, and get comfortable. Not bring them up on the edge of their seats with the opening title and the opening scenes of the picture, but put them back in their seats. We made sure that we never got any big laughing routines in that first reel. We only wanted a few snickers, little incidental pieces of business that were not important, while we planted the plot and the characters. Then, we'd let that come.

To this day, I can't talk a modern producer into seeing it from that angle. It's so much easier for me to bring that man sitting in his seat up onto the edge of his seat, than to give him a breathing spell and bring him back up there for the finale. If I'm going to spring him right up there for the very start, how am I going to keep him there for an hour and forty minutes? You can't do it.

R. FRANKLIN: *Don't you think that people want to laugh today?*
KEATON: Just as much as they ever did.

R. FRANKLIN: *Producers say they don't want to.*
KEATON: Oh, that's nonsense.

R. FRANKLIN: *Every one of your films, when they are brought back, plays to packed houses. Even* The Jazz Singer, *when it is brought back, and this is pretty crummy, is playing to big houses. For example, on television your stuff is put on at two o'clock in the morning, and it is constantly written up that people—I know we do and we are certainly not the only ones. You must say that anybody that is willing to stay up to two o'clock or three-thirty in the morning must love something a great deal. What do you think the Hollywood idea is? Or, do you think that comedians just aren't around anymore?*

KEATON: They're around. They come and go. You lose one, and a new one comes along to take his place. But for this type of material, your new batch has never been trained that way. They haven't had that experience.

R. FRANKLIN: *It seems inconceivable that some producer doesn't ask you to make three comedies. You've obviously lost none of your touch. Like this little girl who is sitting here is going to grow up in it, and at least I grew up in it with Raymond Hatton and Wallace Beery. These were the first pictures that I can remember,* In the Army *and* In the Navy.[14] *Don't you think that it is pretty horrible that these little children are going to grow up and not see any Buster Keatons or Harold Lloyds?*

KEATON: Things change so fast and go in circles: three or four years from now, they're all liable to be doing Sennett comedies. You can't predict that. You never know how they are going to change. But you find yourself back doing them. They say pantomime's a lost art. It's never been a lost art and never will be, because it's too natural to do. Every now and then, even today, Jackie Gleason does a whole fifteen-minute sequence. Sid Caesar's been doing it on and off, ever since he's been in television. Every now and then, Skelton does one. They all do it. He brought over a clown from France . . .

R. FRANKLIN: *Jacques Tati.*

KEATON: Yes.

---

[14] The two films starring Raymond Hatton and Wallace Beery, both directed by Edward Sutherland, were *Behind the Front* (1926) and *We're in the Navy Now* (1927).

JOAN FRANKLIN: *Marcel Marceau.*

R. FRANKLIN: *What do you think of him?*

KEATON: The way he works? He's marvelous, as far as that goes. But that's a different type of pantomime. I don't do what they call old English or French pantomime. I never did—like you point this finger, and that means, "I want to put a ring on your finger," or you put your hand over your heart and it means, "I love you." Your finger to your lips means, "One little kiss." I never did that in my life. But body action pretty near told the story for me. You could almost tell by the way I turned and walked whether I was happy or mad or . . .

R. FRANKLIN: *That's right, without any expression.*

KEATON: Yeah. I didn't have to worry about expression—just simply body action told you that.

R. FRANKLIN: *What changes have you seen come about in Hollywood. Let's just have a closing thought on that. We have about a minute.*

KEATON: Well, it's hard to say what's happened there because television has wrecked it—all your studios. The picture business to me right now is as dead as it can be. You've got to spend five or six million dollars to get a picture that's worth going to see. Program pictures just simply don't draw, and you're a cinch to lose money if you make one. Well, that's not a very good situation to have. I'd like to see them merged, the way it should be done, and pay television . . . and pay for your television the same as you pay for your phone or your gas or your electricity or your water bill. The man comes and reads the meter, and you're charged accordingly. He can also tell by the channels what you've been watching, so they know the ratings. With that done, you could afford to make motion pictures for television that would get you your money back. But it's impossible at present to ever go out and spend a million dollars for a picture for television, because you can't get that kind of money back.

R. FRANKLIN: *Now one last question. Hollywood has been called the cruelest city in the world. Let's have your thought on that.*

KEATON: Oh, it can be. Well no, New York can be that too. You can be a Broadway star here one night, and something happens, and out—nobody knows you on the street. They forget you ever lived. That can happen in Hollywood, too.

R. FRANKLIN: *Is it a new kind of Hollywood now, a business Hollywood, more so than in the old days?*
KEATON: No, it hasn't changed. There's only been one radical change in Hollywood, and that was when sound first came in, because it brought a whole new cycle, I mean whole new factions: songwriters, dialogue directors, stage directors, stage producers. A whole new faction moved into Hollywood, and from then on, for some silly reason, there was class distinction. People who got $500 a week were seldom seen with somebody getting $1000 a week—you'd never see them at their house. Whereas in the old days, it was a common thing for a prop man in our studio to say, "Good morning, Joe," when the boss of the studio came walking past. We didn't used to have to put policemen on the gates to stop each other from going to the other one's studio.

R. FRANKLIN: *It was a more personal thing then.*
KEATON: Oh, sure. I'm liable to go to Mr. Schenck's house and there'd be the assistant cameraman, invited to the party. Then. But that doesn't happen today!

R. FRANKLIN: *Sound brought the big change, the big transition.*
KEATON: Yeah.

R. FRANKLIN: *I guess we've done it.*

Interview with Buster Keaton

TONY THOMAS / 1960

KEATON: I was born on a one-night stand in Kansas in a little town called Piqua. My mother . . . the show traveled on, and my mother stayed there for two weeks and then rejoined the show with me.

THOMAS: *Obviously, your people were "show biz." What exactly did they do?*

KEATON: My dad was a comedian and a great eccentric dancer—tricks. He wasn't exactly an acrobat, but darn near. And my mother played musical instruments and danced with him. Of course, when I came into the act, then they got the idea of trying to show the audience how to bring up children correctly. And every time I did something he didn't like, he'd either take me by the back of the neck and throw me through a piece of scenery or kick me clean off the stage, through chairs, tables, or anything that would be in the way. I grew up getting knocked around.

THOMAS: *Isn't there a story that a Society for the Prevention of Cruelty to Children complained about your parents?*

KEATON: Yes. Well—yeah—well, we ran into that trouble every place when I joined the act. They took me into New York when I was around five years old. Number one is that . . . at that time the Gerry Society Law in New York which hadn't been very important yet—it was more to

Recorded at Keaton's home in Woodland Hills, California, March 1960; transcript from *Voices from the Hollywood Past*, with Tony Thomas, Delos Records, F 25412, Track 8 (1975). Printed by permission of Delos Records.

buck child labor, than anything else, in the factories. But the law there says no child under the age of seven can even walk on the stage then. Well, we got around that because they lied about my age. They said I was seven when I was just five.

THOMAS: *That's when you started to perform, at the age of five?*
KEATON: No, I had been getting a salary since I was four years old. And the next thing was that the law said that no child under the age of sixteen can walk wire, juggle, do acrobatics, roller-skate, play musical instruments—all of those—an awful list of things. But none of them said that you couldn't kick him in the face.

THOMAS: *No.*
KEATON: And for that technicality, we were permitted to work, but we did get stopped often.

THOMAS: *This was the heyday of vaudeville—American vaudeville?*
KEATON: Your heyday of vaudeville started around the turn of the century, around 1900. B. F. Keith was the first man to glorify his theaters and made them as high class as any of the legit theaters we had in the country. The theater he built in Boston first, it cost him a million dollars to build, and when you go back sixty years a million dollars was an awful lot of money.

THOMAS: *A lot.*
KEATON: Then, one in Philadelphia he built was almost as expensive. And, he took vaudeville and raised it from the ten, twenty, and thirty-cent class up to the dollar-and-a-half class, and really added class to vaudeville. Well, I saw that!

THOMAS: *Was it fun in those days?*
KEATON: Yes. Your high-class vaudeville theaters did the best business of any type of theaters in the country. And I knew all the greats acts and a lot of great people. I've worked with . . . you can imagine. Now to you, it sounds like ancient history. I've even worked with Lillian Russell.

THOMAS: *Was she really beautiful?*
KEATON: The most gorgeous woman I ever saw in my life.

THOMAS: *But you would also travel in vaudeville all over the United States?*
KEATON: That's right.

THOMAS: *Canada, too?*
KEATON: That's right.

THOMAS: *Now, that must have been a pretty hard way to make a living?*
KEATON: Well, no. The traveling part didn't bother us. We were used to hotels and trains and boats, and we had a summer home. We didn't work in the summer. Our summer home was in Muskegon, Michigan. There was a whole actors' colony there. We got to spend three months a year there. We used to look forward to so many towns, too, you see. For instance, we had a German boarding house in New York that was a home to us, because we'd be in New York more often than any-place else. And even when we laid off a week—or something like that— we'd generally get on a train and go to New York, spend that week there.

THOMAS: *Now, wasn't 1915 the year that you started your career in pictures?*
KEATON: No, '17.

THOMAS: *How did that come about?*
KEATON: Well, we had trouble with the United Booking Office—my father did—and there was a strike coming up, an actors' strike, which didn't happen often, but this was one of the first attempts. And I sent my folks home, and I went to New York alone and went up to our rep-resentative and said I want to work alone—I put Pa and Ma in the home in Muskegon. He says, "All right." He took me over to the Shuberts' office, and the Shuberts signed me immediately to go into *The Passing Show of* 1917, at the Winter Garden. And while I was leaving that office, walking down the street, I ran into an old vaudeville performer who was with Fatty Arbuckle at the Keystone, first thing. And Arbuckle's

contract with Sennett was up, and he had just signed with Joe Schenck, an independent producer at that time. He was making pictures with his wife, Norma Talmadge, and her sister, Constance Talmadge, and he signed Arbuckle.

Arbuckle says, "Have you ever been in a motion picture?"

And I says, "No, I've never even been in a studio."

He'd seen me work on the stage. He says, "Well, come on down to our studio, the Norma Talmadge studio over on Forty-eighth Street, and do a bit with me. See how you like it."

I says, "When are you shooting?"

He says, "Tomorrow morning we start."

I says, "Right. I'll be there."

So, I'm waiting for rehearsals to start in the Winter Garden. I get down [to the studio]. I did that picture, and I was fascinated by everything there was about motion pictures. The first thing I did, I wanted to get in the cutting room, see how they put the scenes together, in the projecting room, and tear a camera to pieces, and everything else.

THOMAS: *It was love at first sight with pictures?*

KEATON: Yes. And digging up material, I was a veteran at this. I didn't know it at the time, but I turned out to be Arbuckle's whole writing staff for gags.

THOMAS: *Not only that, but your background on the stage prior to that had been visual comedy . . .*

KEATON: That's right, all visual.

THOMAS: *. . . which adapted itself very well to pictures.*

KEATON: That's right.

THOMAS: *Slapstick.*

KEATON: So, I only . . . instead of doing the one bit in the picture, I stayed there and worked the whole week and went all the way through the picture. And I went up to my representative and said, "I don't want to go to the Winter Garden. I want to stay in pictures."

THOMAS: *What was your impression of Hollywood when you came out here for the first time to work?*
KEATON: It was marvelous. Well, we actually worked harder. We didn't mind it.

THOMAS: *All hours of the day?*
KEATON: Oh, you never knew. We were liable to decide to work all night or . . . and we never had schedules, not an office like ours. Number one, I owned my own studio. I owned all the equipment—the studio owned it all. So, if we said, "Let's set up the camera," it didn't cost us a cent because the cameraman was under salary for the year. The cameras we owned—we were not paying rental on anything. And when I finally got into feature-length pictures in '22, all they wanted from me was two pictures a year—and that wasn't taking life easy. We'd have been really pressed if we had tried to turn out a third picture a year. Two was ideal—give you a spring and a fall release.

THOMAS: *Tell me, how did the business of the frozen face come about, the dead pan?*
KEATON: That came from the stage. As I grew up, I was the type of comedian that the minute I laughed at what I did the audience didn't. So I just automatically learned to take everything seriously, and by the time I was—oh, something like—ten or eleven years old working with a sober face was mechanical with me—never even thought about it. So, when I went into pictures I was twenty-one, and I got the reputation immediately [of being] called "frozen face," "blank pan," and things like that. We went into the projection room and ran our first two pictures to see if I'd smiled.

THOMAS: *You made sure you didn't.*
KEATON: Well, I hadn't paid any attention to it. We found out I hadn't. It was just a natural way of acting.

THOMAS: *Would you hope for anything more out of your career than what you've had?*
KEATON: No, I had a very interesting career. In other words, I have no complaints.

Interview with Buster Keaton

STUDS TERKEL/1960

TERKEL: *The world of entertainment has come a long way. There have been new inventions, new devices, and yet the art of acting is still an eternal one. A few nights ago, I was in a movie house in the neighborhood seeing the film, When Comedy Was King, and it re-created . . . excerpts of some of the fantastically ingenious two-reelers of some of the geniuses of the past—not of now, but of the silent film. There was a piece of Chaplin, a piece of Langdon, and a piece of Buster Keaton, who is our . . . we are delighted to have as our guest this morning. Buster Keaton, I think of you—aside from this film I saw the other night—I think of you in terms of some of these critics who speak of Keaton, one of the geniuses of the silent film. Your approach in so many of these films, these two-reelers, these feature films you did, was the man never spoke, of course, but how was it done? There were subtitles.*

KEATON: That's right. Oh yeah. No, your lips moved. You spoke, and in the cutting room you simply ran the film through your fingers down to where . . . just where your mouth opened, and the second syllable you'd cut, slapping your subtitles—it explains what you are talking about. And, when you come back, you pick it up just as your mouth is about to close. So that's the way it was done.

TERKEL: *But you had to say, you had to communicate to the audience. There was only one way—through action, through pantomime.*

Archived at the Chicago Historical Society (T0201); interview conducted September 5, 1960, transcribed by Kevin W. Sweeney (2004). Printed by permission of the Chicago Historical Society. A much abbreviated version of this interview was published in Studs Terkel, *The Spectator: Talk about Movies and Plays with the People Who Make Them* (New York: The New Press, 1999), pp. 30–37.

KEATON: That's right. We eliminated subtitles just as fast as we could, if we could possibly tell it in action.

TERKEL: *I remember you once told me something about ten years ago, about you and Charlie Chaplin having friendly contests of who could do the feature film with the least amount of subtitles.*
KEATON: I think Chaplin won that. One of his pictures [had] something like twenty-one titles, and I had twenty-three.

TERKEL: *And this is for an hour and a half film, something like that.*
KEATON: Yeah, a seven-reel picture. We started off with . . . our features were only five-reelers, but I think around . . . um see '25, we're into seven reels. It became a standard length for all feature pictures.

TERKEL: *Thinking about . . .*
KEATON: But another thing too, you got to call attention to, is the average picture used two hundred and forty titles. That was about the average.

TERKEL: *Two hundred and forty was the average.*
KEATON: Yes, and the most I ever used was fifty-six.

TERKEL: *Fifty-six, and one time you used twenty-three or so. Again, we think of you saying something to. . . . At this theater, at this movie house, there were young kids, couples, who weren't even born—perhaps their parents weren't born—at the times these films were made. Yet, they were laughing, they were howling. And, it gives me the impression that this humor is eternal, that there seems to be a hunger for it now too, there is so little of it today. So I was wondering about your feelings as you watch TV. You notice that some of the gags are repeated, aren't they?*
KEATON: They have to; you can't dig material up that fast. I refused to do a weekly show because it is the fastest way to a sanitarium that I know of. Drive you absolutely out of your mind, trying to dig up. . . . Well, I always tried to dig up new material, and it's just impossible.

TERKEL: *Well, back in the days of the silents, when you invented a gag, a sight gag, it had to be for each film or for that matter for each reel of the film. It had to be fresh and different each time.*

KEATON: Yes. We didn't repeat gags, and we didn't steal from each other either.

TERKEL: *Well, I'm thinking about this film I saw the other night. You were a moving man. You were Buster Keaton without the smile, and you had the pancake hat on—I'll ask you about that in a moment—and you were the moving man, but you got involved in a big police parade, and there were thousands of police, and it became like a dream. You gummed up the parade, and they were chasing you.*
KEATON: Well, I tried to cut through the parade, and I couldn't do it, so I just joined it. And before anybody could stop me, some anarchist up on top of a building threw a bomb down on the police parade, but it lit in my wagon. So, when it went off, the whole police force was after me.

TERKEL: *And it was like a dream. There were thousands of police who were chasing this one man, never quite caught you. Now we come to your art, the art of . . . the way you moved, your body, the acrobatics. Where did this originate?*
KEATON: Oh, just doing a hit-or-miss routine there, just ducking cops in all directions. Just a common ordinary chase sequence.

TERKEL: *This chase sequence—how much of it was planned way in the beginning and how much came out in the actual doing? How much was improvised, you know?*
KEATON: Well, as a rule, oh about 50 percent you have in your mind before you start the picture, and the rest you develop as you're making it.

TERKEL: *As you are making it . . . the ideas come to mind.*
KEATON: Yes.

TERKEL: *As I look at you now, Buster Keaton, I'm going to . . . I see something here that James Agee, the film critic, wrote about you in his very excellent article, "Comedy's Greatest Era," that appeared in* Life *a couple of years ago. "Keaton's face ranked almost with Lincoln's as an early American archetype; it was haunting, handsome, almost beautiful, yet it was irreducibly*

*funny; he improved matters by topping it off with a deadly horizontal hat, as
flat and thin as a phonograph record. One can never forget Keaton wearing it,
standing erect at the prow as his little boat is being launched. The boat goes
grandly down the skids and, just as grandly, straight on to the bottom.
Keaton never budges. The last you see of him, the water lifts the hat off the
stoic head and it floats away."[1] The hat . . .*
KEATON: That's right.

TERKEL: *You know what film he is talking about?*
KEATON: It's called *The Boat.*

TERKEL: *That was* The Boat. *What of the hat? The paraphernalia first—
how did the paraphernalia . . . ?*
KEATON: Well, I had a similar hat on the stage before I went into pictures. I went into pictures when I was twenty-one years old, in the
spring of 1917.

TERKEL: *And you were part of an acting family.*
KEATON: Yes.

TERKEL: *I understand it was Harry Houdini gave you the name of "Buster."*
KEATON: Well, I was born with the Keaton-Houdini Medicine Show
Company on a one-night stand in Kansas.

TERKEL: *And what was your work at the time when you were the kid in
this act?*
KEATON: Well, my old man was an eccentric comic. And soon as I
could take care of myself at all on my feet, he had slap shoes on me and
big baggy pants, and then just started doing gags with me, especially
kicking me clean across the stage or taking me by the back of the neck
and throwing me. And as I grew used to doing it and knew how to do
it, the throws became longer and by the time I got up to around seven

[1]James Agee, "Comedy's Greatest Era," *Life,* vol. 27, no. 10 (September 5, 1949), p. 82;
reprinted in *Agee on Film: Reviews and Comments* (Boston: Beacon Press, 1958), p. 15.

and eight years old, we were called the roughest act that was ever in the history of the stage.

TERKEL: *And so when the movies came along, you were a veteran now at being tossed about.*

KEATON: I was a veteran when I went into pictures.

TERKEL: *Of course, the question would come up of the approach of you and humor—first your face. The lack of the smile, the sorrowful sad face, of course, made the audience howl all the more.*

KEATON: Well, you see I learned that from the stage . . . that I was the type of comedian that if I laughed at what I did, the audience didn't. So, I just automatically got to that stage where the more seriously I took my work, the better laughs I got.

TERKEL: *You were always, in everything you did, there was always the dead seriousness . . .*

KEATON: Yes, so by the time I went into pictures, not smiling was mechanical with me. I just didn't pay any attention to it.

TERKEL: *Now you just used the word, "mechanical," which brings us to another point. Agee, and Iris Barry (in this excellent book by Griffith and Mayer), speak of you as the master of what they call "the mechanical gag."[2] Chaplin in* Modern Times *was kidding the machine, but there is a difference between the two that Iris Barry points out that I think if you could expand on this: "Buster Keaton moves in the mechanized world of today like the inhabitant of another planet. He gazes with frozen bewilderment at a nightmare reality. Inventions and contrivances like deck chairs and railroad engines seem . . . animate . . . to him, in the same measure that human beings become impersonal. Without friends or relatives, he is generally incapable of associating with his fellow-beings on a 'human basis,' but mechanical devices, though often inimical to him, are . . . the only 'beings' who can*

---

[2] Iris Barry qtd. in Richard Griffith and Arthur Mayer, *The Movies* (New York: Simon & Schuster, 1957), p. 155.

'understand' him" [155]. And then she [Iris Barry] goes on to speak of
Chaplin escaping into the realm of freedom in his films, but you actually
throw your humanity into the machine world, and you make the machine so
much a part of yourself. Could you tell us a little bit about this, you and the
machines? The way you work with . . .

KEATON: Well, I guess I found out that I get my best material working
with something like that. In other words, I was one of your original "do
it yourself" fellas. I may not know how to do a carpenter's job, but I set
out to build a house.

TERKEL: *And then as you build it, it becomes funnier and funnier.*

KEATON: Everybody knows that you are going to get in trouble when
you start that.

TERKEL: *Thinking about today, I mean, why your humor is so alive*
today. Today, with more and more machines, the Keaton humor in those
early two-reelers seems even more pertinent today. Have you thought of . . .
has the idea of re-creating silent films using today as a basis occurred
to you?

KEATON: Oh, I wouldn't try to re-create those films. I'm past the age
of being able to do . . .

TERKEL: *The jumping around?*

KEATON: The wild action stuff that I did. But I still try, but I'm not
going to remake any of those. I'm going to reissue them.

TERKEL: *Oh, you are?*

KEATON: Yes, I'm just back from Europe and went through to Munich
and then passing Paris I found out that this *When Comedy Was King* was
playing in four theaters there. And then I found out that they were
playing at six theaters in London, about three in West Berlin, and even
down into Munich, which is one of their big labs, their studios. An
exhibitor says, "Have you got any pictures we can have, I mean the
silents?" Says, "No, but I'm going to make sure you get 'em." So, in
Munich, I made arrangements to give them dupe negatives because I
found prints. The original negatives . . . practically gone, but finding
good prints of all these old pictures that I could get a good dupe

negative off of, and give 'em to them there in Munich. They will make me new prints, some with the subtitles . . . in French, some in German, some in Italian, some in Spanish, and some in English. And all we would do is put a full orchestration music track to those silent pictures, with no moderator, and leave the old-fashioned subtitles in, but a good musical score behind 'em, and re-release 'em. And this is going to happen within the next couple of months.

TERKEL: *Releasing features, as well as these short ones?*
KEATON: Start in Europe first, because television hasn't wrecked all the neighborhood motion picture theaters there. So, you got an awful lot of theaters. Well, soon as I see what they are going to do there, then I'll have prints made for here.

TERKEL: *Are* The Navigator *and* The General *among them?*
KEATON: Yes. I'll have eighteen two-reelers and ten features.

TERKEL: *One thing is pretty clear, apparently, from what you tell me—that the art of the silent film is universal. Doesn't matter what, there is no language barrier involved.*
KEATON: No. We found out that long ago. Now, mind, is this picture you saw *Cops?*

TERKEL: *Yes.*
KEATON: It is exactly forty years old.

TERKEL: *It is hard to believe.*
KEATON: Made in 1920. The youngest picture of the silents that I'll have will be a . . . '27, which will be thirty-three years old. That should be the youngest.

TERKEL: *The most recent. Thinking about you and parodying, kidding some of the serious silent films too, I noticed in this book of Griffith and Mayer, there's Keaton as Hamlet [159]. But here you are as the cowboy hero. What happened?*
KEATON: I tried to be Bill Hart in that picture.

TERKEL: *The Frozen North.*
KEATON: Yeah. I had a little trouble, but I tried my best to be Bill Hart, so much so that Bill Hart didn't speak to me for a couple of years after I made it. He thought I was kidding him. I said, "I didn't kid you, Bill, I was just trying to be an actor like you, and I didn't quite make it."

TERKEL: *[A little chuckle] Would you mind telling us about that William S. Hart, the strong silent hero, who always loses the girl, and noble hero?*
KEATON: That was only the last part of his career. For some reason, he kind of turned ham on us. He was a great actor, but he got hammy at the end of his career. He always looked for the opportunity to . . . cry, even with two guns strapped to his side out in the desert. If the girl turned and looked at another man, tears ran down his cheeks. There's nothing you could do about it. He was his own producer.

TERKEL: *So what did you do in your film?*
KEATON: Oh, I cried too, glycerin tears.

TERKEL: *But down one eye, you told me.*
KEATON: Yeah.

TERKEL: *What of . . . you take off Cecil B. DeMille too in the big extravaganzas back then?*
KEATON: Oh, anytime I had a bathroom scene or a bedroom scene I tried to make a DeMille set out of it.

TERKEL: *I'm looking at a picture or a photograph of you, the film, which I don't know, called Daydreams in 1922 . . . and you dreamt of being a famous surgeon.*[3]
KEATON: Well, this was a vision.

TERKEL: *Of Hamlet.*
KEATON: In that picture, there is like a dream, a dream sequence. I imagine myself as a great physician.

---

[3] Griffith and Mayer, p. 158.

TERKEL: *I'm thinking since you mentioned dream . . . coming back to the movie involving the cops, the one in* When Comedy Was King. *Did the thought occur to you it was like a dream? That all your movies were like a wild dream? Now, we dream of strange things.*

KEATON: Some of the two-reelers were. We got so wild and crazy in 'em. We lost all of that when we started making feature pictures. We had to stop doing impossible gags and what we call cartoon gags. They had to be believable or your story wouldn't hold up.

TERKEL: *Now let's see if I can follow that. For a feature picture, then, you had to abandon the wild gags.*

KEATON: That's right. For instance, I'm the fellow that got up on a high diving platform at a country club and did a swan dive off of it and missed the pool and went through the ground. People come running up and look down the hole and the scene fades out and the title comes in and says, "Years later." I faded back in on the country club, the pool was empty and grass growing into it, and the whole place neglected, nobody around, and I came up out of the hole with a Chinese wife and two kids. That was a fade-out of a two-reeler. We wouldn't have dared use that in a feature picture.

TERKEL: *But still you have . . . you still use a lot of imagination though, as in* The General *or* Sherlock Jr.

KEATON: Oh yes.

TERKEL: *A lot of the critics love to talk about your chases, the imagination of a chase. Today, when we see a chase, it is one word, one dimension. Someone chases around and there's a verbal gag. But when you were being chased. . . . There is talk of a film. Is it* Sherlock Jr.? *You miss the girl and the girl misses you, and this goes on for—it seems for hours, and yet each time it seems something different. Finally, you fall down a chute and you land on a . . . I think the plank breaks and you drop right in her arms.*

KEATON: Yes, that's in *The Navigator.*

TERKEL: The Navigator. *How did a gag like this come into being?*

KEATON: Well, those . . . we sit around and talk about it for quite a while before we start the picture and then take advantage of anything that happens to add to it. This is a shock to anybody who is in the motion picture business today—I mean your veterans of the pictures of the last twenty-five years or so that didn't know the silent days. A feature-length picture . . . neither Chaplin, Harold Lloyd, or myself ever had a script. That sounds impossible to anyone today in the picture business. We never even thought of writing a script; we didn't need to. By the time we had talked and worked out what we thought was a picture, for instance . . . we always got a start. People always come up with a start. Says, that's funny, that's a good start. All right, we want to know the finish right then and there, see. There's nothing else to work on but the finish, and if we can't round it out to something we like, we throw that one away and start on a new one. But when we get the start and the finish, we've got it, because the middle we can always take care of. That's easy.

So, by the time we get through talking about it and you got this all set, enough to start, my prop man knows the props he's going to have to get, the wardrobe man knows the wardrobe, the guy that builds the sets he knows what sets you want, and you help him design 'em. There's no need for a script. We all know what we are going to do. And if I build a nice set here, says, we got to make this an important set, make it look good and so forth. We find out that the routine I intended to do in there is laying an egg, is not holding up, but a broom closet off of it got me in trouble. So I end up shooting only two minutes of film in the big set and half a reel in the broom closet. So what good would a script have been to me? We just throw gags out right and left when we're shooting because they don't stand out and they don't work well, and the accidental ones come.

TERKEL: *Here's the case of the actual freshness, the fresh routine coming out of the accident. This is, I suppose, the accidental art you might cause. Nothing—you have a beginning and an end and that's all.*
KEATON: That's right.

TERKEL: *And let what happens happen, depending upon your imagination.*
KEATON: We could always go into any story and pad and fill in the middle. That was the easy part.

TERKEL: *You would direct some of these films, too.*
KEATON: Quite a few pictures, I would take a director with me and just co-direct with him, but the majority I did alone.

TERKEL: *What about . . . this would also make the other actors, too, be more imaginative, challenge them, too. They would do something . . .*
KEATON: Oh yes, oh yes. We want to. Another thing we didn't do in those days that they do today is that we didn't rehearse a scene to perfection. We didn't want that because it was mechanical then. We'd much rather . . . for any of our big rough-house scenes where there is a lot of falls and people hitting each other, we never rehearsed those. We only just sat down and talked about it, and, says, now he drops that chair, you come through that door and come through fast, and this person here sees you come and throws up their hands and from the center door you can see it. Now you come through and just about hit him. If you miss him, get her.

Now that's the way we laid those scenes out because when we did those rough-house scenes, if you had to do it the second time, invariably somebody skinned up an elbow or bumped a knee or something like that, and now they will shy away from it the next take or they will favor it. See, you seldom got a scene like that as good the second time. You generally got them that first one, and anybody in that scene is free to do as he pleases as long as he keeps that action going. So, even your extras can use their imagination.

TERKEL: *Even the extras can use their imagination . . .*
KEATON: Yeah.

TERKEL: *. . . 'cause what you are saying here to me is a very pertinent point: even the extras can use . . . we're so accustomed to have everything planned today . . . a multimillion dollar project. Everything is planned.*
KEATON: They rehearse scenes to perfection before they ever turn the camera over. And with us, it used to be the other way. We tried to eliminate that. We didn't want anything to look mechanical.

TERKEL: *Maybe that is one of the reasons there was so much laughter in the house the other night at* When Comedy Was King, *is that you had the feeling—I mean the younger people and I had this feeling—that what we were seeing was happening now. That it had happened only once. It was not something that was pre-done and done and done.*

KEATON: I'll show you. For instance, Hank Mann one time when he was a newcomer . . . Sennett had never heard of him, nobody else had, but he happened to get in as an extra in one of the [Keystone] Kop chase scenes. And he wanted to do something, and he hadn't the slightest idea of what to do, until the last second. He was standing outside of a building that had caught fire and the police had sent for the fire department, so he's got the fire department and the police department in the scene. Hank Mann came out of the burning building, took a look around and put a cigarette in his mouth and lit it off of the burning building, and walked off. And in the projecting room, Sennett saw it, and he says, "Who was that so and so?"

Says, "Well, it was one of the extra guys."

"Well, get him. He's all right. We keep him here for a while."

TERKEL: *It was as simple as that: Sennett saw an unknown using his imagination.*

KEATON: With a cigarette off of a burning building.

TERKEL: *Since you've mentioned Mack Sennett, we think of the Keystone Kops. I guess one of the reasons there's so much laughter, too, in these early films is pomposity is being kidded or authority, a cop, say. A cop was always . . . kidded, but there was always a great deal of laughter involved here. Was this part of the pattern of these films?*

KEATON: Well . . .

TERKEL: *You know, a snow-ball-at-the-top-hat idea.*

KEATON: Oh yes, sure. Or, like throwing a pie. There's another thing there too. You can hit the wrong people with a pie, get an audience mad at you.

TERKEL: *Wow, what do you mean?*

KEATON: There are certain characters you just don't hit with a pie. We found that out a long time ago.

TERKEL: *Whom don't you hit with a pie? The girls were hit with a pie.*

KEATON: Oh, they don't mind that at all. I remember a lot of people who wanted to hit Lillian Gish so bad because she was always so sweet and innocent. But now, for instance in television—this is about eight years ago, something like that—Milton Berle got Ed Sullivan over to make an appearance on his show, and he hit Ed Sullivan with a pie, and that audience froze up on him, and Milton didn't get another laugh while he was on that stage.

TERKEL: *Well, now, that's a very strange thing. I'm just trying to think about that. Offhand, it would seem to be funny. You are hitting someone who is deadpan, you know, with a pie. Wouldn't that be funny? Why? He became a sacred figure in the meantime, is that the idea? Someone who is so serious you can't kid?*
KEATON: No, there are just certain people you just don't hit with a pie. That's all there is to it.

TERKEL: *Would this have happened in silent films, I wonder?*
KEATON: Oh sure.

TERKEL: *There are certain people you can't hit with a pie.*
KEATON: If I had a *grande dame* who is dogging it, putting it on. She's a grey-haired woman but she was so overbearing and everything else that the audience would like to hit her, then you could hit her with a pie and they'd laugh their heads off. But if she was a legitimate—an old lady and a sincere character—you wouldn't dare hit her.

TERKEL: *I haven't thought of that.*
KEATON: If she's a phony, that's different. The same thing goes with the men.

TERKEL: *In almost all those films, though, there were enough people to hit because you were kidding all the frailties that are in . . .*
KEATON: I'll show you how seriously they used to take our stories. In *The Navigator*, with an ocean liner with nobody on but the girl and myself, we had drifted across the Pacific Ocean on a dead ship—no water running, no lights, no nothing. So we are just like being on a desert island, trying to survive. And we run aground stern first off a cannibal island, and through the binoculars I can see that they are the

wild type of cannibals, they are headhunters. Well, it was just a matter of time that they are going to come out there and get onto this ship. And we spring a leak in the stuffing box, which means we can see this water pouring in around the driving shaft. It can't be plugged from the inside; it's got to be done from outside. Well, automatically there's deep-sea diving equipment right there in the set with us. So, the girl helps me put it on, and she's up there to pump air to me.

Well, we laid out this gag in advance and had it built by the Llewellyn Iron Works in Los Angeles. We got about twelve hundred solid rubber fish about a foot long and hung 'em on cat gut, violin strings that are transparent under water. And then hung 'em from this rigging so that a school of fish . . . we could make a school of fish go past, circle around back of the camera and continue, and with one spot to break it when we wanted to. So my gag was, while I'm down there trying to fix that stuffing box, that a big fish came up and tried to go through the school and couldn't make it. And I see a starfish clinging to a rock, so I got the starfish off of the rock and let it grab my breastplate. I stepped into the middle of the school of fish and brought it to a stop, and then turned and brought the big fish through, and then turned—I directed traffic—and then went back to my job.

Well, the gag photographed beautifully. We preview the picture, and it lays a beautiful egg, not a giggle from the audience. We can't figure it out. We get home. Says, it might be one of those things, the mechanics of it, that the audience tried to figure out how-the-thunder we ever got a shot like that. We're actually photographing around twenty feet deep. Well, says, we'll try it at the next preview and see. Next preview, the same thing. It finally dawned on us what it was. I went down there to stuff that stuffing box to keep the girl and me from falling into the hands of these cannibals, and I had no license in the world to stop to go help a fish go through the traffic.

TERKEL: *It was simple as that.*
KEATON: Simple as that.

TERKEL: *They took seriously the whole situation.*
KEATON: That's how seriously . . . although I'm getting laughs trying to stuff the stuffing box, but as long as I kept to my job . . .

TERKEL: *But their mind was on the situation you and the girl were in.*
KEATON: That's right. Now to prove it, we take it out of the picture and of course our picture travels the way it is supposed to and finished great. And I took that sequence and put it in with what they call the trailers. In other words . . . "Coming next week, Keaton in *The Navigator*"—a few of the scenes, high spots, I just show a couple of flashes of this and that. And this scene was in it, and it got an out-and-out belly laugh.

TERKEL: *That got the belly laugh, when it was out of context because they weren't worried about the actual trouble you and the girl were in.*
KEATON: That's right. I did a picture called *The Cameraman*, one of the silents. A newsreel cameraman, I got into a tong war down in Chinatown in New York trying to photograph things, and I got cornered by them. And they didn't want any pictures to go out, so they started after me. So, I'm down at the last reel of the picture, and it was a very good picture for us. It was a big laughing picture. And I got down to the finish there, and when they started for me I ran down fire escapes and rooftops and everything else to get away from them, and to the finish of the picture. We previewed that, and our last reel takes a nose dive.

TERKEL: *What was wrong?*
KEATON: The rest being swell, see.

TERKEL: *What happened?*
KEATON: We finally figured that one out. I deserted that camera. The audience didn't like it.

TERKEL: *You say you deserted the camera.*
KEATON: I left the camera there, when the Chinamen started after me. So we have to go back and retake that sequence. I don't desert the camera. I kept it with me, and then it was all right.

TERKEL: *I see. It had to be with you all the time.*
KEATON: Yes. I didn't dare desert it.

TERKEL: *Because they were identifying themselves with you all the way.*
KEATON: The camera was too important to me, for me to just desert it.

TERKEL: *What about the matter of laughs, building for a laugh?*
KEATON: So, if you don't think they took our stories seriously . . .

TERKEL: *What are the ways you would build for the end, which was the belly laugh? Would you plan, you know? First it was a titter, a giggle or . . .*
KEATON: No. We always tried to construct from that . . . always tried for that. And none of us ever made a picture that we didn't go back and set that camera up for at least three days, sometimes longer. It wasn't a case of adding laughs here or there that failed us, as it was to help the high spots. We needed something else to happen, about now, to help build that laugh bigger.

TERKEL: *But it has to be part of the whole. It can't be brought in from nowhere. It has to be part of that whole design.*
KEATON: No. A poison thing to us was a misplaced gag—a great gag, but it didn't belong there.

TERKEL: *Even though you have a beginning and an end and that is all, at the same time there is a unity throughout, even though that thing happens accidentally.*
KEATON: Well, when I say the padding in the middle is easy, because once you got the start and you know where you are going, that's the easiest part to go in and gag up and keep your story alive.

TERKEL: *Mr. Keaton, you know you said something about today you wouldn't be able to do certain of the routines you did some forty years ago, yet a funny thing happened.* Limelight *is not too old. You and Chester Conklin, I believe, were in Charlie Chaplin's* Limelight.
KEATON: That's right.

TERKEL: *When that tremendous vaudeville acrobatic routine . . . and you bounced around like a rubber ball there. The three of you did.*
KEATON: Oh, I still turn over, as far as that goes.

TERKEL: *What of the art of Chaplin? I think when I met you ten years ago, you mentioned* A Woman of Paris, *a film he directed, I think,* A Woman of Paris.
KEATON: That's right.

TERKEL: *His greatness as a director there. What was it about him as a director?*
KEATON: Well, Charlie was one of the best directors ever in the picture business. *A Woman of Paris* with Adolphe Menjou, his first motion picture.

TERKEL: *Edna Purviance.*
KEATON: Edna Purviance was the girl who had always been Chaplin's leading lady. And he made this high-society drama, the background, Paris. He just directed it, and for the first time on the screen, in that dramatic story, he kept doing things by suggestion. Well, every director in pictures went to see that picture more than once just to study that technique. He absolutely revolutionized the direction of pictures.

TERKEL: *You say, "by suggestion." Could you sort of give an example?*
KEATON: Well, he wanted Adolphe Menjou . . . that he wanted the audience to know that Menjou paid for the apartment that Edna Purviance was living in. And the way he did it was that he called on her one evening to take her out, give her a little bouquet or something like that, and he looked in a mirror and saw a spot on his collar. He took the collar off, went over to a bureau drawer, and took out a clean one.

TERKEL: *That tells the whole story right there.*
KEATON: That told the whole situation.

TERKEL: *This was the first time something of this sort happened in films. It was not diagram but suggestion.*
KEATON: Yes. That's right.

TERKEL: A Woman of Paris *was one of the films that revolutionized the directing.*
KEATON: There's something that leads into that. I went into pictures with Roscoe Arbuckle. I mean, his pictures were the first ones

that I appeared in. And I'd only been with him a short time, and he says, "Here's something you want to bear in mind, that the average mind of the motion picture audience is twelve years old. It's a twelve-year-old mind that you're entertaining." I was only with him about another couple of months or something like that, and I says, "Roscoe, something tells me that those who continue to make pictures for twelve-year-old minds ain't going to be with us long." Well, it was only a couple of years later that a scene like this of Chaplin's kind of proved that. The minds jumped much faster than we were making pictures.

TERKEL: *That's marvelous. The same principle applies of course . . . we hear it today applying to television and radio. The same false belief that the public isn't ready for adult . . . or use of the imagination. What Chaplin did, and what you appeared to do in so many . . . was allow the imagination of the audience to flow freely.*
KEATON: Sure. I always tried to do that. I always wanted an audience to outguess me, then I'd double-cross them sometimes.

TERKEL: *Just to return to* Limelight *for a second. Here's a film that deals with old-time English vaudeville musical hall, and Chaplin called on you— and was it Chester Conklin? I'm trying to remember.*
KEATON: Yes.

TERKEL: *With this routine, and yet all three of you were pretty mature men by then.*
KEATON: That's right.

TERKEL: *Yet, what was it? We think of the ability the three of you had, the physical ability and the imagination to do it there. It threw everybody in see-ing . . . I remember seeing that particular sequence.*
KEATON: Oh I don't know, just all lucky that we can move fast, and still can, I mean.

TERKEL: *How do you find working with a live audience?*
KEATON: Oh, I always like a live audience. When I first tried a television show, when it was a young business, we were working to an

audience. Then later on they talked me into doing 'em just to a silent motion picture camera. Well, it didn't work, because no matter what you did, it looked like something that had been shot thirty years ago. It didn't look up to date. It just looked old-fashioned, but the same material done in front of a live audience. . . .

TERKEL: *A new reaction, a fresh reaction.*
KEATON: Yeah. People sitting in their living room where there are only three or four people—well, they just wouldn't hear—don't laugh out loud to start the others laughing. It is not like being in a motion picture theater where you got a couple thousand people there to help you laugh. You're looking at just a dead machine when you do it with just a silent camera. And the canned laughs are absolutely no good at all. They don't ring true at all.

TERKEL: *You can tell those a mile away.*
KEATON: There's a false note all the way through when there's mechanical canned laughs in there. But the live audience, that's a different proposition. And the same material, I only need two-thirds of it—I can eliminate a third of the material—to do a half-hour show. Work it to a silent camera . . . all right, now do the same material to a live audience, and I can throw one-third of that material away and save it for the next show.

TERKEL: *Because of the audience reaction.*
KEATON: Because of their laughs. Their reaction will make you work to 'em, which you don't do to a silent camera. You don't work to a silent camera, but you do to an audience.

TERKEL: *You mean hearing their laughs.*
KEATON: They space it for you. When you spy a laugh is going to come up, you don't hurt that laugh, you help build it. I slide right past it to a silent camera.

TERKEL: *Hearing that reaction, you actually add something. It's like a wave.*
KEATON: That's right.

TERKEL: *One wave on top of another.*

KEATON: That's right.

TERKEL: *Mr. Keaton, thank you very much for giving us just this bit, a touch of that period known as the "Golden Era of Comedy." Anything else you'd care to add? Some reminiscence?*

KEATON: I think you covered it pretty good.

TERKEL: *And perhaps some day you'll see my little horse again. I'll do Charlie to your Erwin. Ten years ago it was.*[4]

KEATON: That's right.

TERKEL: *In any event, thank you very much for being our guest and being the artist you are. Thanks a lot.*

KEATON: Adios.

---

[4] Studs Terkel recalls his and Keaton's sharing the stage in a 1949 summer stock production of George Abbott and John Cecil Holm's "straw hat" classic, *Three Men on a Horse.* Keaton played the protagonist, Erwin Trowbridge, who has the psychic ability to predict the winning horses at the local race track. Terkel played Charlie, one of the gangsters who kidnap Erwin, hoping to cash in on Erwin's uncanny gift. See Studs Terkel, *The Spectator: Talk about Movies and Plays with the People Who Make Them* (New York: The New Press, 1999), pp. 27, 30–31, 37.

Buster Keaton: An Interview

HERBERT FEINSTEIN / 1960

FEINSTEIN: *Mr. Keaton, is it true that Harry Houdini first named you Buster?*

KEATON: Yeah, that's right. The show I was born with was a one-night stand in Pickway (*sic*), Kansas, in 1895, the Keaton and Houdini medicine show company. That's Harry Houdini, the handcuff king. My father was a grotesque comedian and my mother was the ingénue-soubrette, a singer and dancer in the show.

FEINSTEIN: *How come Houdini called you Buster?*

KEATON: I fell down a flight of stairs when I was around six months old. They picked me up . . . no bruises, didn't seem to hurt myself and Houdini said, "That was a Buster." And the old man says, "That's a good name; we'll call him that."

FEINSTEIN: *How did you write yourself into your parents' act, and become The Three Keatons?*

KEATON: Oh, a kid born backstage, the parents slap a makeup on 'im as soon as he can walk, just as . . . I don't know, sometimes just for the fun of it, and their own amusement, and also to see if the kid takes to an audience at a young age.

Feinstein interviewed Keaton on October 6, 1960, in San Francisco, and taped the interview for the Pacifica Foundation. The interview was subsequently published as Herbert Feinstein, "Buster Keaton: An Interview," in the *Massachusetts Review*, vol. 4, no. 2 (Winter 1963): 392–407. Reprinted by permission from the *Massachusetts Review*.

FEINSTEIN: *What sort of bits did you play?*

KEATON: Oh, my father put grotesque clothes on me, similar to the ones he was wearing. So I had big pants, and big shoes on immediately, and they started playing me in matinees only when I was around three years old. Time I got about four some manager says, "You keep him in for the night show and we raise your salary ten dollars a week." From the time I was five years old, I had played Tony Pastor's Theatre in New York. I was here in January 1901, at the Orpheum Theatre in San Francisco. My first salaried week is in 1899. I have completed sixty-one years.

FEINSTEIN: *And what was the show that Fatty Arbuckle enticed you away from that was going to play at the Winter Garden?*

KEATON: It was the *Passing Show* in 1917. Every summer show that the Shuberts put in at the Winter Garden was the *Passing Show* of that year. All-star cast, the show was supposed to be for the summer of 1917.

FEINSTEIN: *Was it like the straw-hat review we see now?*

KEATON: Oh no, it was one of the biggest shows that was in New York, equally as big as Ziegfeld's Follies.

FEINSTEIN: *And what drew you away from* The Passing Show *of 1917?*

KEATON: I don't know. I'd been watching motion pictures when I was touring the country. I liked to watch the movies there, and when Arbuckle says, "Have you ever been in a motion picture?" I told him, "I've never even been in a studio." Well, he says, "Come on down to Colony and try a bit with me and see how you like it." Well, everything about the studio I liked; the first thing I did was make a friend with the cameraman and get in the cutting room and tear a camera to pieces and everything else and find out how I can get trick photography and things I could do with a camera that I couldn't do on the stage. Well, it's a fascinating business when you're as young as I was then.

FEINSTEIN: *It's still a fascinating business, isn't it? I saw* Huckleberry Finn *[1960] not too long ago; it seemed to me you hadn't forgotten any of the tricks. You had no dialogue in* Huckleberry Finn.

KEATON: Very little. I just talked to my lion; Orville, his name was.

FEINSTEIN: *That episode isn't in Mark Twain's novel as far as I can
remember. The circus is, but not the lion tamer. But that's not important.*
KEATON: Well, the writers, I guess, wanted the scene where the two
villains accidentally fell into the lion's cage. Tony Randall [the King]
and Mickey Shaughnessy [the Duke], I think.

FEINSTEIN: *To go back to 1917, how long did you stay at the Colony
Studios?*
KEATON: Well, Arbuckle had just left Mack Sennett, and he was used
to making pictures in the Keystone fashion and most of our pictures,
oh . . . two-thirds of it would be exteriors. And it was a little too tough
to try to do those chases and scenes anywhere around the studios in
New York. So he made Joe Schenck, the producer, ship us to California
after we made about six two-reelers there.

FEINSTEIN: *What about the Buster Keaton Studio? When did that get started?*
KEATON: I stayed with Arbuckle out on the Coast for about six more
pictures, and got into the army, the Fortieth Division, and I was a
doughboy in France for seven months. I was only in the army a year.
When I got back, I only made two more pictures with Roscoe [Fatty
Arbuckle], and Joe Schenck had sold his contract to Paramount. And
the minute Schenck did that, he turned the company over to me and
then went and bought me a studio. Fact, he bought me Chaplin's old
studio, and named it the Keaton Studio. And all he did as the producer,
he says, "You're to make eight two-reelers a year we're going to release
through the new outfit that Marcus Loew has just bought, called
Metro." So Schenck never knew when I was shooting, or what I was
shooting. I just set out to make those eight pictures a year. Well, I did
that for about two and a half years, and then Marcus Loew decided I
should do features. Well, then, when we started in the features, you
only make two a year, a spring release and a fall release. The dates on
this here are a little off. I started my two-reelers in '22.

FEINSTEIN: *Isn't one reason you went into feature pictures that you were
getting top billing for the two-reelers, but not the money for them?*
KEATON: Yeah, the majority of the exhibitors would advertise our
picture above the featured picture. You see, we never got on the same

program with Bill Hart or Doug Fairbanks or Mary Pickford or Gloria Swanson or Mabel Normand or any of the big stars of the day. We always got, well, I'd better not name the names, but the exhibitor was practically paying as much for our two-reelers as he did for the feature.

FEINSTEIN: *What did a feature picture cost in the early 1920s?*
KEATON: I ran the lowest of the three making them. I ran around $225,000˘ to the picture. That would include my salary. Harold Lloyd, he would go a little more than that, up to $350,000. And Chaplin went higher still. Of course, Charlie was a little independent, and a little lazy at times. He stopped immediately trying to make two pictures a year, satisfied to make one; then after he'd made a couple like that, he'd skip a year, make one, then he'd skip three years, and make one; he got very lazy.

FEINSTEIN: *I've seen you quoted too, I think, as saying that Chaplin would sometimes go to Europe in the middle of making a picture.*
KEATON: Oh, sure! Take a trip. Take off somewheres.

FEINSTEIN: *In* Sunset Boulevard *[1950], one of the many pictures you've made in the last decade, Gloria Swanson, as the memorable Norma Desmond, says about the movies that they've ruined themselves, that they've gone downhill: as a silent actress, the star could say anything she wanted to with her eyes, and that all most contemporary films do is talk, talk, talk. Would you care to comment on Miss Swanson-Desmond's statement? Have the talkies plunged films artistically downhill?*
KEATON: Oh, I don't think so. But there's only a certain type of people that work like I did, or any of the people who were so successful during the silent days. Trouble is in laying out a story. When you've got spots in there where you can do things in action without dialogue, you should take advantage of it. And the average company don't do that. It was the same as when I started making silent pictures. First instructions with the new writers we were getting from Broadway; see, everything with them was based on a joke, funny saying, people shouting. But we'd tell our story, our plot with our characters, and we talk when necessary. But we don't go out of our way to talk. Let's see how much material we can get where dialogue is not needed.

FEINSTEIN: *How would you account for the fact, though, that since the advent of talkies, with the probable exceptions of W. C. Fields, Mae West, and Laurel and Hardy, there have been no great comic stars that I can think of?*
KEATON: Well, my pet is Red Skelton. And I like Lou Costello, too. Both of these boys would have done well in the silent days. I don't doubt but what that Jerry Lewis would have, too.

FEINSTEIN: *Lewis has made a silent film,* The Bellboy.
KEATON: I haven't seen it, so I don't know. Jackie Gleason's another one that if he'd been turned loose in the silent days, he would have come out all right.

FEINSTEIN: *Do you think any of these people have reached the stature—just to leave Buster Keaton aside—of Charlie Chaplin?*
KEATON: No. I classify Chaplin as the greatest motion picture comedian of all time.

FEINSTEIN: *What about a verbal comic? For instance, I like Bob Hope, and I've read somewhere that you like Hope, too. But do you think that Hope depends too much on dialogue?*
KEATON: Why no! That's his style and his way of working. I don't like to see Hope in action. His body movements are not funny to me. He don't seem natural when he starts looking for laughs in action.

FEINSTEIN: *He does mug.*
KEATON: Oh, yes . . .

FEINSTEIN: *By body movements do you mean the entire body?*
KEATON: Yeah, I'll send W. C. Fields in there just to get me the telephone book and look up a number for me. For some reason or other, he'll just have trouble finding it. He'll get ten laughs where Hope won't get one. But I've always had my pet, but I have to go back through the field. My favorite clown was Marceline at the Hippodrome, and Slivers Oakley of the Barnum and Bailey show. And third choice, Poodles Hanneford. Now I go in for blackface comedians. My pet was Bert Williams, who was actually a colored man, but used to put burnt cork

on, black up . . . the same as Moran and Mack, or Lew Dockstader, Frank Tinney; we had some great blackface comedians. We have lost them completely.

FEINSTEIN: *I notice you left Al Jolson off your list.*
KEATON: Well, Al Jolson is an entertainer. Same as Eddie Cantor. I never classified Jolson as a comedian. He did comedy, but those other people who were in minstrel shows, they were character comedians. I go for the tramp comedians; one of our great monologists and a funny man was Nat Wills. W. C. Fields was a tramp. And you went for your light comedians like Raymond Hitchcock. That's a Bob Hope or a Jack Benny.

FEINSTEIN: *What about another favorite of yours whom we very rarely see nowadays, Lloyd Hamilton; what was his work like?*
KEATON: Well, Lloyd was one of the funniest men in silent pictures. He just looked like a big overgrown kid. That's all.

FEINSTEIN: *Was it Harry Langdon who looked like a big baby?*
KEATON: Well, Langdon was younger. Langdon worked like he was about six years old. Lloyd had grown up, but still was a kid.

FEINSTEIN: *Don't Bob Hope and Jerry Lewis have juvenile elements about them, too? They act like boys rather than men. This business of comedy . . . I wonder . . .*
KEATON: Of course, I do lose my pets: my German comedians, my Jewish comedians, and Italian.

FEINSTEIN: *How do you mean, "You lose them"?*
KEATON: Well, you don't see them anymore. They're afraid to do it.

FEINSTEIN: *You mean because of social pressures from sensitive minority groups?*
KEATON: You get a good Joe Welch today, a Jewish comedian—half of Israel would turn over, see, objecting to it. You don't dare show a low Irish character.

FEINSTEIN: *You think this limits the area of comedy because people are sensitive and can't take a joke?*
KEATON: So those comedians are afraid of offending somebody, and they just haven't developed in the last, oh, I'll say, thirty-five years.

FEINSTEIN: *Do you remember a character named Stepin Fetchit?*
KEATON: Very much.

FEINSTEIN: *Do you think Stepin Fetchit was very funny?*
KEATON: Sure, he was a funny guy!

FEINSTEIN: *But you can see why some Negro groups might object to him as a phony stereotype?*
KEATON: Oh, well, sure, because he plays a stupid.

FEINSTEIN: *That's it. And he might be used by some anti-Negro groups to say* this *is what the Negro is.*
KEATON: Well, that's the wrong way to look at it from the theatrical viewpoint, because you've got stupid people in every walk of life and in every country. Our American rube used to be a very funny character. And very witty, in the bargain. We've lost him. We don't have him anymore either.

FEINSTEIN: *Who would that be? Can you think of any . . .*
KEATON: Go back to Will M. Cressy, Eddie Buzzell, Judy Canova, and a few rube characters who were very funny. The nearest thing you've got to them today is the hillbilly who is lazy and sloppy, but that wasn't the rube.

FEINSTEIN: *Was Bob Burns a rube character?*
KEATON: He was an Arkansas rube, almost the hillbilly, but he was a rube character. Like Chic Sale.

FEINSTEIN: *What about Will Rogers?*
KEATON: Will Rogers—out and out—well, he was a high class rube, an Okie. That's about all you can say. I don't know how else you can classify him.

FEINSTEIN: *Perhaps there's a category called Will Rogers. Mr. Keaton, it has been said by many that the secret source of humor is not anything pleasant, but pain or pathos. Commentators like Sigmund Freud and Mark Twain have made that same point. Freud called humor "the loftiest of the defense functions"; and Mark Twain says somewhere in* Pudd'nhead Wilson's New Calendar *that "Everything human is pathetic. The secret source of humor itself is not joy, but sorrow. There is no humor in heaven." And since you mentioned Yiddish humorists, a lot of Yiddish humor has been explained by way of its intrinsic sadness. To come to the medium of film, one humorist, Al Capp, has written about another, Charlie Chaplin, that Chaplin is only funny because his tramp is a professional victim and is so truly pathetic. Capp says we laugh at Chaplin's* City Lights *[1931], "because we are eternally delighted at the inhumanity of man to man." Now, in view of your own brand of dour, deadpan humor, Mr. Keaton, would you agree that human pain, not pleasure, is at the bottom of most successful humor?*

KEATON: Yes, I'm afraid I do to a certain extent, a great deal of it because an audience will laugh at things happening to you, and they certainly wouldn't laugh if it happened to them.

FEINSTEIN: *Take your recent performance as King Sextimus in the play,* Once Upon a Mattress *[1960]. Here's a man who is terribly afflicted, and yet it's hilarious to everybody that he can't talk.*

KEATON: Now, neither Harold Lloyd, nor myself, as a rule, started out looking for sympathy. We may have been poorly dressed, but we generally had a job to do and a way of living.

FEINSTEIN: *You were rich in* The Navigator *[1924], weren't you?*

KEATON: In *The Navigator*, I started out as a multimillionaire. I had troubles other ways in life.

FEINSTEIN: *In* The General *[1927], the boy is a* schlemiel.

KEATON: In *The General*, I'm an engineer.

FEINSTEIN: *As I remember, he had his troubles, too. Didn't he want to get in the army, the Confederate Army?*

KEATON: Well, I had only one plot. I had a girl and when the Civil War broke out, I tried to enlist, but the minute they found out I was a locomotive engineer, they wouldn't enlist me. The old Colonel tells the man, he says, "He's more valuable as an engineer to the South, so don't enlist him." But they don't tell me that when they turn me down. So I don't know why. And because I don't get in uniform, the girl won't speak to me.

FEINSTEIN: *I remember, yes. Then isn't pathos a source of humor? I sup-pose there is considerable pathos at the heart of* The General. *Some people would count themselves lucky if they couldn't get into the army, but in your picture the fellow got the cold shoulder, got the brush from his girl. So he is pathetic. Do you think, however, that there are other kinds of humor—that some humor is just plain fun?*
KEATON: Oh, sure. Now, you go for another type of comedian and material. There is the Marx Brothers. There was no sense to anything they did.

FEINSTEIN: *Pretty far out. But do you think . . . ?*
KEATON: But pathos there had nothing to do with them. They never even got into a situation where you felt sorry for somebody.

FEINSTEIN: *Everybody else, but not them.*
KEATON: Course, they'd kid themselves in and out of everything. Same as the Ritz Brothers.

FEINSTEIN: *Very good at conmanship, that's right. You know the Marx Brothers made a picture about a railroad, too. Do you remember their* Go West *[1940], with the same title as your own* Go West *[1925], though with a different story? When the Marx Brothers needed firewood to keep the engine running, they chopped up the train and escaped from the Indians that way.*
KEATON: That's right.

FEINSTEIN: *Many funny films have locomotive chases in them—for instance,* My Little Chickadee *[1940], the movie with Mae West and W. C. Fields—and others have in some sense derived from* The General. *Did you direct and produce* The General?
KEATON: Yes.

FEINSTEIN: *Was it a solo job?*

KEATON: That was . . . well, I was more proud of that picture, I suppose, than any other picture I ever made because I took an actual happening out of the Civil War, out of the history book. And I told it in detail, too. I told the story of the Northerners coming into the South as civilians and stealing that engine with the intent of burning bridges behind them to cripple Confederate supply trains moving north to the Southern armies. And then the chase was on. Well, I stuck to the detail of that, and then, where their story ended, I added on—to get a finish to the picture.

FEINSTEIN: *What did you add?*

KEATON: What I laid out was my own continuity. I cut the picture, directed it. And I had a successful picture. And Mr. Walt Disney, something like twenty-nine years later, made a picture called *The Great Locomotive Chase* [1956]. He was told maybe he better go run my picture first—and he wouldn't do it. Well, he made a mistake. Disney made a very bad mistake in it.

FEINSTEIN: *In what way?*

KEATON: Well, he told the story from a Northerner's standpoint. Well, his leading man is a Northerner [Jeffrey Hunter] and it's awfully hard to a motion picture audience, for some reason, to make heroes out of the Northerners.

FEINSTEIN: *I agree with you, it was an aesthetic failure. It wasn't funny. It wasn't even particularly interesting.*

KEATON: Well, Disney wasn't trying to make it funny. He was trying to show you the real thing in the dramatics.

FEINSTEIN: *The picture wound up as a spy story.*

KEATON: That's right. Another thing he didn't tell you, too, see, because he couldn't put it on the screen and get a happy ending to it. In the real story, all eight of those men were captured by the Southerners and they dropped one big pine tree and put eight horses under there with eight ropes and dropped all eight at once.

FEINSTEIN: *That wouldn't make a very good kid's picture, would it?*

KEATON: No, that wouldn't make a very good finish, but that was the real finish to the story.

FEINSTEIN: *What do you think, Mr. Keaton, of some of the work of some other present-day comedians? We've spoken about Lewis and Hope, but what about the ladies, say, Marilyn Monroe or Lucille Ball?*

KEATON: Lucille Ball is my top. The greatest character comedienne, Marie Dressler. Light comedienne, Lucille Ball.

FEINSTEIN: *What are your reasons for thinking so?*

KEATON: I mean of all time, as far as I can remember. Nothing Lucille can't do.

FEINSTEIN: *You get the impression that she's a great sport, that she has a wonderful sense of humor, that she can kid herself.*

KEATON: Yeah, she can do anything.

FEINSTEIN: *What about Marilyn Monroe? Have you seen any of her films?*

KEATON: I saw *Some Like It Hot* [1959].

FEINSTEIN: *What did you think of that?*

KEATON: Oh, I liked the picture very, very much. It was awful hard to do what that man [Billy Wilder] did in that picture . . . directing it.

FEINSTEIN: *How do you mean?*

KEATON: Because, well, the minute a man puts on women's clothes, you've got a farce comedy on your hands. It's awfully hard to tell a legitimate story, and he darned near did with that picture.

FEINSTEIN: *"Darned near" anyway.*

KEATON: Darned near!

FEINSTEIN: *Don't you think that a lot of the great impact of that picture comes from the fact that George Raft and Pat O'Brien and Joe E. Brown are all in it playing themselves . . . to perfection.*

KEATON: Sure thing. I loved Joe E. Brown in it.

FEINSTEIN: *What about Jack Lemmon? Does he have the potential to be a great comic?*
KEATON: I think he has. You get the certain types of material that he—that you can put him in; he's a light comedian. You don't call him a character comedian, or a low comedian, such as I am.

FEINSTEIN: *Well, I wouldn't say you were a low comedian.*
KEATON: Well, no, when you say a low comedian it *is* a character comedian.

FEINSTEIN: *Did you see* The Apartment *[1960], the picture Lemmon did with Billy Wilder, in which he plays a serious character, a sad sack?*
KEATON: No, I didn't see it. I've never seen him except in *Some Like It Hot.*

FEINSTEIN: *Do you think he's spasmodic; does Lemmon move too much?*
KEATON: No, I think he did a great job with *Some Like It Hot.*

FEINSTEIN: *Might I ask you—I'll give up if you don't answer this time— what you think of Marilyn Monroe's performance?*
KEATON: Well, it was great in that picture.

FEINSTEIN: *Yes, I'm sure it was. What about some of the British comedians? Have you seen, do you enjoy the films that Alec Guinness makes, for instance?*
KEATON: Oh, I've got one pet over there.

FEINSTEIN: *Who's that?*
KEATON: Richard Hearne, Mr. Pastry. He's been on the Ed Sullivan Show a dozen times. He's a young fellow that makes up as an old man, and he does a routine where he's supposed to be at a dance, and he dances with imaginary characters. And he does another one where they initiate him into a drinking club of some kind or other, where they jump up on chairs and take a drink between every jump.

FEINSTEIN: *Is he a character comedian, would you say?*
KEATON: Yeah, he's a character comedian.

FEINSTEIN: *What about a Frenchman, Jacques Tati—the guy who did* My Uncle *[1958] and* Mister Hulot's Holiday *[1952]? He's a mime. He doesn't talk.*

KEATON: Oh yes. I like him. Very, very much.

FEINSTEIN: *He uses physical equipment the way—though not quite the way—you used to, but the way Tati uses an apartment house in* My Uncle, *I think, is similar to the way you used the ship, say, in* The Navigator, *as a setting.*

KEATON: Yeah.

FEINSTEIN: *If we can go back for a moment to* The Navigator, *the most spectacular scene was the one in which the boy and the girl keep on missing each other—how did you set that up? Do you remember . . .*

KEATON: Yeah, we set the camera out on the bow of the ship so it could take in the three decks, and just set down and talk it over with the girl—tell her how fast to travel, where to look, how to come down the stairs and look, and go back up and so forth, until we laid out the chase, and then go 'head and shoot it.

FEINSTEIN: *How many cuts were in that? I don't remember.*

KEATON: I don't remember the cuts.

FEINSTEIN: *You'd have to remember an awful lot in order to keep on missing one another, because you could have run into each other so easily. . . . You were in Europe, I take it, for several years, with Mrs. Keaton?*

KEATON: Oh, I've been over there quite often.

FEINSTEIN: *Did you observe the work of, say, Jean-Louis Barrault, the mime, or Marcel Marceau, the French mime—men who use no dialogue at all?*

KEATON: No.

FEINSTEIN: *What about the French comedians, besides Tati? Do any of them appeal to you?*

KEATON: Very much. I like him. I like the Clown.

FEINSTEIN: *What about Fernandel, say, the guy who looks like a horse?*
KEATON: Oh, he's a great character!

FEINSTEIN: *What about the idea of a one-man show?* An Evening with
Beatrice Lillie, Elsa Lanchester Herself, *solo stage performances by Yves
Montand, Maurice Chevalier, etc. Have you ever thought of putting on your
own one-man show?*
KEATON: I've been asked to. But I turned it down. I could probably dig
up the material and the sets, but—too hard a work. I work too hard
when I start doing those things.

FEINSTEIN: *You mean, to do an hour and a half of mime. If you were on all
the time I think it would be rough. . . . I wonder, what do you think of the
possibilities of television as a medium? Rossellini and Jean Renoir, the Italian
and French directors, have suggested that perhaps TV is the coming medium
because production isn't too expensive, and that therefore there can be experiments on television. Do you agree?*
KEATON: That's what he said?

FEINSTEIN: *Jean Renoir and Rossellini.*
KEATON: They weren't expensive?

FEINSTEIN: *Well, a television show is less expensive than making a feature
picture, anyway.*
KEATON: Yes, that's true.

FEINSTEIN: *And of course, they're talking about Italy and France where
maybe—*
KEATON: Yeah, I know.

FEINSTEIN: *Well, do you think TV is too expensive?*
KEATON: TV hasn't reached anywheres near the proportions it is in
the United States—nowhere in Europe. Their sets are beautiful, and the
French have the number one, the best television. I believe we have,
what is it, five hundred lines in our picture? There's 750 in the French.
They got a much finer grain picture on their screen than we do. . . .

FEINSTEIN: *What about your own experiences in doing shows specifically for TV?*

KEATON: I like to work in TV, but I like the live audience. I don't like to do anything on film for television.

FEINSTEIN: *That's unusual. It's very often the reverse. Many artists feel that they may make mistakes on a live show, mistakes without the chance for retakes.*

KEATON: No, because the minute I see something that was done to a silent camera then it looks like something that was done thirty years ago. But the minute you've got an audience's reaction right along with the work—I don't mean canned laughs. . . .

FEINSTEIN: *I understand.*

KEATON: They are poison to me. I hate to watch anything that's got canned laughs to it.

FEINSTEIN: *Do you ever change your style? Suppose you feel you're not getting a response from the audience and you are doing a live TV show, will you alter your routine on the spot?*

KEATON: As a rule, I automatically speed up until I start getting laughs some place. Then I slow down again. And another thing I found, too. The biggest thing that any comedian has got in television is diggin' up material. I'll give you an idea; it's that I used to make eight two-reelers a year. Well, a two-reeler was a half-hour show. Well, now when television comes along, they want thirty-nine of those a year. Well, there's only one way you can get material. I mean just hiring writers and gag men don't solve the problem. You've just got to start repeating and stealing. Anything you can think of. Like, "Well, we did that three or four weeks ago in a drug store; the next time we'll do it in a butcher shop. And we change the backgrounds for gags or steal gags right and left!"

FEINSTEIN: *That's death to an original comedian. Harry Langdon repeated himself to a quick end.*

KEATON: I don't know how Red Skelton manages to do TV at all.

FEINSTEIN: *Didn't you write gags or help him with his gags for a while?*
Weren't you a consultant for Skelton?
KEATON: It's the quickest way to Forest Lawn that I know of. Trying to
dig up material for that weekly show. The first few are easy. Then it
starts to get tough!

FEINSTEIN: *What sorts of things did you do for Red Skelton, when you*
worked with him?
KEATON: Any of the pictures that he was . . . He remade three of mine
at MGM.

FEINSTEIN: *What were they?*
KEATON: Picture called *The Cameraman* [1928], which was the last of
the silents. That and a picture called *Spite Marriage* [1929] were the last
two silents made—that *I* made. Well, Skelton remade both of those.
One was called *Watch the Birdie* [1951], and the other was called *I Dood It*
[1943].

FEINSTEIN: *Were they successful, do you think?*
KEATON: They were for Skelton, yes.

FEINSTEIN: *Were they in the same class as your pictures?*
KEATON: If you sat through the two pictures you wouldn't know it
was the same story.

FEINSTEIN: *Is that because of the difference in personality between you two?*
KEATON: No! By the time the writers got through improving it, they
killed half the laughs in it. Skelton had to dig up his own to put in
there.

FEINSTEIN: *In your book* [My Wonderful World of Slapstick, *with Charles*
Samuels, 1960], you talk about "the worst mistake" you made in your life, and
that was in moving to Metro. And you suggest that the MGM stable of gag
writers didn't do you any good. What did happen when you went to Metro?
KEATON: Too many cooks. Not that there wasn't brains at MGM.
Plenty of writers and high-salaried men, but *too many!* And they warp
your judgment.

FEINSTEIN: *How do you mean that?*

KEATON: Well, now here is rule number one with us when we were making our pictures: simplicity in story. And as few characters as possible, too. Well, that was the reverse English when I went to MGM. Irving Thalberg was in charge of production and he wanted—oh—I wasn't in trouble enough trying to manipulate a camera as a cameraman, trying to photograph current events as a news weekly cameraman. In *The Cameraman*, Thalberg wanted me involved with gangsters, and then get in trouble with this one and that one, and that was my fight—to eliminate those extra things.

FEINSTEIN: *Thalberg wanted too much complexity.*

KEATON: Uh huh.

FEINSTEIN: *What about Metro's being star-happy? Did MGM pictures become top-heavy because there were too many personalities roaming around on the screen?*

KEATON: Oh, they did that. For instance, I was in the first *Hollywood Revue [of 1929]*. That was Metro's first big musical. And they put every star in the studio into that, to do a bit. But in my own pictures, they would just give me a good supporting cast, but the first picture I made there [*Free and Easy*, 1930], who do you think my villain was?

FEINSTEIN: *Wallace Beery?*

KEATON: Bob Montgomery.

FEINSTEIN: *He's come a long way. What about the leading ladies of the time: Joan Crawford and Marion Davies. Did you ever make pictures with them?*

KEATON: No. Never worked with them [save in MGM's *Hollywood Revue of 1929*].

FEINSTEIN: *How about Marie Dressler?*

KEATON: No. And that's one, oh that's one I wish I had.

FEINSTEIN: *You suggested earlier that you consider her one of the greatest comediennes of all time.*

KEATON: The greatest character comedienne I ever saw.

FEINSTEIN: *Do you want to expand on that? Is it because of the way she looked?*
KEATON: No, her way of working. She was marvelous.

FEINSTEIN: *In* Tillie's Punctured Romance *[1914], as I understand it, Mabel Normand was the star, although you couldn't tell that when you were through watching the picture.*
KEATON: *Oh no! No, no!*

FEINSTEIN: *The other way around?*
KEATON: No, the other way around. You see Marie Dressler was already a Broadway star when [Mack] Sennett got her to do that picture. But he wanted to help Charlie Chaplin's career then, 'cause Charlie looked like he was gonna wrap up the picture business overnight. So he got Dressler into it to star her, supported by Charlie Chaplin. And then Mabel Normand and Chester Conklin and . . .

FEINSTEIN: *Who was the big bully? I've forgotten now.*
KEATON: Chaplin was the villain.

FEINSTEIN: *He was the villain, but there was a big guy, Tillie's papa.*
KEATON: Oh, there's always big guys in the Keystones to scare you to death.

FEINSTEIN: *Did you ever play with Chaplin?*
KEATON: Only in *Limelight*. . . .

FEINSTEIN: *Have you ever had a desire to play something as straight as Shakespeare or Molière?*
KEATON: Shakespeare I don't want to play, no. I've never wanted to do *Hamlet*. But I have done dramatic parts.

FEINSTEIN: *What about those dramatic parts?*
KEATON: Oh, people get an idea, like Doug Fairbanks Jr., did here about three years ago. I went to London and did one of his shows. And it was a straight dramatic part. No laughs in it; not even a giggle in it.

FEINSTEIN: *Was it a film, a motion picture?*
KEATON: No, it was for television there.

FEINSTEIN: *I have read in your autobiography that you once did smile on screen; that just once, for a moment, the Great Stone Face smiled.*
KEATON: No—oh, I tried it!

FEINSTEIN: *But you couldn't bring it off. What happened?*
KEATON: Well, I did it to satisfy MGM, and Irving Thalberg especially, who insisted that I try it. So I did. A big fadeout at the finish of the picture, the girl in my arms or something—a big smile. We previewed the picture, and instead of the audience saying, "Oh, look, he smiled. Hooray!" they said, "Oh, the bum smiled." And they actually got mad at me.

FEINSTEIN: *What happened? Did they cut your smile out of the picture?*
KEATON: We went right back to the studio, to the cutting room, took that scene out and put the one in where I didn't smile through the fadeout.

A Dinner with Keaton

GEORGES SADOUL/1962

HE HAD ALREADY ARRIVED before me in the lobby of his sumptuous hotel. I recognized him right off, this little man in his over-coat of white leather: Buster Keaton, the greatest American comic after Charles Chaplin. He had just arrived straight from Munich with his wife, tall, blond, and congenial. The journey had been tiring, the air-plane deafening. He looked done in, absent. He arrived not saying more than a few words to the special correspondent from *France-soir*. Then, obtaining his key from the front desk, he asked our permission to go up to his room to freshen up for a half hour.

He was so visibly fatigued that I hesitated dining with him, as I had been urged to do by Henri Langlois, the organizer of a monumental Keaton retrospective at the *Cinémathèque Française*. With my uncertain English, would I be able to engage in conversation with this great man, whom I was afraid of overwhelming with questions?

He came down twenty-five minutes later, looking twenty-five years younger. And right away he started telling stories. The meaning of certain words escaped me, but his gestures, his amazing expression, expli-cated to me by their mimicry what I would otherwise not have understood.

KEATON: We've been traveling though Germany for fifteen days non-stop, my wife and I. We went there to revive my old film from 1925, *The General*. In ten towns at a time. And everywhere a terrific success. Turning people away. Tens of thousands of spectators every day.

From *Les Lettres Françaises* 916 (March 1–7, 1962): 1, 6. Translated from French by Kevin W. Sweeney.

This success obliged me to do a quick tour of each of these ten towns. Except Berlin, where we stayed forty-eight hours, we had to leave before a single day would pass. No time even to wash our clothes. We were as dirty as Bohemians. Our next-to-last stop had been Hamburg. Then the flooding rains began. In our hotel, they continued to prepare meals in kitchens filling with water, cooking until the water rose to mid-thigh on the staff. Our plane was the last able to leave the town and an airport where helicopters converged bringing in relief supplies, aid, and medicine.

Everywhere we have been assailed by reporters and the public. My film, *The General*, is now thirty-two years old. I was happy to add some sounds and music to it, sometimes adding a piano and sometimes a symphony orchestra. No dialogue or commentary. Only some subtitles. The success has been fantastic. People were scrambling everywhere in Germany just to see it. Soon it's going to start a new run in France.

The archive of the *Cinémathèque Française* has put together a showing of the complete films of this great comic. By a rare chance in the cinema, this great filmmaker has been able to become the owner of all his old films. He is in control of them. And without a doubt, the success achieved by *The General* will soon bring about the reissue of his other feature-length masterpieces: *Three Ages*, *Our Hospitality*, *The Navigator*, and *The Cameraman* (1923–28).

Keaton wanted to get to bed early, so we dined at seven o'clock that evening. The restaurant was very close to his luxurious grand hotel whose lobby was adorned with Gobelin tapestries and Sèvres porcelains.

We arrived at the restaurant. It was still entirely empty. We chose a table, and we were going to sit down when many loud thumps rang out. It was a patron that we had not noticed who was banging on the table. However, it was Buster Keaton, who had arrived by running ahead of us by another route, and who had thought up this gag to make us laugh.

Keaton laughs often, and he smiles even more. They say however that long ago, instigated by the publicity of the moniker, "the man who never smiles," he had forbidden himself ever to smile in public. And that the constraint had been so terrible that he would be driven mad for a number of years.

His filmography, the one of the second period, alone refutes that. He had not stopped working during the 1930s, where they speak about his being unbalanced. As far as his first period of film production is concerned, why not ask the question of him? He must have often heard the question and his smile was a little annoyed.

KEATON: All of that is stupidity. A myth. Certainly, in my films, I had this impassible expression. But I did not abstain from laughing or smiling out in public places or in my private life.

I told him that I had the honor, in 1952, of meeting and interviewing Mack Sennett, the creator of American slapstick film, who takes pride in having discovered all the great comics of the great silent era. Was it he who gave you your start, as he has sometimes allowed people to write?

KEATON: No, that's not true. Sennett, I knew him before he himself would make films. I was still a boy, but I was already a comic actor in vaudeville. With my father and mother, we made up a vaudeville act that was a great success: The Three Keatons, with Joe, Myra, and Buster. They gave me the nickname of Buster one day when I had fallen down a flight of stairs on my rear without hurting myself. In my childhood, I had learned acrobatics, and how to do pratfalls, the art of falling without hurting oneself.

It was not Sennett who gave me my start in film, but Roscoe Arbuckle, then universally renowned as "Fatty." In 1916—I was just twenty years old—I had turned down a good contract with a variety review, a thousand dollars a week perhaps, in order to become, for forty dollars a week, a supporting actor for Fatty along with our friend Al Saint John, in the films that he was then turning out.

That continued until 1918. And then, at the beginning of that year, I was drafted into the army. They sent me as a soldier to France. I spent eight months there. After the Armistice, on the way back, coming from Lyon, I stopped in Paris. I was given a marvelous Roquefort cheese. And I bought some red wine. But I lacked bread, and at that time one couldn't get bread without ration coupons, as a sign on the door of a bakery reminded me. All the same I knocked on the door. The baker, a large stout man with a big thick black mustache . . .

With a gesture, Keaton depicted the mustache in the same way as the comedians had in his films and those of Chaplin around 1918. And throughout the story, he related it less with words than with gestures. What a mime! Trained from childhood in this precise and difficult art, this dance of the hands and fingers. The years vanished from his face. We see him again just as he was in 1918, explaining his predicament for better or worse (he never knew French) with a Parisian baker two times larger than he was. We see the baker start to grumble, be moved by compassion, make a sign to Keaton to go to the back door, give him without a coupon a long piece of bread that the young Keaton conceals, vertically, under his coat which he rebuttons. The baker wants by all means that he leave by the back door. Because of his other customers and because of a cop who is passing by in the street. But the young soldier persists in leaving by the front door, giving a "Vive la France!" salute to mock the police officer.

This story of the bread summons up another one:

KEATON: In 1946, I spent two months in Paris, starring at the Cirque Médrano. I was staying in the same hotel as I am now staying in. But it was terrible, then, the food rationing in town: no butter, no oil, hideous yellow bread (with ration coupons), almost no meat. But, happily, I'd met up with my old friend Chico Marx, one of the Marx Brothers, who, alas, died six weeks ago. It was he who pointed out to me this restaurant where we now are. And there, at that time, no coupons were necessary, but plenty of butter, meat, a profusion of olive oil, and a marvelous cuisine, as good as their present cooking . . .

We had hesitated to speak to him about the Médrano. That was stupid. Why would one want him to consider his 1946 season as a disgrace, this son following in his father's footsteps for whom the variety stage or the circus are modes of expression as noble as the cinema. As soon as he had left Paris, Buster Keaton inquired of Monsieur Médrano, who no longer controls the establishment as he did formerly. And he remembers with pleasure the great success that he had then in Paris.

KEATON: They had asked me to appear on television, almost at the same time as my act at the circus. So that I had to change in a taxi, and

I mixed up my clothes and my costume, and I entered my hotel in my regular clothes but with my enormous clown shoes on from the circus. Everyone laughed on seeing me, and I realized that I had forgotten my regular shoes in the taxi. I told them this. And it became the latest news published the next day on the front page, in three columns, in many of the large Parisian newspapers: Buster Keaton lost his shoes in a taxi. That made the taxicab driver afraid. He had not recognized me and feared that people would take him for a dishonest man. He had my shoes taken to a police station by a little boy who said they had been found in the street. And the police returned them to me.

We returned to older times. To the era when the French film distributors had baptized him sometimes as "Frigo," sometimes as "Malec," which must be the anagram from the French word "calme" (calm). Because his comedy was based on the most absolute impassivity in the face of the most extravagant situations, before the worst catastrophes, the permanent revolt of objects and machines as soon as he touched them.

KEATON: Yes, I had a blank-page countenance when you would call me "Malec."

His countenance again took on, without thinking about it, his former expression, that of Malec, long since a classic. And Keaton naturally assumed this countenance as soon as he stopped participating in the conversation or stopped eating. He had little appetite, and although his wife begged him to finish his duck with red cabbage, he left his plate almost full.

"A blank-page countenance" . . . This signature phrase haunted me as a definition of his comedy. Soon after having left Buster Keaton, I reread the classic lines where he defined the characteristics of his art.

They often have asked me why I uniformly keep, all through my films, this particularly desolated look. The fact is that I noticed about my appearances in vaudeville that when one finished a routine more or less funny, I provoked a much greater laugh when I remained indifferent, than being astonished at the public laughter. There are other comics, on the other hand, who always seemed to take the side of the spectators and put themselves in their confidence. That was the way that Fatty worked. The public laughed with him, whereas as far as I was concerned, the public laughed at me. After all, comedy consists in "playing the fool," and the more serious one makes it, the funnier it will be. One of the best comics that I ever saw in vaudeville was Patsy Dole, "the big sad man." I see him again, standing on the stage with his doleful demeanor, telling his worries to the public with a sorrowful voice. The audience was rolling in the aisles, laughing themselves to death. All that would have failed if Patsy had permitted himself a smile.*

I questioned him now about his career.

KEATON: After my demobilization from the army, I started working again with Fatty, but only for a few short films. And then I became my own boss, in 1920, with my own company, whereas elsewhere my friend and old partner Al Saint John (whom you called "Picratt") had no luck.

During the years 1920 to 1930, I was always in charge of making my films. Even if I did not happen to be the producer, I, of course, played in them. I was also their principal scene planner, chief gag writer, and director, with the collaboration of many other co-directors (Eddie Cline, above all). At the start of the 1920s, the film distributors asked us—after the success of Chaplin and poor Fatty—to change over from short to feature-length films, which would be from two reels (which then lasted a half hour) to five reels (seventy-five minutes) and even to seven reels (an hour and three quarters).

To make a successful short comedy was already very difficult. I have often repeated that it was even more complicated to make a two-reel slapstick film than a drama of five or six parts. At that time I would work without a preliminary shooting script, just a simple sketch. It was essential to come up with good gags. And I would shoot material for five or six two-reel films in order to make a successful single film, because in assembling the film I would cut out four-fifths of the scenes in order to keep only the best.

---

* Buster Keaton, "Le métier du faire rire" (1932), *Anthologie du Cinéma: Rétrospective par les Textes de l'Art Muet qui Devint Parlant, ed.* Marcel Lapierre (Paris: La Nouvelle Edition, 1946), pp. 355–60. Sadoul only paraphrases sections of the article.

To change from short to feature-length films posed some very difficult problems for me to resolve. And I continue to think that it is almost impossible for a comic film to last longer than an hour and a quarter (five reels in the silent era). My two greatest successes, after all, have been films of that longer length: *Our Hospitality* and *The Navigator*. And if *The General* has as much success now, it is due to its being a sound film whose projection speed is a half times faster, bringing this seven-reel film to only an hour and ten minutes. I had the good luck not to have made dramatic films in the silent era. Because today, at the projection speed of twenty-four frames a second instead of sixteen, the tragic scenes often become ludicrous, as has happened in the masterpieces of those of D. W. Griffith. Whereas comedies of that era can very well support that increased speed.

That comedy is a difficult and meticulous art, no one (except Chaplin) could have said it any better than this exemplary man, intelligent, exceptionally gifted, who created a "personage" having an intense poetic face with a certain sense of the absurdity of the world, and who would have been "Kafkaesque" (before Kafka) if he had not always had, underneath his "blank-page countenance," a warmth of heart, a noble tenacity of spirit, a faith in men, yet none of this with a smug boy-scout style optimism . . . In 1920–30, Keaton was prodigiously modern, and he has stayed that way, this cantor of the irrational, this lyric eccentric, this grand poet who the surrealists would place in their pantheon besides heroes from Lautréamont to Jarry. He has written formerly, this master of a very difficult art:

> Comic effects are fleeting. They must be initiated at a very precise moment, allow the audience the time to recover themselves, then following that circumstance, to be pushed to the brink or to recover their progression. In their rhythm, it is necessary for them to have a mathematical precision, and this rhythm is a science whose responsibility is entirely dependent on the film director. A film comedy is assembled with the same precision as the inner workings of a watch.
>
> Executed too quickly or too slowly, the simplest thing can produce a disastrous effect. And for having been polished off or played too quickly, certain scenes, which in themselves are extremely funny, will not produce any effect on the audience.

Of course a science of rhythm is employed in the planning of all slapstick film, but there is also a great sense of human psychology that one should not in any case ignore.

I, however, had so many other questions I still wanted to ask him. I was only able to touch lightly with him on the Tati question. He admires the great French comic and scoffs at the American distributors who did not at first believe in *Monsieur Hulot*, found his rhythm too slow, greatly hesitated in presenting the film and showed great surprise at the big success that it finally achieved in New York.

In 1932, Keaton, a man exceptionally intelligent and lucid, wrote these lines that are at the same time severe and melancholic: "A film comedian is not able to last many years and, above all, always produce a number of consistent quality films. Four years is about all the length of time for progress and inspiration. After that one ceases to innovate."

Is this iron law only valid in film for its most difficult genre, comedy? There are very few *auteurs* of the cinema who, since 1900, have been able to "last," I certainly wouldn't say four years, but ten or twelve years. The greatest *auteurs* (Méliès himself) have very rarely been able to exceed this terrible time frame.

"For the past twelve years," said Keaton with a certain melancholy, "I have only appeared two times on the screen: in *Limelight*, the film of my friend Chaplin, and in a cameo role in *Around the World in Eighty Days*.

But for several years now he has achieved a terrific success in television: In comic sketches that he plays in, writes, and himself directs, in dramas that are more or less detective stories, also in TV commercials. He owns a beautiful house not far from Hollywood: not a fake Spanish, Italian, or Chinese palace, but an 1860 ranch house that he has restored and tastefully remodeled. If he has had to stop being a film *auteur*, at least advancing in years he has known neither misery nor failure as have so many of his friends, those who established, by their talent and their personality, a prodigious Hollywood fortune.

Finally and above all, his masterpiece films have not died. Their recent success proves (if it was necessary to do that) that his films, from now on and forever, have a place of honor reserved in the cinema archives of the entire world.

Telescope: Deadpan

FLETCHER MARKLE/1964

In his backyard, Buster Keaton walks past his wife, Eleanor, on a swing, past his St. Bernard puppy, to a patio table where Fletcher Markle is sitting in a chair. Keaton sits opposite him at the table and the interview begins.

FM: *Tell us about the custard pie and its ingredients.*

BK: Yeah, well, number one is we don't use a regular baker's pie, and throwing the pie in a cardboard plate is no good because that plate flying off detracts. So, what we used to do is our prop man would get our baker—whoever is closest to the studio—to make pie crust, two of them, with nothing in them, and take just a little flour and water to make a paste, just enough to glue the two together. That was so that your fingers wouldn't go through the bottom of it. Now you fill it, about an inch, with just flour and water mixed, which clings like glue and stretches. Now, on top of it, if I'm going to hit somebody in dark clothes, a brunette, you put a lemon meringue type of topping to it and garnish with whipped cream, you see. When it was a light costume, a blond, something like that, you put in blueberry, and then enough whipped cream just to splatter.

FM: *So you'd have a contrast.*

BK: Then, when you threw the pie, you shot put up to a distance of about eight feet. But from there on back, you brought that pie from

---

This television interview for Canadian Broadcasting Company took place at Keaton's home in Woodland Hills, California, April 29, 1964. Printed by permission of CBC Television.

here [*points to shoulder*] right overhand, 'cause with a little practice you can learn to make that pie come in this way [*vertically*] and not crossways.

FM: *So you get a real splatter.*
BK: Yes. It comes in that way at you.

FM: *Yes. I notice here in your autobiography that at one stage of the custard pie era you threw a pie—twenty-seven feet was it? —and hit the target right on.*
BK: Caught the villain plum in the pus with it.

FM: *How did you learn to control your body during the many difficult stunts that you performed in all those films? I'm not a gymnastic type myself, so I'd appreciate hearing exactly what you mean . . .*
BK: Any time that you leave the ground, your head will steer you.

FM: *And you don't think about your feet or your knees or your elbows or whatever? It's . . .*
BK: Well, you generally like to know where you are going.

FM: *Yes, that's true. Well, that is part and parcel of the surprising fact . . .*
BK: And doing falls—I do those in my sleep—'cause I was brought up being thrown all over the stage—and not just rollovers. I mean the length of the stage, and through chairs, tables, scenery. I used to do a thing coming out of the set house door of the stage, and we're grabbing the piece of scenery here and holding the door here and my own hand on my neck. And from the front, it looks like somebody has got me by the neck. And I'd yell blue murder and shake the scenery and everything— and with my feet going in all directions. And my old man comes up there to free me. And he used to kick over my head, and his foot would come down there and knock me loose from there. And as I'd slid back across the stage this way, he saw that it was me who had a hold of myself, and he'd chase me right out of the theater, see.

FM: *This was when you were a youngster?*
BK: Yeah. And this one night—I was only about eight or nine years old—at the Poli Theater in New Haven, when he kicked over my head, he misjudged it, and his kneecap caught me right there—back of the

head. And I stiffened and went out and fell straight back—and he didn't realize what was wrong—and my head hit the floor first. I'm out eighteen hours.

FM: *Why did you never smile on stage or in your films?*
BK: Because as a kid, growing up with an audience, I'd simply learned that I was the type of comic that if I laughed at what I did the audience didn't. And the more seriously I took my work or whatever I'd done, the bigger laughs I got. Well, by the time I was something like nine and ten years old, it was mechanical with me to work without smiling. So by the time I went in . . . the proof of it . . . going into pictures when I'm twenty-one years old . . . I started to get the name of "Frozen Face" and "Blank Pan" and things like that. We went into the projecting room and ran our first two pictures to see if I'd smiled. So you see, nobody, including my company, ever was conscious of it.

FM: *When did this marvelous hat come into your life?*
BK: It was very similar to the one I had on the stage, only the one I had on the stage was beaten up so bad, it didn't have much shape left. But when I went into pictures, every comedian wore a Derby hat. So, I says: "If there is one thing I won't wear, it's a Derby hat." So . . .

FM: *Did you invent . . . ?*
BK: I got my hat back out there to make sure that that brim stayed that way [*BK raises the hat to show a straight brim*], pretty near flat. Take sugar and water, soak the brim with it, and let it dry. It stiffens it enough so that you can do a lot with that hat, and it won't get out of shape.

FM: *Did the hat evolve over a period of time, or did you invent the flattened version of it first time out?*
BK: No. It is the same hat. I mean the same type.

FM: *. . . so that the top of the hat was brought right down to the brim.*
BK: No, well . . . it was easy to handle. That was one reason I did it that way, see, because the first thing I learned when I got into pictures was: Never leave that scene without your hat. I didn't know why 'til I finally . . . . Well, we'd shoot a scene here, and we'd shoot a scene a

week from now, [which] will be on the screen ahead of the scene we did yesterday. Well, in that scene I left my hat in there and here I've got my hat back on and nothing matches. So, never leave a scene without your hat. The girl may be tied to the railroad tracks and anything else, and you run into the cops. Get your hat first and then go save her. See.

FM: *Marvelous.*

BK: So, all right. Lloyd liked his straw hat.

FM: *And Charlie had his bowler.*

BK: Yeah, but every time he gets in a roughhouse scene, that's a hat gone. It's crushed. That's gone.

FM: *This one . . .*

BK: This one went through fire, earthquakes, floods, everything.

FM: *How did you plot your jokes? By talking it out among yourselves?*

BK: Yeah. Well, always when we set out to lay out a picture, says, "Jean here's got a good start." "What is it?" "This . . . so forth and so on." I had three men in my scenario department. Chaplin had about the same, but Lloyd had five or six. Well, we just . . . in our own little studio . . . so, the head cameraman, the head electrician, the prop man, they're in the conferences, the same as we [are], talking about whether they like it or not.

FM: *You're trying it out on each other.*

BK: Sure. And the minute we found something we liked, we said, "That's a fine start. Now, what's the finish?" Well, when we found a finish—how to round that out—we never worked on the middle. We always figured the middle would take care of itself.

FM: *Just let that happen.*

BK: We'd get off to a good start and have a good finish.

FM: *Was there any particular time when your best ideas came to you during a picture?*

BK: Generally in the bathroom.

FM: *Really!*
BK: Shaving was a great time to round out a routine.

FM: *And the bathtub is always a great source of inspiration.*
BK: Oh yeah. You can daydream in the bathtub.

FM: *And of course as a comedian on film, you had to depend, indeed, on your experiences with audiences in the theater.*
BK: Well, that's just automatic with me. If I picked up something here [*he picks up a coffee cup*], and the coffee ran out of the bottom here, I'd probably hold it [awhile thinking] . . . about what I thought they'd giggle at, before I tried to find out what happened to the cup.

[Scene of collapsing buildings from *Steamboat Bill, Jr.*]

BK: I played Shea's Theatre in Toronto when it was an upstairs theater.

FM: *Upstairs, was it?*
BK: Yes, and the one in Buffalo was called Shea's Garden Theater, and the footlights were gas jets.

FM: *What period was that?*
BK: Electric lights hadn't come into 'em yet. I played there one of my first years. So, it would have been about 1900.

FM: *What was your first professional appearance? That was the year before that, wasn't it? Eighteen . . . ?*
BK: The year before that in Wilmington, Delaware was my first official opening as a pro.

FM: *At what age?*
BK: Four years old.

FM: *That pretty much makes you the dean of Hollywood film stars, I would say.*
BK: Pretty near. I don't know of anybody that passes me. In other words, I'm older professionally than Francis X. Bushman, Maurice Chevalier, Charlie Chaplin, Mary Pickford, Ed Wynn . . .

FM: *Our own Canadian Mary Pickford.*
BK: Yes. Older professionally than these people.

FM: *I certainly think there ought to be a special title to go along with that, one way or another.*
BK: Like they do it with umpires in the big leagues? I could become the "Beans" Reardon of the . . .

FM: *We'll hope somebody thinks of an adequate one for you soon enough.*
BK: "Deacon" Keaton. I like that. Be perfect.

FM: *Yes. What was that first film that attracted you the year of* The Passing Show?
BK: *The Butcher Boy*, and my first scene in front of the camera was when I come into that grocery store with Arbuckle behind the counter to buy a little bucket—twenty-five cents worth—of molasses.

FM: *Oh, this was finding the coin . . .*
BK: That's right, in the bucket.

FM: *. . . in the bucket.*
BK: And spilt molasses all over and got my feet stuck in it and my hat got stuck on my head because he poured the molasses in my hat to find the quarter. When I put my hat back on to leave and got the bucket of molasses, he tipped his hat and said, "Good day," and I start . . . and the hat won't move.

FM: *Well now, you mentioned Roscoe—or Fatty—Arbuckle, as audiences know him, and I notice in your autobiography that you describe him as your best friend.*
BK: Well, number one, you see he—next to Chaplin—he was considered the best comedy director in pictures. For instance, Sennett's *Tillie's Punctured Romance*—well, Arbuckle directed about half of that picture.

FM: *. . . but didn't get credit for it.*
BK: No.

FM: *You made a great many films, actually, with Arbuckle, didn't you?*

BK: He was second to Chaplin as far as the box office was [concerned, for] a comedian. Lloyd passed him, when Lloyd put on the glasses and hat and stopped being "Lonesome Luke," which is about 1919—some place in there, 1918. He climbed overnight, up 'til then he didn't mean anything.

FM: *And Red Skelton was your favorite among associates of that time?*

BK: Yeah, I used to get mad at Skelton as well as anybody else. . . Skelton's first love was radio, and yet nobody could do a better scene on the screen than Skelton without opening his trap, but he'd do it anyhow—ad lib. When I say radio was his love at the time, he'd go to his dressing room on the stage between scenes and he wasn't worrying about what he was going to do in the next scene. He'd go in there and write gags for Little Junior to say or something for his radio script.

The Marx Brothers—it was an event when you could get all three of them on the set at the same time. The minute you started a picture with the Marx Brothers, you hired three assistant directors, one for each Marx brother. Get two of them, while you sent to look for the third, one of the first two would disappear. And they were the same thing. They never worried what the next setup was going to be or what the routine . . . or anything else. We'll ad lib it when we get there. Or Chico always had his bookie on the phone. Groucho had some other excuse to be missing. Harpo was visiting the other sets to see who was working.

Abbott and Costello—never gave the story a second thought. They'd say, "When do we come and what do we where?" Then they find out the day they start to shoot the picture what the script's about. Didn't worry about it. Didn't try to. Well, that used to get my goat because, my God, when we made pictures, we ate, slept, and dreamed them!

FM: *The story you tell in your book about a parody you wanted to make of one of the great MGM films,* Grand Hotel. *Tell us about that.*

BK: Well, there's people connected to MGM and [reasoning] that they could get the entire cast, and we'd set out and tell the same story that the *Grand Hotel* told—only our hotel would be down on bum's row, see. I don't know what we would call it, but then I wanted Marie Dressler to do Garbo's part. So, her opening scene is getting in front of the full-length mirror and taking off that long mink coat—and she's got a ballet costume on including toe slippers—and she says, "I think I'm getting too old to dance." And behind the curtain is the count. The phony count that was played by John Barrymore would have been Jimmy Durante. And I was going to play Crinoline: I'm dying of hiccups, and the doctors only give me thirty-five years to live, so I want to see life before I die. I've taken my . . .

FM: *That was originally the Lionel Barrymore part.*
BK: The Lionel Barrymore part. Then I wanted Babe Hardy to play Wally Beery's part, the German manufacturer. And he manufactures collar buttons, but he only manufactures the front ones. And he's trying to merge with Stan Laurel who manufactures back collar buttons. You get those two together.

FM: *Yes. Which among the shorts and the features did you like the best?*
BK: My biggest money maker was a feature picture, *The Navigator.* Next to that was one called [*Our*] *Hospitality*, and the third one was *The General.*

FM: *I don't know* Hospitality, *but I've seen* The General *and* The Navigator. The Navigator *is my favorite, I must say.*
BK: *Hospitality* would have out-grossed *The General.* It did out-gross it.

FM: *Well, Mr. Keaton, when you left MGM, the dark years of the thirties began.*
BK: Oh, I was going to answer that question you put to me, when I said that everything seemed to happen, including sound coming in. About this time, Chaplin is too lazy. Lloyd had got all that he needed, and he was retiring. I had trouble. So, there is none of us making pictures, and this would start in the early thirties. So, the first one to come along and make anything that looked like one of those pictures had the field to himself. There is no competition.

FM: *What do you think was it that brought the wonderful era, the golden age of comedy, to an end?*
BK: I don't know. It seemed like everything happened at once. Sound came in. New York stage directors, New York writers—dialogue writers— and musicians' union, all moved to Hollywood. So, the minute they

started laying out a script, they're looking for those funny lines, puns, little jokes, anything else. And my fight with Thalberg at MGM was: lay out a script with me the same as you always did. You come to that sequence where a man's working here on this part of the thing and I'm working on something else. We don't talk back and forth; we work. Now, you go out of your way when you have us talk. Work the same as we always did. We avoid talking when it's not necessary.

FM: *You were making moving pictures not talking pictures.*
BK: That's it, and we won't have any trouble. We talk when we're supposed to talk, but we lay out material that doesn't call for dialogue.

[Scenes from *College* and *The Playhouse*]

FM: *Mr. Keaton, how did you come to get the name, "Buster"?*
BK: Well, I was born with a tent show in a one-night stand in Kansas. My mother joined the show when I was two weeks old, and it was called "The Keaton & Houdini Medicine Show Company." Now, that's Harry Houdini, the handcuff king. He was the doctor and trickster of the outfit, and my old man was the entertainer and comic. And when I was six months old, we are in some little town, a small hotel, and I fell down a full flight of stairs to the bottom. They came running up, and I sat up and just shook my head. Shook it off and didn't cry. So they knew I wasn't hurt, and Houdini says, "That was sure a 'buster,' meaning a fall, 'cause that was the only time it was used. It meant a bronco buster or a fall. It was never used as a name. My father said: "That would be a good name for him. It doesn't sound bad." So, that's the way I got it.

[Shot of Eleanor Keaton on a swing in the foreground with Buster Keaton and Fletcher Markle at the table in the background]

FM: *You yourself had a very difficult period in that decade. You were divorced; you lost a great deal of money.*
BK: And I drank too. That helped.
[*The videotape of the interview ends abruptly at this point.*]

Buster Keaton

PENELOPE GILLIAT/1964

"WHEN YOU TAKE A FALL," the ailing Buster Keaton explains to me from the top of a bookcase as he is nearing seventy, proceeding then to zoom towards the window, "you use your head as the joystick." The poetic human airship grounds delicately and coughs.

He often seems to see himself rather distantly and as if he were some mechanical object. I suppose this is partly because of the physicality of a stage career that began in vaudeville as a man-handled toddler called "The Human Mop," and partly because he has an exceptionally modest notion of himself, including his suffering. Hollywood after the talkies treated the decorous genius like a goat.

"You don't go out of your way *not* to talk in a silent film," he says, "but you only talk if it's necessary." Two-minute pause. He is sitting in his rather poor ranch house in the San Fernando Valley, quite a drive from the stars' hangout in Beverly Hills. He always talks about work done long ago in the present tense. You wouldn't use any other.

He has been less canny than Chaplin or Harold Lloyd about retaining possession of his pictures and preserving himself from the new producers, and after the halcyon time his working conditions were ruthlessly taken from him, followed by the sack from Louis B. Mayer and the boot from a chilling wife, who changed their son's surname when the gloss went off it. But with his back to the wall and drinking enough to kill himself he still seems to have been practical and rather dashing, with much the same spirit as his fighting Irish father, who once dealt with

From Penelope Gilliat, *Unholy Fools* (New York: Viking, 1973), pp. 45–54.

an impresario's humiliating order to cut eight minutes out of the family vaudeville act by setting an alarm clock to go off on stage in the middle of the routine. It seems entirely characteristic of Buster that he should once have escaped from a straitjacket during the anguish of DTs by a music-hall trick learned from Houdini. As an infant he was plucked out of the window of his parents' digs by the eye of a cyclone and deposited intact a street away. Maybe it was this incident that planted in his father's head the theatrical possibilities of throwing the baby around. Joe Keaton started by hurling him through the scenery and dropping him onto the bass drum. When the child bounced, he began wiping the floor with him. One of his costumes had a suitcase handle on the back of the jacket so that he could be swung into the wings. Joe's wife, Myra, a lady saxophonist who seems always to have been at the end of her tether, used to refer thinly to the human-mop rehearsals as "Buster's story hour."

Buster is now sitting down, his back away from the back of the chair. The pause goes on. He is trying to explain, on the basis of what he started learning this way in vaudeville when he was rising three, the machinery of silent jokes. The beautiful head looks out of the back window, on to the plot of land where he has built his hens a henhouse that has the space of an aviary and the architecture of a New England schoolhouse. The great master of comedy, who is one of the true masters of cinema, suddenly gets up again and climbs onto a dresser and does a very neat fall, turning over onto his hands and pretending that he has a sore right thumb. He keeps it raised, and then stands stock-still and looks at it, acting. "Suppose I'm a carpenter's apprentice," he says after a while. Chest out, manly look, like a Victorian boy with his hands in his pockets having his photograph taken. "Suppose the carpenter hits my thumb with his hammer. Suppose I think, God damn, and leap out the window. Well, I'm not going to *say* my thumb hurts, am I? That's the trouble with the talkies."

He sits down in his chair again and thinks. He is wearing a jersey with piratical insignia on the front, and the sort of jaunty trousers that people sported on smart yachts in the 1930s. "The thing is not to be ridiculous. The one mistake the Marx Brothers ever make is that they're sometimes ridiculous. Sometimes *we're* in the middle of building a gag that turns out to be ridiculous. So, well, we have to think of something else. Sit it out. The cameras are our own, aren't they? We never hire our cameras. And we've got a start, and we've got a finish, because we don't begin on a film if we haven't, so all we've got to get now is the middle."

He lays out a game of solitaire. The room has a pool table in it, and a lot of old photographs. On the table between us there is a card that a studio magnate left stuck in his dressing-table mirror one day soon after the talkies came in, giving him the sack in three lines. "In the thirties, if there's a silence," says Buster, "they say there's a dead spot." Stills from his films come to mind: images of that noble gaze, austere and distinctive even when the head is up to the ears in water after a shipwreck, or when Buster is in mid-flight of some sort. Partly because of his vaudeville experience and partly because of his temperament, he obviously reserves great respect for those who retain a stoic attitude toward calamity and imminent death in the middle of being flung from one side of life to the other. He admires the character of a performing animal—a chimpanzee, as I remember, called Peter the Great—who expressed a Senecan-sounding serenity as he was being thrown around the stage of Buster's childhood.

Keaton's first film entrance was in *The Butcher Boy*. His character is clear at once. We are in a world of slapstick chaos, but he emits a sense of wary order. The scene is a village store. Everyone else moves around a lot, to put it mildly. When Keaton enters, the unmistakable calm asserts itself. He is wearing shabby overalls and big shoes with a hole in one sole (which later turns out to be usefully open to some spilled molasses) and already the famous flat hat. He then goes quietly through a scene of almost aeronautic catastrophe and subsidence, the whole parabola photographed in one take. Only a child brought up in music-hall riot from toddling age cold have done it. The shop—hung with posters promising "Fresh Sausages Made Every Month," run by a Roscoe Arbuckle who puts on a fur coat to go into the freezer locker (Keaton never calls him Fatty; it is always Roscoe), and inhabited by a club of aloof cardplayers with Abe Lincoln faces clustered around a stove—turns into a whirlwind. Molasses sticks, and bodies fly, and flour powders the air. We are in a world of agile apprentices and flung custard pies and badly made brooms that Buster scathingly plucks by the individual bristle as if they were suspect poultry. And through it all there is the Keaton presence: the beautiful eyes, the nose running straight down from the forehead, the raised, speculative eyebrows, the profile that seems simplified into a line as classical as the line of a Picasso figure drawing. After a bit, Roscoe Arbuckle throws a sack of flour at him. Throughout his life, to many people, Buster has repeated his admiration of the force and address of that throw.

In spite of the peculiarly heroic austerity of his comic temperament, Keaton maintains firmly that he is a low comedian. This is a simple piece of old vaudeville nomenclature. "The moment you get into character clothes, you're a low comedian," he says. There are also, among others, tramp comedians and blackface comedians—a category that was stylized for purely technical reasons but that drew some of Keaton's shorts into looking Uncle Tom-ish. "What you have to do is create a character. Then the character just does his best, and there's your comedy. No begging." This is the difference between him and Chaplin, though he doesn't invite comparisons and talks a lot more eagerly about technical things. The system of vaudeville comedy that he works by is methodical, physically taxing, and professionally interpreted. "Once you've got your realistic character, you've classed yourself. Any time you put a man into a woman's outfit, you're out of the realism class and you're in *Charley's Aunt*." There are one or two films of Keaton's, early in his career, in which someone wears drag; leaving aside modern unease about transvestism, the device goes against what Keaton can do.

Keaton's logical and vitally realist nature gradually got rid of the farfetched, or what he amiably calls just "the ridiculous." His whole comic character is too sobering for that, though infinitely and consolingly funny. Nothing much changes, it says. Things don't get easier. He will be courting a girl, for instance, and have to make way for a puppy, which the etiquette of the girl's demonstrativeness demands that she hug; the proposal that he meant to make to her goes dry in his mouth. He leaves with an air. Seasons pass, the puppy grows to frightful size, and he is still outwitted by her intervening love of pets. Finally, against every sort of odds, and only by great deftness, he manages to marry her, but the chance of kissing her is still obligatorily yielded to others—to the minister, to the in-laws, to the rival suitor, and to the now monstrous slobberer, who ends the picture by sitting between the wedding couple on a garden seat and licking the bride's face. All the same, whatever the mortification, Keaton is never a pathetic figure. His heroes stare out any plight. Perhaps because he has an instinctive dislike of crawling to an audience by exploiting any affliction in a character, including any capacity for being victimized, his figures never seem beaten men, and after a few experiments in his early work he never plays a simpleton. He has perfected, uniquely, a sort of comedy that is about heroes of native highbrow intelligence, just as he is almost the only man who has ever managed to establish qualities of delicate dignity in characters with money. Comedians don't generally play the high-born. The fortunate, debonair, tongue-tied central character of *The Navigator* is one of the rarer creations of comedy: rich, decorous, possessed of a chauffeur and a fine car that makes a U-turn across the street to his fiancée's house, infinitely capable of dealing with the exchange and mart of high-flown social marriage, jerking no heart-strings, Keaton's world is a world of swells and toffs as well as butcher boys, and mixed up in it are memories of his hardy past in vaudeville that give some of his films a mood of the surreal. In *The Playhouse*, which he made after breaking his ankle on another picture, he plays not only nine musicians and seven orchestra members but also a music-hall aquatic star, an entire minstrel show, a dowager and her bedeviled husband, a pair of soft-shoe dancers, a stagehand, an Irish char, and her awful child, among others. We see the Keaton brat dropping a lollipop onto the Keaton *grande dame* in the box below; the dowager then abstractedly uses the lollipop as a lorgnette. He also plays a monkey who shins up the proscenium arch—something that must have been rough on the broken ankle. The film has a peculiar aura, not quite like anything else he made. It is dreamlike and touching, with roots in a singular infancy that he takes for granted. Vaudeville is what he comes from, as powerfully as Shakespeare's Hal comes from boon nights spent with Falstaff. In *Go West*, there is a music-hall set piece about a slightly ramshackle top hat that is kept brilliantly in the air by repeated gun shots. "It has to be an old hat," says Buster. "You couldn't use a new hat. Otherwise, you don't get your laugh. Audiences don't like to see things getting spoiled."

Keaton has a passion for props. Especially for stylish-things like top hats, for sailing-boats and paddle steamers, and for all brainy machinery. He finds ships irresistible. A short called *The Boat* forecasts *The Navigator;* there is also *Steamboat Bill, Jr.*. Facing many calamities, Buster as a sailor works with a sad, composed gaze and a resourcefulness that never wilts. In *Steamboat Bill, Jr.*, he leans on a life preserver that first jars his elbow by falling off the boat and then immediately sinks; Keaton's alert face, looking at it, is beautiful and without reproach. In *The Boat*, where he is shipbuilding, though deflected a good many times by one or another of a set of unsmiling small sons, his wife dents the stern of his creation with an unbreakable bottle of Coke while she is launching it; Keaton helps by leaning over the side to smash the thing with a hammer, and then stands erect while the boat sinks quickly up to his neck, leaving us to watch the august head turning around in contained and unresentful bafflement. In *Steamboat Bill, Jr.*, his last independently produced film, he turns up, looking chipper, to join a long-lost father who runs a steamboat. The son will be recognized by a white carnation, Buster has bravely said in a telegram delivered fours days late. He keeps authoritatively turning the carnation in his lapel toward people as if it were a police badge. No one is interested. His father eventually proves to be a big, benign bruiser, and not the man his son would have expected; nor is Buster the sort of man his father instantly warms to. He is much put off by the beautiful uniform of an admiral that Buster wears to help on the steamboat. It is not, maybe, fit for running a paddle steamer, but it is profoundly hopeful. It represents an apparently mistaken dapperness and an admission of instinctive class that turns out to be as correct in the end as the same out-of-place aristocratism is in *The Navigator*, that poetic masterpiece of world cinema.

There is nothing anywhere quite to equal the comic, desperate beauty of the long shots in *The Navigator* when Buster, the rich sap, is looking for his girl on the otherwise deserted liner that has gone adrift. The rows of cabin doors swing open and closed in turn, port and starboard in rhythm, on deck after deck; the noble, tiny figure with the strict face and passionate character runs round and round to find his dizzy girl, who is looking for him in her own quite sweet but less heartfelt way. The flower-faced fiancée played by Kathryn McGuire is a typical Keaton heroine. She is rather nice to him when he has got into his diving suit to free the rudder and has forgotten, with the helmet closed, that there is a lighted cigarette in his mouth. (This is a mistake that apparently happened while Keaton was shooting. "They've closed the suit on me," he says, coughing, the memory bringing on his present bronchitis, "and everyone just thinks I'm working up a gag.")

Keaton's characters are outsiders in the sense of spectators, not of nihilists or anarchists. He isn't at his best when he hates people (unlike W. C. Fields, for instance—whom he talks about with regard, doing a brotherly imitation of the voice of men who are martyrs to drinkers' catarrh). A short called *My Wife's Relations* has some of the Fields ingredients, but Keaton muffs the loathing. The picture has its moments, though. The wife is a virago with Irish relations who are devout but greedy; the only way to get a steak, Buster discovers, is to turn the calendar to a Friday. The blows that he manages to give her in bed when she thinks he is only thrashing in his sleep are pretty funny. So are the hordes of rapacious brides in *Seven Chances*, rushing after him on roller skates and wearing improvised bridal veils to make a grab for him because he will inherit a mint if he marries by seven o'clock.

But Keaton is really at his best when he is being rather courtly. He has great charm in a feature called *The Three Ages*—about love in the Stone Age, the Roman Age, and the Modern Age—when he stands around among primordial rocks in a fur singlet and huge fur bedroom slippers chivalrously helping enormous girls up boulders. In that Age, prospective in-laws assess the suitors by strenuous blows with clubs, and people ride around on mastodons that are clearly elephants decked out with rococo tusks by Keaton's happy prop men. In the Roman Age episodes, Wallace Beery as the Adventurer has a fine chariot, and Keaton has a sort of orange crate drawn by a hopeless collection of four indescribable animals. The Romans throw him into a lion's den, but he thinks of only the pleasantest things to remember about lions, which is that they behave well if you do something or other nice to their paws. He takes a paw, washes it, manicures it, and dries it. The interested beast responds affably. We switch back to the Stone Age. Keaton, looking more than usually small in the surroundings, is dealing courageously with the colossal opposite sex while hoping privately for more lyric times. He gets them for a moment in the Roman sequences; there is a wonderful shot of a girl's worshipful face as she thinks of Buster when she is in the middle of being pulled by the hair in some impossible Roman torment. But nothing vile in antiquity, Keaton implies by the sudden pinching end of this revue-film, can equal the meagerspiritedness of Los Angeles; the Stone Age and the Roman Age episodes both finish with shots of Buster and his bride surrounded by hordes of

kids in baby fur tunics and baby togas, but the Modern Age episode fin-
ishes with the happy couple walking out of a Beverly Hills house followed by a very small, spoiled dog. Such minutes of tart melancholy are
often there in Keaton. They go by fleetingly and without bitterness, like
the sad flash in *The Scarecrow* when a girl takes it that his kneeling to do
up a shoelace means that he is proposing. His beloveds sometimes have
overwhelming mothers; one battle-ax, in *The Three Ages*, causes a pang
when she makes him produce his bank balance, which is in a passbook
labeled "Last National Bank" and obviously not up to scratch. One
thinks, inevitably, of the hard time that Keaton was to have with his
ambitious actress wife, Natalie Talmadge, which left him flat broke
when the talkies came in. The Keaton hero, with the scale he is built
on, and with his fastidious sense of humor, is obviously the born physical enemy of all awesome women. The girls he loves are shy and funny,
with faces that they raise to him like wineglasses. But his idyllic scenes
are very unsentimental. There is a nice moment when his loved one in
The Navigator says to him, in reply to a proposal of marriage, "Certainly
not!" Chaplin was once said to have given comedy its soul; if so, it was
Keaton who gave it its spine and spirit.

"They have too many people working on pictures now, you know,"
says the aging, unsoured man whom the talkies threw on the dustheap
although he could probably have gone on making great films in any
new circumstance, and on a minute budget, and editing in a cupboard.
"We had a head electrician, a head carpenter, and a head blacksmith."
The blacksmith seems to have been crucial. There was a lot of welding
to do. Keaton himself did his stunt work, magically and beautifully.
Who else? He could loop through the air like a lasso. When he is playing the cox in *College* and the tiller falls off the boat, it is entirely in
character that he should dip himself into the water and use his own
body as the tiller. The end of *Seven Chances* is an amazing piece of stunt
invention, inspired by cascades of falling boulders, that would have
killed Keaton if he hadn't been an acrobat. Most of his stunt stuff isn't
the sort of thing that can be retaken, and Keaton doesn't care much for
inserts. "I like long takes, in long shot," he says. "Close-ups hurt comedy. I like to work full figure. All comedians want their feet in."

He has just been asked to the première of *It's a Mad, Mad, Mad, Mad
World*, which he has a part in after spending decades doing nothing

172 BUSTER KEATON: INTERVIEWS

much but commercials. *Mad World* is in the mode of wide screens with a vengeance, Buster has seen the picture. It can't be much to his taste, but he doesn't say so. He likes working, even making commercials doesn't strike him as such a cruel outcome to a life. He wants to go to the premiere. He looks vigilant and spry.

The wife of his last years thinks he shouldn't go to the premiere, because he might get a coughing fit and have to leave.

"We have aisle seats," he says.

"You're not well," she says.

"I can take my cough mixture," he says. "I can take a small container. I can get ready to move in a hurry."

Buster Keaton

KEVIN BROWNLOW/1964

TOM WEBSTER DROVE me out to Woodland Hills, and we got
to Buster Keaton's on schedule. It was a small, ordinary-looking house
named "The Keatons," a change from his huge Hollywood place later
owned by James Mason. Mrs. Keaton opened the door. She seemed
about forty-five years old and a real covered-wagon, shoot-from-the-hip
western wife. (I later found out that Eleanor had been born in L.A., not
on a ranch.) Their dog filled the doorway, an enormous brown, soft
St. Bernard. Mrs. Keaton said she had no place to call us; otherwise she'd
have cancelled the visit. The studio had put him on standby, but they'd
cancelled it. Out came a short, stout elderly man; the light was behind
him, so I couldn't see his face. Then he stepped into close-up, and I
caught my first glimpse of those wonderful features. Keaton had a voice
like an anchor chain running out. He had a very expressive face, even
when supposedly deadpan, but in reality he laughed a lot. He talked
freely, as though he were enjoying it, and several times roared with
delighted laughter at a remembered situation and had to go out from
behind the table and act it out for me. The first was a story about filming a scene for *Sherlock Jr.* in a lion's cage, when he did that marvelously
assured nonchalant walk, whistling. Hearing him whistle was a surprise.
The second was when he said Eleanor thought he'd been remiss in not
feeding his chickens, and he gave an imitation of a red chicken glower-
ing and tapping its claw in irritation.

This interview was conducted at Keaton's home in Woodland Hills, California, on
December 18, 1964. Also participating in the conversation were Keaton's wife, Eleanor
Keaton, and a young man, Tom Webster, who drove Brownlow around Los Angeles.
Brownlow introduces the interview. Printed by permission of Kevin Brownlow.

The interview was carried out in a room at a lower level than the entrance hall. Along the walls were the only stills Keaton had left after Rudi Blesh took the others in trunkloads for his book: a smiling picture of Roscoe Arbuckle dominated one wall; a framed sheet of notepaper for The Three Keatons; a picture of The Three Keatons taken in 1899 ("my second salaried year"); a photo of his father with the locomotive used in *Our Hospitality*; a photo of Keaton, Harold Lloyd, and Jacques Tati; a hilarious picture of Buster with Zsa Zsa Gabor outside the Moulin Rouge, with Buster on his knees doing a Toulouse-Lautrec.

The interview was very rewarding, for Keaton loved to talk about the mechanical problems involved in staging his comedies. Eleanor sat with him and filled in facts when he got stuck. I realized that this was not only a highlight of the trip, but would be a highlight of my life, but there always has to be some nagging worry to mar perfection. I was concerned about our next interview. I called Allan Dwan from Keaton's telephone, but he was just going out. This broke the continuity of the interview. Keaton offered us beer from a little bar he had devised with an ingenious cooling device, behind tiny barroom doors and a sign saying SALOON. I usually dislike beer, but I accepted his and liked it a lot. Eleanor showed us a new book they'd been sent by an old friend, the writer Paul Gallico (author of *The Snow Goose*), and Buster went back to a cowboy series on TV.

BROWNLOW: *About the control that you had on your pictures—the actual way you worked with Eddie Cline and with Clyde Bruckman and the rest of them—now they would presumably be on the set behind the camera, but who would in fact select the take?*
KEATON: I would select the takes in the projecting room, sure, 'cause I cut 'em.

BROWNLOW: *You actually cut them?*
KEATON: Oh, yes.

BROWNLOW: *I was going to ask you who your editor was. I didn't realize that you were responsible for that.*
KEATON: We all did it. Lloyd and me just talked to a cutter. I doubt if Lloyd ever handled his own film because he also didn't like . . . he didn't direct.

BROWNLOW: *Lloyd didn't?*

KEATON: No. He *was* a co-director as far as that goes, but he never set out to make a picture by himself. Well, I did, see. Chaplin never had a director. Well, that was against his principles—to just let anybody else have anything to do with any picture he made, see.

BROWNLOW: *But you gave credit to your directors.*

KEATON: Oh, I'd put one of my writers' names—or something like that—on there. Says directed by. . . . Give 'em a promotion. I did that with . . . Clyde Bruckman because Lloyd didn't know any better and hired him and kept him for about four pictures—four or five pictures. He was there for about three years, or something like that. But he turned out good for Lloyd, so there was no harm done. Made him a good director. But up to then he had no experience of directing at all.

BROWNLOW: *Didn't Roach also fall for Clyde Bruckman as a director?*

KEATON: I guess later on, yes, but by that time he was a director.

BROWNLOW: *Yeah, well now, I've looked at the pictures of Eddie Cline, that Eddie Cline made on his own . . .*

KEATON: When I first started making two-reelers, I had Eddie Cline—I just co-directed with him. What we'd do, of course, we always carried three men on our scenario staff and worked with them, and by the time we decided on a . . . we were ready to start a picture, my head technical man that builds my sets, my head prop man, my head electrician, assistant director, everybody knows what we've been talking about for weeks. So, we never had anything on paper.

BROWNLOW: *You never had a script?*

KEATON: Neither Chaplin, Lloyd, nor myself—even when we got into feature-length pictures—ever had a script.

BROWNLOW: *Well, what did Carl Harbaugh write then when he wrote your scenarios?*

KEATON: He didn't write nothing. He was one of the most useless men I ever had on the scenario department. He wasn't a good gag man; he wasn't a good title writer; he wasn't a good story constructionist.

BROWNLOW: *Well, how come he's got sole screen credit for* Steamboat Bill, Jr.?
KEATON: Well, we had to put somebody's name up that wrote 'em, and did this. . . .

BROWNLOW: *You really had us historians on a . . .*
KEATON: He was on a salary with us. He was one of the weakest—the two best I ever had were Jean Havez and Clyde Bruckman. Especially after we stopped making wild two-reelers and got into feature-length pictures, our scenario boys had to be story conscious because we couldn't tell any far-fetched stories. We couldn't do farce comedy, for instance. It'd have been poison to us. An audience wanted to believe any story we told them. Well, that eliminates farce comedy and burlesque and everything else, see. The only time you could do something out of the ordinary—it had to be in a dream sequence or something or a vision, something like that. So story construction became very important to us.

For instance, somebody comes up with an idea. Says, "Now, here's a good start." We skip the middle immediately—we never paid any attention to the middle. Immediately went to the finish. We work on the finish, and if we get a finish that we're all satisfied with, then we'll go back and work on the middle, because the middle for some reason always takes care of itself. You get the start and a finish, you're all right.

Now here's the difference in independent companies in those days. It would be the same thing today as far as that goes. When you owned your own studio and you're the only company in there, well, you're making feature-length pictures. Well, you make two a year—a spring release and a fall release. Your skeleton outfit of the company—that's your technical man, your head cameraman and his assistant, and the prop man, your head electrician—these people, they're on salary with you for fifty-two weeks of the year. So, if I'm sitting in the cutting room, and the picture's been finished, I'm going through it, and I say: "I'd like to take this sequence out, and if I'd turned to the left in that alley there, I could drop that whole sequence and pick it up right here. So, we'll get the cameras out this afternoon and we'll go back to that alley and shoot it." Now, to do that, that'd cost me the gasoline for the cars that we owned and the amount of film that we bought from Eastman to put in the camera to take that—which, when it all adds up, means about $2.39.

You try that at any major studio today, and I'll tell you the least you could get that scene for—just go out and grab that scene and get back—would be around $12,000. Because everything is rented. Everything! And of course you don't move a company today but the union has to take so many prop men, so many . . . this has to go, this has to go . . . the commissary truck goes, the dressing-room truck goes.

BROWNLOW: *Now, you had Fred Gabourie doing your sets, didn't you?*
KEATON: Yes. Fred Gabourie was my technical man, built all our sets.

BROWNLOW: *Now, he would also be responsible for special effects?*
KEATON: Yes.

BROWNLOW: *Now, who was the production manager?*
KEATON: Production manager would have been my studio head, who was Lou Anger, whose name would never have been on the screen. And most of the time I used Gabourie as a production manager.

BROWNLOW: *Did you have a property man as well as Gabourie?*
KEATON: Oh, yes.

BROWNLOW: *Who was that, can you recall? Who was the property man?*
KEATON: His name was Bert Jackson. And a head electrician . . .

BROWNLOW: *Did you have Reve Houck ever work . . . because I know you had Byron?*
KEATON: Byron Houck . . . Byron Houck was a second cameraman with me.

BROWNLOW: *Was he the brother of Reve Houck at the Ince studios?*
KEATON: No. Byron Houck was a baseball player with the Philadelphia Athletics at one time. He was with the famous team of [Frank] "Home Run" Baker, Eddie Collins, Chief Bender—that outfit.

BROWNLOW: *And you had Elgin Lessley, I believe, who was Arbuckle's . . .*
KEATON: He was my first cameraman.

BROWNLOW: *Who was also with Arbuckle, wasn't he?*

KEATON: He was with Arbuckle originally, because I had the Arbuckle Company when I started. Because when I got back out of the army in 1919, I only made two more pictures with Arbuckle when Schenck sold Arbuckle's contract to Paramount for feature-length pictures and gave me that company to start my own. And then he got me the studio. The studio was the old Chaplin studio before Charlie built the place on La Brea. So I had a city lot there, a good-size block for a studio. We had all the room in the world for one company—plenty of room.

BROWNLOW: *Did you shoot most of the stuff on the lot or did you use location?*

KEATON: For our type of pictures, we used location an awful lot.

BROWNLOW: *It's difficult to tell in your pictures which is location and which is shot exterior on the lot. You have, for instance, the scene in* Sherlock Jr. *when you come off the roof into the back of the vehicle—you remember that—which would be on location.*

KEATON: That's location, yeah.

BROWNLOW: *You have something built on the lot where you leap through the window into that . . .*

KEATON: Oh yeah. The set . . . we divided the set. That had to be built.

BROWNLOW: *And that's on the lot, but it is hard to tell which is which.*

KEATON: That's right.

BROWNLOW: *Presumably, you must have been worried by the amount of people that would get in the way during the shooting of a location scene?*

KEATON: No. We didn't used to have so much trouble. If we were going to be in a congested section, we'd always tell the police department, and they'd send down two or three motorcycle cops to control any traffic or whatever we needed.

BROWNLOW: *In those days, did you get good cooperation from the police?*

KEATON: Oh, anything we wanted.

BROWNLOW: *Did you have to pay them?*

KEATON: No. But we used to deliberately give the . . . for instance, if we used police, we'd give them an extra's check or a stunt check. In other words, probably about $10 or something like that.

BROWNLOW: *Wasn't it true after a time the police department refused to let their men be used in pictures?*

KEATON: I don't know. I guess they did, but in those days we didn't pay any attention to that at all. We'd simply tell them what we wanted. If we wanted the fire department, they said, "Which one do you want?" We went down and got it and sent them out on a call. Cost us nothing, never did. None of our railroad things ever cost us anything.

BROWNLOW: *How was that?*

KEATON: The Santa Fe people were tickled to death to see on the screen, "SANTA FE RAILROAD." It was on their boxcars; it was on their engines and trains and everything. They were perfectly satisfied. They can't get cheaper advertising than that!

BROWNLOW: *Which was the railroad you did* The General *on, then?*

KEATON: Well, that was nobody's railroad. Number one, I went to the original location, from Atlanta, Georgia, up to Chattanooga, and the scenery didn't look very good. It looked terrible. The railroad tracks I couldn't use at all because the Civil War trains were narrow gauge, and those railroad beds of that time were pretty crude. They didn't have so much gravel rock to put between the ties, and then you saw grass growing between the ties every place you saw the railroad, darn near. And of course, I had to have narrow-gauge railroads, so I went to Oregon. And in Oregon, it is honeycombed . . . the whole state is honeycombed with narrow-gauge railroads for all the lumber mills, 'cause they handle all their trees and things like that with narrow-gauge railroads.[1] Well, so I

---

[1] Brownlow points out: "In interviews, Keaton always maintained that he needed narrow-gauge railroads and that was why he went to Oregon. For a railroad enthusiast to make such an error is odd—perhaps Keaton was muddling the trains in this film with that of *Our Hospitality*. For neither Civil War railroads nor the lumber lines in Oregon were narrow-gauge" ("The Search for Buster Keaton" [unpublished manuscript], p. 109).

found trains going through valleys, mountains, by little lakes or mountain streams—anything I wanted.

BROWNLOW: *Huge viaducts?*
KEATON: Or anything I wanted. So, we got rolling equipment—wheels and trucks and stuff like that. We built our freight train and our passenger train, and remodeled three locomotives.

BROWNLOW: *You remodeled them. You didn't get the originals out of the . . . ?*
KEATON: Oh no, but the engines working in these lumber camps were all so doggone old, it was an easy job. They were all wood burners, all of them. [Pointing to a photograph on the wall, Keaton says,] The same engine, that's the General. That's the way she is at the present time. She's at the World's Fair in New York, but they keep it in a showcase down in Atlanta, Georgia, where the start of that chase was supposed to be from, see. And at that period they didn't pay much attention to numbers of engines—they named them all. That's what accounts for the General—and the one I chased it with was the Texas. It's the Texas I threw through the burning bridge.

BROWNLOW: *How . . . that incredible scene?*
KEATON: Well, we built that bridge.

BROWNLOW: *How many extras did you have in that?*
KEATON: We also dammed up water underneath it so that there would be more water, so that the stream would look better.

BROWNLOW: *How did you get down to planning a thing like this? You had Gabourie, and who else did you work with on a scene like that?*
KEATON: Just Gabourie—he and a couple of his right-hand men, one a blacksmith, because we had a forge and a blacksmith's shop right on the lot!

TOM WEBSTER: *Where did you operate out of in Oregon?*
KEATON: In a place called Cottage Grove, just a little south of Eugene—only about thirty-five miles from Eugene, Oregon. And when I wanted

the battle scenes, I managed to get extra people. No experienced people there, being extra people, we just had to train 'em to be extra people.

BROWNLOW: *Did you ship them up from . . . ?*
KEATON: No, they were just all around. They came from miles around in Oregon to get in there, see. And when we did the battle scenes, I got the National Guard of Oregon.

BROWNLOW: *But where did you get your uniforms?*
KEATON: From here.

BROWNLOW: *You shipped them all up from . . .*
KEATON: Yes, all the uniforms. Now that location, from Hollywood, is around twelve hundred miles.

BROWNLOW: *Now, how many cameras did you have on that?*
KEATON: Always had three, and a fourth one when I needed it. Because in the silent days, there's always two cameras on every shot, right alongside of each other—not to give you different angles but right alongside of each other, because the one generally on the cameraman's left was [for] the foreign negative. Because when you completed your picture, you cut your picture, we said that's it. Now, they cut the same scenes from the other camera. Well, they match that negative and ship that [second negative] to Europe, and in Europe all the foreign prints were made off of that. Otherwise a couple of hundred reels of film would have to be shipped over there—so much cheaper to do it that way. That's why you always had a foreign [negative] print.

BROWNLOW: *So, when you had other camera positions, you'd have two in each place?*
KEATON: Well, no, then we'd start spotting cameras for odd angle shots. If this one was good, this [other] one would have to be satisfied with our angle. That's all there was to it. Europe didn't see that one. Of course, later on when we got rolling and [had] new inventions, we got so we could take and duplicate an odd shot and make a foreign negative out of it, a dupe negative we called it. [In the] early days, they weren't very good. A dupe negative was always grainy and milky—it wasn't good

photography, see. But in later years, they had practically perfected it, so you could hardly tell a dupe negative shot from the real one.

BROWNLOW: *These were the days, of course, when you had to do your own opticals in the camera.*
KEATON: Oh, yes.

BROWNLOW: *Your chief cameraman was Dev Jennings?*
KEATON: Both Lessley and Jennings.

BROWNLOW: *Well now, to go back a little further, what I want to try to discover is how you learned about motion pictures yourself, because . . .*
KEATON: I was going to go into a show in New York. I was going into the Winter Garden for *The Passing Show of 1917,* when I met Arbuckle on the street with an old friend of mine, who introduced me to Arbuckle. Arbuckle asked me if I'd ever been in a motion picture. I said I hadn't even been in a studio. He said, "Come on down to the Norma Talmadge Studio on Forty-eighth Street on Monday. Get there early and do a scene with me and see how you like it." Well, rehearsals hadn't started yet, so I said, "all right." I went down and did it.

Well, the making of a motion picture started to fascinate me immediately. So I stuck with them and went in and out of that picture. First thing I did was I asked a thousand questions about the camera and got into the camera. Then I went into the projecting room to see things cut. It just fascinated me. For a finish I asked them to break my contract, let me out of the show, and I stayed with Arbuckle. And Arbuckle at that time was considered, next to Chaplin, to be the best comedy director in pictures.

BROWNLOW: *Director? He was directing?*
KEATON: Oh yes. He directed all his own. He was a good man to watch. Well, I was only with him about maybe three pictures when I became his assistant director. I don't mean in the sense of an assistant director like we have today who sees that the people are on the set. I mean when he was doing a scene and I wasn't in it, I was alongside the camera to watch him. I directed when he was in the scene. So by

the time I'd spent a year with him, it was no problem at all, when I set out to make my own, to direct.

BROWNLOW: *So, a picture like* Coney Island *would have been co-directed by you and him?*
KEATON: Yeah.

BROWNLOW: *Was Al St. John ever interested in directing?*
KEATON: No. He never was.

BROWNLOW: *Did Arbuckle really have the knowledge and the feel . . . ?*
KEATON: Yeah. Do you remember Sennett's famous picture, *Tillie's Punctured Romance?* Well, Arbuckle did an awful lot of that, although his name wasn't on the screen for it. I think Freddie Fishbach was the director of that, but Arbuckle did an awful lot of work on it for Sennett.

BROWNLOW: *Well, now in those days, cutting wasn't done in animated viewers. You held it up to the light and . . .*
KEATON: Well, we had the little cranks too, but they were a nuisance. Once we've seen that scene on the screen, we knew about what it is. We can get in the projection room and run down to where the action that we want is. "There, just as he goes out that door. Rip it. That's it. Pick up. Give the next shot. Get down to where he's just coming through the door." Edit them and spliced together. Now you've started, see. And stopping to thread those things up for that. . . . The only thing that happens today is you got a sound track on there.

BROWNLOW: *Yeah, but how did you get the pacing on it?*
KEATON: Oh, that comes from experience . . . of assembling.

BROWNLOW: *Experience? This is what I can't understand. Your pictures, right from the start, were so technically perfect. And you say you did it by experience, but, you know, this is . . . I've been in the editing business for years, and I can't get this experience just by going into the cutting room and doing it like you did. This is something that comes from a knowledge and handling of film, but it comes after many years. But with you, you did it like this!*
KEATON: Yeah, I don't know.
MRS. KEATON: It must have been the timing of actors.

KEATON: It must have . . .

MRS. KEATON: Having worked all his life, he's always had this mathe-matical timing as far as actors moving around.

BROWNLOW: *True.*

KEATON: See, I was a veteran before I went into pictures. I was twenty-one years old then. So, pacing . . . for instance, in fast action you'll cut scenes a little closer together than just normal action. And when you've got a dramatic scene, you lengthen out a little bit more on those, so you don't get a fast pace.

BROWNLOW: *But you know that every film is based on . . . the cutting of it is based on the rhythm, and you've got to cut right on that. And if you take one of your pictures and you run it at the correct speed and you just sit back and you go [clicks fingers] . . . like that, every cut comes up right to the frame. That scene where you are running out in* Cops *to grab hold of that car as it goes past—the driving mirror, as it goes up—right to the very frame, it's correct. It's perfect. And this is something which very few editors today could do.*

TOM WEBSTER: It's a cut on action.

BROWNLOW: *Yes, it's a cut on action, but it's more than that. Did you have any assistants in the cutting room who were looking after the filing of trims and so on?*

KEATON: Oh yes. We called him my cutter.

BROWNLOW: *Who was that?*

KEATON: He's the fellow that broke your film down and put it all in the racks there and had them all there. I'd say, "Give me that long shot of the ballroom" or whatever, and he'd hand it to you, and start through it . . . you'd start off with this. "Give me the close-up now of the butler announcing the arrival of his lordship." All right.

BROWNLOW: *Who was the cutter; do you remember?*

KEATON: As I cut them, he splices them together, running them onto the reel as fast as I hand them to him.

BROWNLOW: *What was his name; do you remember?*

KEATON: "Father Sherman" [J. Sherman Kell], he was with us. Sherman was his last name; we never did know his first name. "Father," we called him—he looked like a priest.

BROWNLOW: *You had those glass things on the cutting room table that you could see . . .*

KEATON: Oh yes, and indirect lighting underneath it.

BROWNLOW: *What about the fire risk in those cutting rooms?*

KEATON: We never paid any attention to it. No, if a match ever got near one of those films, brother, it went up fast.

BROWNLOW: *Now, some of those pictures—or nearly all of your pictures—are based round some large piece of mechanism or some important stabilizing fact. Now in* One Week, *which I have a print of but which I probably shouldn't have, but never mind, the house which starts going round, which was really shot on your lot: How did you evolve the mechanism for getting the wind machines going, the leaves coming in front of it, and the house going round at the same time?*

KEATON: We built it on a turntable and buried the control belt or rod or whatever it was.

BROWNLOW: *That would have been a very expensive thing to have . . .*

KEATON: Oh no. You just dig a ditch down about that far and lay your stuff in there and then put boards over it and then shovel dirt and grass on top of it. And that's it.

BROWNLOW: *You make it sound so simple!*

KEATON: You're sure to do that in nothing flat.

BROWNLOW: *Gabourie would have built this turntable?*

KEATON: Oh sure.

BROWNLOW: *How long would it have taken him to have done something like that?*

KEATON: If he set a couple of men to work on that, it would take about three days. If he had to hurry it, he'd put more men on it, that's all. If he knew what was coming in advance, he'd have built it. You [remember] a picture of mine called *Steamboat Bill, Jr.*, with that cyclone in it and those houses going through the air and everything else? That's all Gabe Gabourie. That's the one where the house falls on me.

BROWNLOW: *With the attic window going through . . .*
KEATON: Yeah, when I go through the window.

BROWNLOW: *How many takes did that take?*
KEATON: That's a one-take scene. All of those scenes are one-takes.

BROWNLOW: *The hospital scene?*
KEATON: The whole hospital went off of me.

BROWNLOW: *Cranes?*
KEATON: Cranes.

BROWNLOW: *Location or on the lot?*
KEATON: Oh, that was location . . . all along the Sacramento River up at Sacramento, 'cause that river looks like the Mississippi up there, see.

BROWNLOW: *So that was Chuck Reisner, wasn't it?*
KEATON: Chuck Reisner co-directed with me on that one, yes.[2]

BROWNLOW: *How was he as a comedy director? How would you rate him?*
KEATON: He was a good one.

BROWNLOW: *What did you ask of these directors when you hired them, because you changed around quite a lot?*
KEATON: Oh, work with me, that's all.
TOM WEBSTER: *Do you mind telling us the budget on that film, of* Steamboat Bill, Jr.?
KEATON: Oh yes, that was an expensive picture. That picture cost as much as *The General*, believe it or not—around $330,000. That was

---

[2] Although listed on the credits of *Steamboat Bill, Jr.* as 'Chas. F. Reisner,' the director's real name was 'Charles F. Riesner' (1887–1962).

another thing the average person, even in the picture business, never realized. Take any program feature-length picture, I mean your standard stars such as Gloria Swanson, Norma Talmadge, Rudolph Valentino—not Doug Fairbanks doing *Robin Hood* or those big elaborate expensive pictures—but the average program picture. For instance, Norma Talmadge makes, with an all-star cast, *Within the Law* (1923). The budget of *Within the Law* was $180,000. *The Navigator* with me was $220,000. Our pictures always ran almost a third more in price than the dramatic pictures.

BROWNLOW: *Because they took longer to make?*
KEATON: Automatically, we couldn't help ourselves. We got too many tricks to do. We not only take longer, but those things are all a little expensive when you start doing those things. So our pictures as a rule cost about a third more. Chaplin would go higher yet, and Lloyd would go more than I did.

BROWNLOW: *The average crew when you went out on location—did you take the gag men with you?*
KEATON: Sometimes we asked them to come on up. They wanted to do it anyhow. Quite often I took them with me—maybe not all three of them. Anybody who wanted to stay home, we let them stay home. With our studio manager, Lou Anger, they can see our dailies come in.

BROWNLOW: *So your average crew would be pretty large because you'd have carpenters, grips, electricians. You'd have how many?*
KEATON: We took what we knew we needed, not like a union rule today.

BROWNLOW: *But if you hadn't written anything, how did you know what props to take?*
KEATON: Oh, they all knew. The prop man, he'd know everything you needed. Wardrobe department would too. Gabourie knew what to build. Didn't need anything on paper. To commence with, with us, you'd say, "When they get into this hotel lobby. . . ." I'd say, "Build a pretty good-looking set. I think I may want to shoot a lot of stuff in there." We go to shoot, and the first couple of routines we try are not working out right. And yet, over here was a breakfast nook. We got into trouble here, and we ended up shooting more in this breakfast nook

than we did in the hotel lobby. That happened to us all the time. Well, if we're going by script, there goes the script right there and then.

BROWNLOW: *What about the footage ratio? What was the ratio of footage you shot on these pictures? What would you allow yourself?*
KEATON: We didn't pay any attention to it. We knew our picture. First, we were making five-reelers, and around 1924 or '25—about 1925—we went to seven-reelers, because everybody else did. And the amount of raw stock we used—we never paid the slightest bit of attention to it. But we could generally tell when we were over footage, which we didn't mind, because it was much better to be able to cut and throw things away than to go short.

BROWNLOW: *But this couldn't apply in the early two-reelers. You must have been much more economical because you were just starting.*
KEATON: Shot 'em the same way, exactly. We generally knew when we had enough footage for . . .

BROWNLOW: *So sometimes you'd run into a hell of a lot of takes on one . . .*
KEATON: Oh I didn't pay any attention to . . . that's just throwing that film away, that's all.

BROWNLOW: *You didn't print it. You didn't print everything.*
KEATON: No. We generally picked out a couple of takes. We shot a scene eight times. Says, "The second and the fourth one were pretty good—just print those two, that's all." The others were thrown away.

BROWNLOW: *On* Our Hospitality, *you had a prop which was a fantastic train, "The Rocket." Now, did you let Arbuckle have this for* The Iron Mule *(1925)?*
KEATON: Yes. I'm the only one in the picture business ever built that railroad. The whole thing was built in the Keaton Studio—that whole train.

BROWNLOW: *It was built from scratch? It wasn't a conversion?*
KEATON: No, it was built from scratch. The only thing we did was stick to the original thing. Your first railroad was stage coaches with flanged wheels put on them and coupling links . . . and the wagon tongue taken

off. And of course put braces on the front wheels so they can't turn. Well, that was the original coaches of the original train. So that was easy to do with us. Now the baggage car, which was just a little short flat car—like that—with a little roof over it, and the tender and engine were all built from scratch. But we duplicated the drawings that we could get of the Stephenson Rocket. It was the English engine, or was it the DeWitt?

BROWNLOW: *No, the Stephenson Rocket.*
KEATON: The Stephenson Rocket was the English. Well, that's the one we built. We built it to measurement, to scale and everything.[3]

BROWNLOW: *And the rail, the line was on your lot?*
KEATON: Oh no. That was up in . . . from Lake Tahoe down to Truckee, which again was a narrow-gauge railroad, see.

BROWNLOW: *So, Arbuckle's* The Iron Mule . . .
KEATON: Sure, when he had to do it, he had to go find a narrow-gauge railroad someplace and do it.

BROWNLOW: *He took your engine and your . . . ?*
KEATON: Yeah, I gave it to him to make a two-reeler with Al St. John. That was years later. I don't remember how long it was.

BROWNLOW: *And they credited that to Grover Jones. They wouldn't give him [Arbuckle] credit as director on that picture.*
KEATON: What?

BROWNLOW: *They gave credit for that film of his,* The Iron Mule, *to Grover Jones. They wouldn't say that William Goodrich or Arbuckle directed it . . . which is rather sad. I only found out that he directed it by coming across a still of that engine and him standing by the camera.*
KEATON: That's right. Oh, he didn't dare use his name at that time. He used "Goodrich."

---

[3] Buster Keaton told John Gillett and James Blue that he chose the English Rocket over the American DeWitt Clinton "because it's funnier looking" ("Keaton at Venice," *Sight and Sound* vol. 35, no. 1, p. 27).

BROWNLOW: *But they wouldn't even put that on it. They put Grover Jones, who was his writer. Do you remember Grover Jones?*

KEATON: That's right. Well, Grover Jones was a two-reel director at one time.

MRS. KEATON: He was some kind of a relation of mine. Or was. My mother's cousin or something. I can remember when I was a little kid we used to go visit them all the time. . . .

BROWNLOW: *You're obviously fascinated by railroads anyway, aren't you—apart from using them in motion pictures?*

KEATON: Oh, well. It was a great prop. I did some awful wild things with the railroads.

BROWNLOW: *The thing is, of course, about your pictures, whatever subject you choose, the accuracy—the way you build the props and the way they are used—is quite extraordinary. I mean, the Civil War was re-created as accurately in your pictures as anybody has ever done it—those Brady-print battle scenes are quite incredible. Incidentally, talking on these prop things, is it true that on* The Buster Keaton Story *(1957) you showed them how to stage that boat sinking and saved them a tremendous amount of money? Remember when the boat launched and . . .*

KEATON: When I made the picture with Donald O'Connor, *The Buster Keaton Story.* Yes, because when we actually did it, it took us three days to get the scene. Just kept running with things, that's all. We got that boat to slide down the waves. Now, we got something like sixteen hundred pounds of pig-iron and T-rails in it to give it weight. We cut it loose and she slows up, slows up so slow that we can't use it. Well, you don't like to undercrank when you're around water. If you undercrank water, immediately you see it shows, that it's jumpy. Well, first thing we do is build a breakaway stern to the boat. So, when it hits the water, it would just collapse and act as a scoop, to scoop water. That worked fine except the nose stayed in the air. We've got an air pocket in the nose. We get it back up and bore holes all through the nose and everyplace else that might form an air pocket. Try her again. And there is a certain amount of buoyancy to wood no matter how much you weight it down. She hesitated, before she'd slowly sink. And our gag's not worth a tinker's dam if she just don't go straight right down to the bottom. So for a finish, we go out in the bay at Balboa and drop a sea anchor with a cable to the stern, a cable out of a pulley over to a tug out of the shot. We've got all the air holes out of it and the rear end to scoop water—I actually *pulled* that boat down. That's the way we got the scene.

So, when I told the construction department of the bugs and how to eliminate them before they built it—and how to prepare it in the first place—they improved on me one way. They went out with a sea anchor, but they put an extension from the launching ramp of timber out there so it couldn't move, and it would be far enough out that the pull on the center of the boat would control it. And [they] brought the cable right back up under the launching ramp to a powerful truck. And the truck pulled this way, and the boat went that way, see.

BROWNLOW: *Did you know that they'd pinched that gag for a Ray Griffith film, and they had to do it in miniature?*
KEATON: Yes, I know that they pinched it, but I never saw it.

BROWNLOW: *They couldn't do it the way you did it. They had to do it in miniature.*
KEATON: Well, it would have cost them too much money, that's why.

BROWNLOW: *That was right after yours. It's a great . . . That's incredible, that story. Again, that would be Gabourie and you working on . . . ?*
KEATON SAYS TO MRS. KEATON: He's done some research when he knows that.

BROWNLOW: *When you meet one's idol, one always tends to know something about him before. . . . Now, the other thing is, did you hire Donald Crisp purely for the dramatic aspect of* The Navigator?
KEATON: That's right, and it didn't work.

BROWNLOW: *Why not?*
KEATON: He had just finished a picture at Paramount. Now, to commence with, he had a reputation as an actor, but he'd directed a couple of small pictures for some independent outfit or something like that, and Paramount gave him a picture with Louise Dresser called *The Goose Woman* (1925). And it was acclaimed at the time as the best dramatic picture of the year.

BROWNLOW: *Now you've put this before in a magazine. This is incorrect.*
Clarence Brown directed The Goose Woman. *Donald Crisp had been direct-*
ing for some time and had been an actor and then had returned to directing
for DeMille, and he was directing little five-reelers like Young April *(1926)*
with Bessie Love and a few things like this.[4] The Goose Woman *was*
Clarence Brown.
KEATON: You sure of that?

BROWNLOW: *Definitely. I have a print of it back in London. That was*
directed by Clarence Brown with Louise Dresser.
KEATON: Well, he had something to do . . . maybe he just acted in it.
I only know that we knew he had been connected with . . . well, we
knew him well as far as that goes.

BROWNLOW: *He was a regular dramatic director.*
KEATON: Yeah, well I said, "I've got a couple of dramatic sequences in
this thing, and I don't want . . . I want 'em straight. And I'm going to a
cannibal island, and I don't want burlesque-looking headhunters and
cannibals out there. I want them legitimate." "Fine," he says. Well,
I had just made *Sherlock Jr.*, and I did that one alone. I started with
Arbuckle.

BROWNLOW: *Really?*
KEATON: Yeah, because Arbuckle had just gotten out of his trouble,
see, and he didn't dare use his name. So, I gave him the name,
"Goodrich." First I wrote it out, "Will B Good." Well, that's all right for
a laugh. "William Goodrich" is a good name.[5] All right, that's it. So we
hire him as a director for me, and at the end of about three days we saw
our mistake. He is now so irritable and impatient and loses his temper
so easily. He's screaming at people, getting flushed and mad, and of
course things don't go so well. In other words, he hadn't recovered yet

---

[4] Prior to *The Navigator*, Donald Crisp had directed a dramatic feature, *Ponjola* (1923), with
Anna Q. Nilsson and James Kirkwood.
[5] Roscoe Arbuckle's father's names was William Goodrich Arbuckle. See Andy Edmonds,
Frame-Up!: The Untold Story of Roscoe "Fatty" Arbuckle (New York: William Morrow and Co.,
1991), p. 16.

from those trials, of being accused of murder and nearly convicted. It just changed his disposition. In other words, it made a nervous wreck out of him, damn near what it did to him. So, I got Hearst—I didn't talk to Hearst, I got Marion Davies. I said, "You're going to make *The Red Mill* (1927). Why don't you use Arbuckle? He'd make a great comedy director for you." She says, "He sure would, wouldn't he?" And she got Hearst to hire him. (Laughter)

BROWNLOW: *For* The Red Mill?
KEATON: For *The Red Mill*, sure. I said, "We hate to lose you, Roscoe, but this is too big an opportunity, working for Hearst."[6] So, then I went ahead, threw the first three days' stuff in the ashcan, started from scratch and made the picture.

BROWNLOW: *And you didn't have anybody co-directing with you on that one?*
KEATON: No.

BROWNLOW: *You took screen credit on that one.*
KEATON: I think I do.

BROWNLOW: *Why didn't you continue?*
KEATON: I don't know.

BROWNLOW: *Did you need assistants?*
KEATON: You see, I'm the guy that made a picture called *The Playhouse*, where I was everything in the world—where I was deliberately kidding most of the guys in motion pictures, especially a guy by the name of Ince—Thomas H. Ince at the Ince Studio which was out in Culver City. His main star I think was . . .

---

[6] Under the name of William Goodrich, Arbuckle was credited with directing *The Red Mill*, although King Vidor eventually took over. However, because *The Red Mill* was released three years after *Sherlock Jr.*, film historians have been reluctant to believe Keaton's account that Arbuckle had to leave off directing *Sherlock Jr.* in order to take on the more prestigious job of directing Marion Davies. See Kevin Brownlow, "The Search for Buster Keaton" (unpublished manuscript), p. 88–90.

BROWNLOW: *Enid Bennett?*
KEATON: Clara Young?

BROWNLOW: *No. She worked for Vitagraph. He had Enid Bennett and . . .*
KEATON: Oh, I forget now. Of course, he originally had Bill Hart. I don't remember now who else. But he was one of those guys [whose pictures would say]: THOMAS H. INCE PRESENTS SO-AND-SO IN *HEMSTITCHING ON THE MEXICAN BORDER.* WRITTEN BY THOMAS H. INCE. DIRECTED BY THOMAS H. INCE. CUT BY THOMAS H. INCE. THIS IS A THOMAS H. INCE PRODUCTION. So, when I made *The Playhouse*—and remember I do all these double exposures—I'm the whole orchestra, I'm the people in the boxes, in the audience, and I'm on the stage. I bought a ticket from myself—I'm the ticket taker who took a ticket from myself. [Laughs.] So, when we put the credit titles up—we put up the cast of characters, they're all Keaton. We used that: Written by Keaton. Directed by Keaton. Costumes by Keaton—and into a separate title—This is a Keaton production, which got a belly laugh from an audience. They laughed like hell at that. We were only kidding people like Ince, you see. Later on, we'd have done it to Zanuck; we'd have done it to Mervyn Leroy and a few like that [who were] trying to see how many times they could get their names on there. Maybe having kidded things like that, I hesitated to put my own name on as a director and writer.[7]

BROWNLOW: *I see, that explains that, but most of your pictures kidded somebody. Didn't* The Navigator *kid Mr. and Mrs. Martin Johnson? Remember those travel pictures on cannibals?*
KEATON: Oh, yeah . . . well, no. I didn't pay much attention to that. We just had a story.

BROWNLOW: *You weren't consciously thinking of Martin Johnson?*
KEATON: No.

---

[7] Georges Méliès played every member of an orchestra and the conductor in *L'Homme Orchestre* (1900). Keaton probably saw Méliès's film when he was in vaudeville. See David Robinson, *Georges Méliès: Father of Film Fantasy* (London: Museum of the Moving Image, 1993), p. 19.

BROWNLOW: *What about* Sherlock Jr.? *Was that kidding the Barrymore film?*

KEATON: No. The reason for that is that we got the one idea of a motion picture operator in a theater. Runs motion pictures. Give him a problem that almost wrecks his young life. Actually, it's got to be over the girl. He goes to sleep in the projection room and automatically visualizes everything on that screen as his character. Well now, from there on we laid out that story. Because that was an invention—every cameraman in the picture business went and saw that picture more than once, trying to figure out how in hell we did some of that. Oh, there were some great shots in that baby! That's the one where I got up on the screen and they threw me off back into the audience. I finally get back up there again and the scenes changed on me.

BROWNLOW: *Didn't you use surveyor's instruments?*

KEATON: Not for that one, no. I did that in another picture.

BROWNLOW: *If you didn't in this, I don't know how you did this one. I thought that was the answer that you used surveyor's poles to get the position . . .*

KEATON: We didn't need surveyor's instruments for that. All we needed was the exact distance, and the cameraman could judge the height. And by using a traveling matte from the other take—which you could do, see—they get me in position here and they crank [a few feet]. They throw [that exposed film] in the darkroom and develop it right there and then and bring it back to him [the cameraman], and he cuts out those frames and puts it in [the camera gate]. When I come to change scenes, he can put me right square where I was, as long as that distance was correct.

But the other thing where I had to use surveyor's instruments was that [in *Seven Chances*] I had an automobile, like a Stutz-Bearcat roadster. I was in front of an office building. Now it's a full-figure shot of that automobile and me. I come down, got into the car—there's a lot of people walking up and down the sidewalks, office building in the background—I release the emergency brake after starting it, sit back to drive—and I didn't move. The scene changed, and I was in front of a little cottage out in the country. I reach forward, pull on the emergency brake, shut my motor off, and went on into the cottage. I come back out after I visit her, get into the automobile, turn it on, sit back there—and I and the automobile never moved—and the scene changed back to the office building in New York, in the city. Now that automobile's got to be exactly the same distance, the same height and everything, to make that work, because the scene overlaps but I don't.

BROWNLOW: *Now, what about lighting on it?*
KEATON: Standard lighting.

BROWNLOW: *It was interior.*
KEATON: No, all exterior.

BROWNLOW: *If it was standard lighting and the sun wasn't in the right place, the shadows would . . .*
KEATON: We made sure of that, same time of day so the shadows would [be in the same place]. But for that baby, we used surveying instruments, so that the front part of the car would be the same distance from [the camera], the whole shooting match.

BROWNLOW: *[In* Sherlock Jr.*], when you stepped into the screen then, you must have built a set behind and lit it as though it was a motion picture.*
KEATON: That's right. It was our lighting that did it because we actually built the stage with a big black cut-out screen, then the front-row seats and orchestra pit and everything else, apron. I climbed out of the front row and climbed right up on the stage and onto the screen—and they threw me out. I'd interfered with them. And, of course, the audience knows I'm in a dream. I've fallen asleep in the projection booth, and all the characters on the screen now are the people I've just had trouble with.

BROWNLOW: *The most incredible scene is when you are about to leap off a cliff and as you go, on the action, you cut to landing in sand, and you are sitting on a rock and that changes to the sea, and all these things . . .*
KEATON: And then the lion's den, too.

BROWNLOW: *That's right, the two lions. The number of times I've looked at that again and again trying to work out how it was done. I'm sure many people have.*

MRS. KEATON: The precarious part of that were the lions.

BROWNLOW: *What happened with the lions?*

MRS. KEATON: Well, the trainer told them to lie quietly. [Keaton starts laughing.] And he told Buster, "Don't go into any corners and don't move fast."

KEATON: I'm in the cage out at Universal where they had all the animals then, and they had a big cage, probably be sixty to eighty feet in diameter, a round cage full of tropical foliage. So, with a whip and a chair and a gun, he [the trainer] gets the two lions [in position]—one here and one facing this way—and then I get down there. Now the cameraman is outside the cage, shooting through one hole. His lens is here. He says, "Now, don't run from them at any time, don't make a fast move and don't go in a corner." Well, there *is* no corner in a round cage, see! [Laughter]

Well, the fast move part is all right because I'm a natural actor, but what happened was . . . the scene overlaps, and I'm with a lion. I start to walk away from him—and lookit, there's [another] one, here! [Keaton starts whistling and walking.] I got about this far, and I glanced back and both of them were *that* far behind me, walking with me! [Keaton is overcome with laughter.] And I don't know these lions personally, see. They're both strangers to me! I start to walk towards the side of the cage to slip out. Then the cameraman says, "We've got to do the scene again for the foreign negative." I said, "Europe ain't gonna see this scene!" Will Rogers years later used that gag, "Europe ain't gonna see this scene!" We made a dupe negative out of that baby! [More laughter and Buster returns to his seat.]

Oh, no. It took him [the trainer] fifteen minutes to get the lions there. They broke a chair on him—they slapped it out of his hands. He had a helluva time getting them into position in the first place. Then, he wants me in [the cage], saying, "Just don't run or make a fast move or go in a corner." Fine! I've worked with lions since, and some nice ones.

BROWNLOW: *There was that lion in* The Three Ages, *but that was somebody dressed up as a lion, wasn't it?*
KEATON: Yes. I manicured his paw.

BROWNLOW: *So, [Sherlock Jr.] is not a parody on Barrymore's film, and [we discussed some] technical details on that. Oh yes, I know what I wanted to ask you. Why did you use Herbert Blaché?*
KEATON: What was that for?

BROWNLOW: *[He directed]* The Saphead.
KEATON: Oh, I had nothing to do with that. God, I'd forgotten the name. I'm back out of uniform, two pictures with Arbuckle, and Schenck in New York tells Marcus Loew that he's going to sell Arbuckle to Paramount to make feature pictures, and he's going to start making two-reelers with me. Well, Marcus Loew knew me from the stage, knew The Three Keatons, see. He'd also probably seen me in a couple of Arbuckle pictures. He says, "We'll contract for him." Now, Marcus Loew had just bought Metro, and the Metro studios were next to the Keaton studio, see. And he's just bought it because he's a theater owner. He buys the Metro Exchange, which exchanges throughout the whole world, and the studio—and takes over all the contracts of their people. And the first thing he did . . . he says, "I'll take the Keaton pictures." So, he's contracted for those before I'd started to make them. He goes to our leading New York producer of shows, called John Golden, for instance *Seventh Heaven, Turn to the Right, Lightnin'*—great shows. He and Belasco were the two leading producers of dramatic shows. John Golden didn't hesitate to do light comedies such as *Officer 666* and a couple of others like that he did.

Loew says, "We want to do *The New Henrietta*." They called it *The Saphead*, but the original show was called *The New Henrietta*. Of course, it's the name "Henrietta" that causes the kid to get in trouble. It's the name of a silver mine in Montana or something, and the original show in New York starred William H. Crane—elderly character man, grey-haired man—and Douglas Fairbanks. So, this is one of Fairbanks's great hit shows on Broadway. This is before he ever sees a studio, and the character in the show is "Bertie the Lamb"—his name is "Bertie." "Bert," I suppose, but everybody calls him "Bertie." His father is a multimillionaire and known as "the Bull of Wall Street." So his son they called "the Lamb." Well now, it was a hit show that ran a couple of years or so. So, Marcus Loew says to Golden,

> "I want one of your famous shows. I want to make a special immediately. I want to improve the quality of pictures if I can at the studio. I'll take *The New Henrietta*."

> [Golden] says, "Fine."

> "Get William H. Crane—you can get him—to play his own part, and cast the rest of them."

> "Of course, you can't get Fairbanks."

Fairbanks was now one of the biggest shots in pictures.

> "Give me the stage director for direction. Any experience in the studio?"

> "No. Winchell Smith has never had any experience in the studio."

> "Well, we'll put a technical director with him. We'll give him a motion-picture director to sit alongside of him. He'll watch the action of the people. This other man will watch the camera angles."

So there's Herbert Blaché.

BROWNLOW: *Who was the cameraman on the* The Saphead—*was it Bert Haines? [It was Harold Wenstrom.]*
KEATON: I don't know who the hell that was. Bert Haines was an assistant cameraman with me. I don't remember. It was one of Metro's regular cameramen. My cameraman didn't shoot it. That was the Metro staff, see. My staff had nothing to do with that picture.

BROWNLOW: *But did you think that Blaché had . . .*
KEATON: Metro made the picture, not the Keaton studio.

BROWNLOW: *Did you think that Blaché had any value as a director?*
KEATON: I didn't pay enough attention to him.

BROWNLOW: *I've asked you about the background of Gabourie. Can you tell me the background of Dev Jennings?*
KEATON: No, I can't.

BROWNLOW: *Did you call him "Dev" Jennings or "Gordon" Jennings?*
KEATON: It was "Dev" Jennings.

BROWNLOW: *Where did he come from?*
KEATON: "Dev" was an abbreviation for what?

BROWNLOW: *Devereaux.*
KEATON: His brother was the head cameraman for Paramount . . . the head cameraman.

BROWNLOW: *What was his name?*
KEATON: Al Jennings, I think it was.

BROWNLOW: *No, it couldn't be Al Jennings. That was the Western star.*
KEATON: An outlaw.

BROWNLOW: *Did you ever know the outlaw, by the way, Al Jennings?*
KEATON: I knew him. He used to come by my studio all the time. Yes, practically four or five times a year he'd drop in and spend a day or so.

BROWNLOW: *Did you ever see any of his pictures?*
KEATON: No.

BROWNLOW: *They were funny. I found one the other day in New York.*
KEATON: I never saw one.

BROWNLOW: *I don't know where Dev Jennings came from—but Lessley had been Arbuckle's favorite cameraman.*
KEATON: Sure, he originally came from the Sennett studio.

BROWNLOW: *A Sennett man and, I believe, originally a projectionist, wasn't he?*
KEATON: That I don't know, but he was a great cameraman. He practically, on a small scale, invented the process screen, for back projection.

And he did it . . . it got to the place where I could take a piece of film where two people are talking, and he could eliminate one and bring me closer and make a close-up of me in that scene. And he did it with back projection, on a small scale.

BROWNLOW: *Did the grain show?*
KEATON: No, clear as a bell.

BROWNLOW: *Now, you had so many innovations on your lot. I don't know what in the motion picture industry . . . you are responsible for this development of. It's quite incredible. For one thing . . .*
KEATON: I developed more stunt men than any studio in Los Angeles.

BROWNLOW: *Who did you have as stunt men out there?*
KEATON: I've taken the goddamndest people and made stunt men out of them.

BROWNLOW: *What did you look for?*
KEATON: You know this Frank McGrath? Do you know the show, *Wagon Train*? The one with the beard, the cook on *Wagon Train*. What do they call him? His name is Frank McGrath. Well, he was my chauffeur.

BROWNLOW: *I saw him at Universal yesterday. If I had known that he was your chauffeur . . .*
KEATON: He was my chauffeur, and I'm on location, and I've run out of actors. I said, "Put a makeup on him—make him get in there." He said, "All right. What do I do?" I said, "You just do what we tell you." Before long, I'd got him in mix-ups, doing stunts. He was successful enough doing bits and roughhouse work.

BROWNLOW: *Well now, you didn't often use a stunt man for yourself, because I know you broke your neck on* Sherlock Jr.
KEATON: Oh no, I didn't use stunt men for me, but I doubled them. There's a scene in *Sherlock Jr.* when I call a motorcycle cop, and I say, "Follow that car." And I jump on his handlebars, we hit a bump in the street, and I lose the cop. Well, the cop that fell off was me. Because what I did was take Ernie Orsatti, an assistant prop man with me, who

was my size. Put my clothes on him. I put the cop's clothes on, drove the motorcycle, hit the bump and fell off the motorcycle.

BROWNLOW: *Well now, that fantastic shot in which you are on the front of those handlebars and the train is coming at you and you are going fast, presumably that was mounted on a truck at that point?*
KEATON: Yes.

BROWNLOW: *But now the shots where you are clearly guiding it like this, you were really doing that?*
KEATON: Yes.

BROWNLOW: *But this is an impossibility!*
KEATON: Yes, hell of a job. Number one. The control of the gas is here [on the handlebars] for speed, but I've got no brakes. You've got to have a strong arm to get your feet back down there, 'cause it was footbrakes, see. Well, I got some beautiful spills before I could get back. Some beauties. I parked right up on top of an automobile once. I hit it head on, and I ended up with my fanny up against the windshield, my feet straight in the air. [Laughter] Parked car!

BROWNLOW: *Now, do you remember that scene where the water tower is switched on and you're escaping on this train in* Sherlock Jr.? *And you broke your neck on that one, didn't you? It forced you onto the rails.*
KEATON: Yeah, there's that volume of water hit me so hard enough, it just tore my hands loose from the rope and I fell. And when I fell, I lit on the track, feet first and then my fanny, and my head fell right across the rail. It's right in here. [He points to his neck.] And I had a headache for a few hours. I remember I had Donald Crisp with me, too, because I was out getting . . . these were last scene shots for that picture, and we had already made a deal with him for *The Navigator.* And he was with me on the location. It was Prohibition, see. I said, "I want a drink." I turned at the next block coming back from location—it was out here in the [San Fernando] Valley someplace. I went into Mildred Harris's— Charlie Chaplin's first wife—and I went into her house, and she gave me a couple of stiff drinks. During Prohibition, see—when you couldn't just stop anyplace to get a drink. So, that numbed me enough that I

woke up the following morning, my head was clear, and I never stopped working. But fourteen years later, I'm in the Soldier's Home [Veterans Hospital] down here in Sawtelle. They won't release you out of that until they've X-rayed everything you've got. If you've got dandruff, they'll keep you there. The doctor calls me in and says, "When did you break your neck?" I said I never broke my neck. He said, "Look at this X-ray. This callus has grown over the crack; it's next to the top vertebra." I didn't know it. I said, "How long ago was this?" "That looks like it could be somewhere between ten and fifteen years ago." That's how old the scar was. I started thinking back. "I know when it happened. It's that goddamn fall on the track. It cracked this vertebra." I never stopped working, never knew it. Well, that's luck. No nerve pinched or anything in the healing—and I never knew it.

BROWNLOW: *And you went on doing stunts after that.*
KEATON: Oh, sure. I never knew it. That's a fluke. That's a beautiful break. That could have ruined you—there are so many things in that vertebra that could cause you trouble.

BROWNLOW: *Well now, you say Crisp didn't work out on this* The Navigator *deal, but you didn't finish telling me why. I know you hired him.*
KEATON: Oh. The main thing is to go through the picture with him. I said to him, "You don't have to worry about the gag department. We'll take care of that." Well, we start and he directed all right, but he wasn't fussy about it. He was only interested in the scenes I was in. He turned gag man overnight on me. He came to work every morning with the goddamndest gags you ever heard of in your life. Wild! We didn't want him as a gag man, for God's sakes! We went through the picture; the only thing is that we let him go before I did the underwater sequence, because that was the last thing I did and that was a tedious job. It caused us a lot of trouble anyhow. A director can't do anything with an underwater sequence anyway. It's just between me and the cameraman and the technical man.

BROWNLOW: *So Crisp was gone by then?*
KEATON: Sure, he wasn't on that sequence.

BROWNLOW: *But he was on all the rest of it?*
KEATON: He was on all the rest of it. Yeah. He was actually annoying as a gag man, see. Actually, after I let him go, I went back and shot a couple of dramatic scenes again.

BROWNLOW: *Which were they—can you remember?*
KEATON: One was the girl . . . after they had dragged her onto the island, the cannibal island, all these black feet were around her and we went to her close-up; she is just surrounded by feet. He shot it in such a way that it looked like all she was doing was smelling feet, which would have been perfectly natural if we were looking for laughs—but we're not looking for laughs there, see. I shot that again so that she wasn't half unconscious and their feet brought her to, or something, see. Just had her [act] scared more. That and another scene in the first part where he let the spies who cut the boat loose . . . he let them do a little over-acting. I was always a little fussy about that. I didn't like overacting.

BROWNLOW: *Did you do the underwater scene in a tank in a studio?*
KEATON: No. We first said we'll use that big tank down at Riverside. By building up so we can get five or six feet more water in the deep end, we may be able to do it there. So they went down and built it, put the water in and the added water forced the bottom of the swimming pool out. Crumbled it like it was a cracker, the added weight of water— the whole bottom. So we had to rebuild the swimming pool for them in Riverside. Next thing, we tested off of Catalina, and we found there was a milk in the water for some reason—the mating season of the fish around the island causes that. Then, of course, the minute you touch the bottom it riles up with mud, it slowly rises up and blacks out your scene on you. Lake Tahoe is the clearest water in the world, and it's always cold because it's up a mile high—and that's an awful big lake. So we went up to Tahoe, and I'm actually working in around twenty feet of water with that.

BROWNLOW: *You were really in that diver's suit?*
KEATON: Oh God yes. I went down there. I set the set. You imagine . . . we built this camera box for two cameras a little bigger than this table— square—with a big iron passage up to the top with a ladder on the inside. Now, it holds two cameras and two cameramen. That box, of

course, was built of planks and sealed good so that there's no leakage. But it's wood and there has to be added weight added to it. Well, I added about a thousand pounds of weight to it. Now we find out the inside's got to be kept at the same temperature as the water outside. So we hang a thermometer out there so the cameraman can look through the glass and read it—and one on the inside. And we got cakes of ice out there. First thing in the morning and the night before is to put ice in there and then add more to make sure to keep the temperature of the camera box the same as the water on the outside, so it won't fog up the glass. Either one side or the other will fog up on you, see. The difference was that when two bodies are in there, the body heat . . . that means add more ice immediately. So, as you put the cameramen in, you also put more ice in. [Laughter.] Dressed them warm enough to take it. So, there's the whole outfit and me with that deep-sea diving outfit going down there, and the cameraman says, "I'm too close. I want to be back further." I moved that camera box under water—*I* moved it! That's how much you can lift when you're down around fifteen or twenty feet deep. The box must have weighed about fourteen hundred pounds or something like that. Two cameramen and two cameras and about two to three hundred pounds of ice, another thousand pounds of weight on it, and I picked it up and moved it.

BROWNLOW: *How long were you down there?*
KEATON: I was one month shooting that, and I was spending around . . . well, to start with, the longest you could stay down would be about half an hour because that cold water goes through into your kidneys. After about half hour, you start to get numb. You want to get up and get out of there. So, you're actually . . . I did so damn much trick stuff under there for God's sake. I did a lot of stuff.

BROWNLOW: *What about the light?*
KEATON: Oh, that's natural. We didn't worry about any artificial light. Natural sunlight penetrates that far.

BROWNLOW: *Who wrote your titles?*
KEATON: The scenario staff and me wrote all of it. *The General* was my pet for me because I had my nerve setting out to tell that story. Because

that was a page out of history when I did it, see. Because it actually happened. But I couldn't use their finish. Walt Disney tried to do it later, and he couldn't use the real finish either.

BROWNLOW: *What was the real finish?*
KEATON: The real finish was that they took all eight of those guys—the Southerners did—and they felled a pine tree into a crotch and with eight horses—they pulled all eight horses out and dropped all eight at once. Hanged all eight. That was the real finish to that. Then, of course, Disney makes the mistake and puts Fess Parker in to play the lead as a Northerner. So he's trying to make villains out of the Confederate Army. Well, you can't do that with a motion picture audience. And the same crack goes if I was in Michigan, Maine, or Massachusetts. You still can't make villains out of the Southerners.

BROWNLOW: *Why not?*
KEATON: The audience resents it. They lost the war anyhow, so the audience resents it. We knew better. Don't tell the story from the Northerners' side—tell it from the Southerners' side. And when my picture ended, the South was winning. Of course, this episode took place in the second year of the war, which would be 1862. And, of course, the Southerners lost in 1864—lost the war. When my picture ended they were winning—which was correct, they were. But I wrote my own finish to get my engine back. From the time I deserted the engine, from there on it becomes the story. Now, I wrote my own story, my own continuity. I directed it and cut it and titled it. So actually it was a pet. It's not my biggest moneymaker.

BROWNLOW: *Which was?*
KEATON: *The Navigator* was the biggest moneymaker I ever made.

BROWNLOW: *Well, one of my pet gags in* The General *is that moment where you throw the plank and the plank knocks the other plank. How many takes?*
KEATON: One.

BROWNLOW: *Oh no. You keep doing this. One take?*
KEATON: A one-take shot.

BROWNLOW: *And the traveling shots alongside? Was there a road alongside the railroad track?*

KEATON: Yeah.

BROWNLOW: *And you had a truck with . . . ? How did you keep pace? Did you have a fixed speed? Practically all of it is these fantastic traveling shots alongside . . .*

KEATON: There was no such thing yet as back projection, see. So, every shot you see is shot on the level.

BROWNLOW: *I know. That is what's so extraordinary about it, but those [shots] are so beautiful and smooth. Did you have a special suspension on the tracking vehicle?*

KEATON: We made sure [those shots were smooth.] We had big Westinghouse shock absorbers on that automobile and everything else. We used a roadscraper. We were pretty fussy about that.

BROWNLOW: *Well it certainly paid off. Were you drafted in World War I?*

KEATON: Yes. I was in the infantry.

BROWNLOW: *Were you in France?*

KEATON: Seven months in France. I was in the army eleven months—seven months of it in France.

BROWNLOW: *Towards the end of the war?*

KEATON: I got there in 1918.

BROWNLOW: *Did you see any fighting?*

KEATON: Just close enough to hear it, but by the time I hit the front, the Germans were in retreat, which was a great thing. I was tickled to death at that. Well, I was a 14-18er—a doughboy.

BROWNLOW: *You also had a policy of having the feminine leads unknown.*

KEATON: Well, for that you have to go to my studio manager's . . . If he could get a leading lady cheap, he did it, because he didn't consider them important. But later on, when we got into features, I didn't worry so much about the price.

BROWNLOW: *You once had Phyllis Haver.*
KEATON: I had Phyllis Haver in one of the two-reelers.

BROWNLOW: *That's quite expensive, I would have thought.*
KEATON: Even Renée Adorée, the girl that was in *The Big Parade*? I had her in one of the two-reelers.

BROWNLOW: *Which one?*
KEATON: *Daydreams.*

BROWNLOW: Daydreams *she's in, is she?*
KEATON: Yes. She's in that.

BROWNLOW: *That's one that isn't around. Do you have a print of that?*
KEATON: Yes. They've got a print of it in Munich.

BROWNLOW: *Were there any pictures of yours which you never released?*
KEATON: No.

BROWNLOW: *Everything that you did was put out?*
KEATON: Yes.

BROWNLOW: *Was it true that you were in* The Round Up, *the Arbuckle picture?*
KEATON: Yeah. I was up hunting, and Arbuckle was on location at Lone Pine out there on the edge of the Mojave Desert. It's good quail country. So, I went up to visit for some quail shooting. They had a shot, and Arbuckle says, "Put an Indian makeup on Keaton, and let me shoot him." George Melford, the director, says, "All right." They got me an Indian's makeup and put a camera shooting over Arbuckle's head. You could see him take aim at me and shoot, and when he shot, I died. But I was going at top speed when he hit me. I just took off this way, so I sailed—I was running as fast as I could and I hit here first. Well, I ploughed dirt. Ever see a rabbit hit in the back of the head? What it does to him? Well, that's what it looked like it did to me. The silly part of it was . . . my mother and father, I hadn't brought them to California yet. This was right after *The Saphead* was made. This was Arbuckle's first picture for Paramount,

The Round Up. She's in Muskegon, Michigan, and because I'd been working with Arbuckle and this picture had come out starring him now, *The Round Up*, my mother had remembered the show from Broadway; so did my father. But they liked Arbuckle, and so they went down to see it. When that Indian died on the screen, she said, "That was Buster." How in God's name she could pick me [out], but she picked me. Nobody had told her I was in the picture. I never thought of writing.

BROWNLOW: *There was no credit for you, was there?*
KEATON: Oh no. I had no connection with the picture at all, nothing with Paramount at all, nothing. And she picked me. She said, "Nobody else could do that. That body action . . ." She knows me that well, that's all. It was a long shot of an Indian running. [Laughter.] No close-up of my face or anything, and she picked me.
TOM WEBSTER: How did you get all the doors to open at the same time in *The Navigator*?
KEATON: We rigged it. [Keaton then talks about how the ship's pitching and rolling were filmed.] The tough part of that was . . . that big ship. We actually had an ocean liner that was five hundred feet long. We got a camera with a big weight hanging on there, and we went down underneath with a piece of chalk and marked a figure 8—like that. Now this is a free head, a ball head, on the camera. Now this man here just takes this thing here and when the scene starts he just follows that [figure 8]. That way you've your [pitching and rolling.]

[Brownlow asks about the certificate on Keaton's den wall connected with the film, *The Baby Cyclone* (1928), directed by Edward Sutherland.]
KEATON: [It was given to me for doubling for] Lew Cody. And she [the Cody character's wife] sent him down to the cellar to turn on the boiler or something. He was in full dress clothes; they were going out for the evening. And the gag was that he comes down there, steps on this cake of soap and took this spill. Well, Cody can't fall off a chair, see. So he got two stunt men there, just common ordinary stunt men . . .

[Mrs. Keaton interrupts to show and talk about an album of snapshots.]
MRS. KEATON: There's *Our Hospitality*, because here's the train, see . . . The crew cuttin' up and lightening up. And here's *The Navigator*, see.

They're on the deck, there. This is Ernie [Orsatti], 'cause he was always in charge of pumping air for Buster. [Here's] Lake Tahoe. Ernie ran into a whole bunch of . . . old negatives that he'd had probably since the year one, and he went and had a batch of them made up just to see what they were. Well, that's the General. [To Keaton] Here you are with the eel.

KEATON :   Uhuh. That's not the General. That's another old locomotive. See the coupling on there? That kills [any impression it is] the Civil War engine right there!

MRS. KEATON: I thought there were more pictures of the crew. There's your dad, the back of his head. It's Joe, see. Joe was the engineer on that train. . . .

BROWNLOW: *You were saying about this Lew Cody story.*

KEATON: Oh, they had two stunt men to do this fall for Cody. Tried one of them, [and] the guy did a good fall, but. . . .

[Mrs. Keaton interrupts again to show and talk about more snapshots. Brownlow asks about other directors who worked for Keaton.]

KEATON: James W. Horne, I used him in a picture and he was absolutely useless to me. Jimmy Horne. Harry Brand got me to use him for *College.* He hadn't done very many important—no important—pictures that I remember, only some quickies and incidental things.[8] I don't know why [I used him], as I did practically [all of] *College* anyway. It didn't make any difference to me

BROWNLOW: *Was this the same with . . . the famous Blystone?*

KEATON: No. Jack Blystone was with me on *Our Hospitality.* He was a good man, excellent.

---

[8] Keaton is being unfair to Horne. James Wesley Horne (1880–1942) directed some important silent features such as *The Yankee Consul* (1924) with Douglas MacLean and the surreal *The Cruise of the Jasper B* (1926) with Rod La Rocque and Mildred Harris. He also directed many serials and some of the best-loved Laurel and Hardy comedies, such as *Big Business* (1929).

BROWNLOW: *I keep seeing two names. He's Jack Blystone, but I keep seeing Jasper Blystone.*

KEATON: That's another one. I don't remember what he did. But Jack Blystone had some very good pictures under his belt. He was a good director.

But I was starting to tell you about watching the two stunt men do this thing, and finally I said, "Sedgwick wouldn't need me for a while [on *The Cameraman*]. Give me Cody's clothes." So, there was no stage dressing room in those days; I just went behind a piece of scenery and put on his full dress suit, that's all. I come down [the stairs], step on the cake of soap, and . . . The trouble with the other stunt men doing it is that they each did good falls, but they weren't funny. And he didn't want a big, dramatic straight fall—it had to look funny or he couldn't use the scene. So, instead of hitting the piece of soap and both feet going out from under me that way, I did it the other way. I hit the soap and took my feet out that way so that it threw me onto my head. And as I came down, I threw a neck roll and lit with the tails of the coat over my head, and I was on my knees like that with the tail of the coat over here, which is an ideal cut with the camera right there. For a double, it hid me immediately when I hit, see. So all I had to do was to move Cody in there, into the exact same spot, move the camera up just a few feet, and he just rose up, got the coattails back off his head, shook his head like that and went on with it. Now, they did it without putting a number board up on the camera or anything. So it was a continuous scene on the screen except for the one little quick blur moving the camera. In the projection room, the producer Irving Thalberg—the great Irving Thalberg—says to poor Eddie Sutherland in there watching his dailies, "You must never let Cody do a thing like that. Do you realize the chance you took? Cody could be laid up for weeks!" Sutherland said, "Well, he wanted to do it." [Thalberg replied,] "Well, never let him do anything like that again!"

To commence with, Cody couldn't fall off this chair without putting himself in the hospital. That is number one and this was the wildest looking fall you ever saw in your life, see. So they gave me a stunt check. I got $7.50 for that. So, I never cashed it. They owe me an awful lot of interest because that was shot in 1928, see.

BROWNLOW: *Do you think that Lupino Lane as a stunt comedian . . . Do you remember his . . . ?*
KEATON: I remember him very well.

BROWNLOW: *You held the field, but I think that Lupino Lane was pretty good on the contortion side.*
KEATON: Oh no. He was an out-and-out musical comedy man—no good for motion pictures. That's different roughhouse work, see. He was out-and-out musical comedy.

BROWNLOW: *What do you think about Raymond Griffith?*
KEATON: He was a good light comedian.

BROWNLOW: *And how would you rate Douglas MacLean?*
KEATON: On the same plane, a good light comedian. [Keaton points to a photograph.] Here's a picture for you—the best still picture I've got. This was a dinner at the Roosevelt Hotel—this was 1925—to welcome Rudolph Valentino into the United Artists. There are eight of the top stars of that day in the picture. The two missing would be Harold Lloyd and Gloria Swanson. Here are William S. Hart, Norma Talmadge, Douglas Fairbanks, myself, Hiram Abrams (the first president of the United Artists and promoter of the United Artists), Mary Pickford, Charlie Chaplin, Joe Schenck, Rudolph Valentino, Mrs. Valentino, Constance Talmadge. There's your eight—one, two, three, four, five, six, seven, eight. That's Natalie Talmadge, my first missus. There are four of my grandchildren. I've got six. I had two sons by her, six grandchildren. Here's Mother Talmadge, Mother Pickford, Charlie's brother Sydney Chaplin, Lottie Pickford (Mary's sister), Johnny Considine. That's a great photograph! Today you couldn't duplicate it, because if you managed to assemble eight of the top stars, by the time you could get them together, a couple of them wouldn't be in the big ten. They go and come too fast.

BROWNLOW: *What was the difference between—you were talking about these falls—between a pratfall and a "108"?*
KEATON: Oh, the 108 was invented by Ben Turpin.[9]

---

[9] Presumably, the name for Turpin's favorite fall comes from the slang expression for being inebriated, being "one over the eight."

BROWNLOW: *Just a term for any sort of fall.*

KEATON: Yeah. In other words, Ben Turpin, even if he just fell that way, or a walkover frontward, a layout, the spread eagle flat, that was his 108. So anytime a director says, "Hey, you come through there, Ben, and take a fall." [Turpin] says, "Which one do you want? The 108, or 52, or one of the small ones, like 7?" "No," [the director] says, "do a 108." [Turpin] would do a regular straight pratfall. It would have no number. Anytime anyone took a wild fall, he always used to say [it was a] 108.

BROWNLOW: *What did you call your fantastic neck roll?*

KEATON: Just called it a neck roll.

BROWNLOW: *Did you do those billiard things in* Sherlock Jr. *yourself?*

KEATON: Yes.

BROWNLOW: *They couldn't be planned?*

KEATON: Oh, it was a wild scene—and it worked.

BROWNLOW: *I imagined you had electric . . .*

KEATON: No. God no! We shot until we got wild scenes like that, and that's all there was to it.

BROWNLOW: *The hand grenade and the explosions . . . ?*

KEATON: Mademoiselle!

MRS. KEATON: Yeah. You didn't feed the girls [meaning the chickens].

KEATON: Yeah, I just did it a minute ago. And they were all standing there stamping their feet at me, too. I was about forty-five minutes late feeding my chickens out there in the back. And they were all standing by the gate like this. [Keaton imitates a chicken.] Come on.

BROWNLOW: *We mustn't hold you up any longer. This has been . . .*

KEATON: I've got some red chickens back there.

BROWNLOW: *Well, thank you very much indeed. Are there any stills that you are looking for that I might come across? I know you are trying to track down . . .*

KEATON: He's got a picture that I should have up in here . . . of that engine half way to the water going through that bridge. I should have that on the wall here someplace.

BROWNLOW: *You can see how scarce they are, if that's the only one that I've been able to find.*
KEATON: Would you like a good glass of beer before you leave? Everybody has a cocktail bar; I go for one of these. It has a spittoon, a brass rail, and draft beer. If you like beer, this is the best in town.

BROWNLOW: *Great, I'd love one. I was just telling your wife, have you seen this new French comedian Pierre Étaix?*
KEATON: I wouldn't know the name. I probably have.

BROWNLOW: *He's just doing you, I mean exactly you. You haven't seen* The Suitor?
KEATON: No. I've only seen a couple of French pictures in the last ten years, I guess. They sent me especially to see Peter Sellers.

BROWNLOW: *This man has the same deadpan and the same way of walking away from something. Do you remember how you used to do it? Exactly these. And the same gags from the old pictures. Some of them are Harry Langdon, the one about dragging the woman up stairs and going up the ladder—do you remember the scene?*
KEATON: Good beer. It's Michelob. This is a seven-and-a-half-gallon tank here. And instead of the old system of running the [beer] out of a wooden keg through coils—and you've got ice on the coils. This is an ice box and these are aluminum barrels, so it's the temperature of the ice box. No coils; no ice.

BROWNLOW: *That hat? Which one is that from?*
KEATON: Oh, they made me a member of the Fire Department in Buffalo, New York. The cattlemen in Fort Worth, Texas, gave me this one. I'm a member of the Cattlemen's Association too. The other [hat] is from Oklahoma.

BROWNLOW: *There are no original props that you have?*
KEATON: Oh no. They gave them to me.

BROWNLOW: *It almost looks like the one you had in the picture.*
KEATON: Oh, no. That was a real one. This is a cardboard hat.

BROWNLOW: *Was that a real one?*

KEATON: Oh, sure . . . old Civil War costumes from all the wardrobe departments in Los Angeles and New York.

BROWNLOW: *They look very authentic.*

KEATON: They were.

BROWNLOW: *[They look] more authentic than the modern films show them to be.*

KEATON: *Go West.*

BROWNLOW: *You must have had trouble with that cow. Did you find that when you developed the very difficult gags that you found that you got more astonished gasps than laughs sometimes?*

KEATON: Yeah, sometimes. Sure.

BROWNLOW: *I found in running* Sherlock Jr. *that people instead of laughing would start gasping.*

KEATON: Yeah. That happened often. That one [in *The General*] where one railroad tie hits the other one—that's one of those. They laugh later a little bit. [Keaton talks about a photograph.] I did that show a couple years ago, *Once Upon a Mattress*. That's Dody Goodman.

BROWNLOW: *What do you think the Beckett film is going to be like?*

KEATON: I don't know. I didn't pay much attention to it. It was a wild daydream he had. I don't think it meant a damn thing.

BROWNLOW: *What were the other ones like,* Pajama Party . . . ? *Were they any good? I heard somebody talking at lunch about them. Blanche Sweet, incidentally, sends you her best regards. She was talking to a script writer who was saying that everyone was seeing this picture and saying that you were the best thing in it. They didn't think very much of the picture, but thought you were superb.* Pajama Party, *what was that like?*

KEATON: [Keaton makes a contemptuous noise.]

BROWNLOW: *How would you like to get back in production with your old team?*

KEATON: Too much work now. I make sure I don't do too much work. I won't get into a television show if it's a weekly show. It's too hard. I turn that down, Christ, eighteen times a season. They keep coming to me with scripts. I won't do a weekly show—way too much work. It's tiring. Do one of these "Pajama" pictures—do it in a week. Then three or four commercials a year, and that's plenty. I don't want to do anymore than that.

BROWNLOW: *That was a pretty good commercial, the Ford thing, the remake of* Cops.

KEATON: [Keaton talks about more of the photographs hanging in the den.] This picture here was my second salaried year. I'd been getting a salary [starting] the year before that. I was four years old, and that would be 1899—my first salaried year. Here, you can see it better. Go in this bathroom here. Here's another good picture, on the wall over there.

BROWNLOW: *Oh gosh! When was that taken? That's about the same time. Is that about* 1899?

KEATON: That would be 1900, 'cause that's the same time that this picture was taken. My first salaried year was the year before that, 1899. I'm older professionally than Maurice Chevalier, Francis X. Bushman, Charlie Chaplin . . . anybody else . . . Ed Wynn . . . you name 'em.

TOM WEBSTER: With so many years behind you, are you glad you never became a doctor or a lawyer?

KEATON: Yes. It's better I didn't.

BROWNLOW: *What's this picture of Norman Kerry doing here?*

KEATON: That's Ward Crane. Allan Dwan made a picture personality out of him. He was a Navy lieutenant. Dwan saw him during the war and invited him to Hollywood and made an actor out of him. He turned out to be excellent. He turned out to do the villain with Norma Talmadge in [*Within the Law.*]

BROWNLOW: *You had him in a picture.*

KEATON: In *Sherlock Jr.* That was an actor or vaudevillian's letterhead that they wrote the managers with. This was before agents were invented, when you were your own agent. You sold yourself.

BROWNLOW: *Well, thank you very much for the beer, and thank you very much for the interview.*
KEATON: [Keaton points out his Eastman House award.] There are only twenty of those in existence: for the five outstanding cameramen in the motion picture business, five greatest directors, five male stars, five female stars. So there are only twenty of those out. The George Eastman Award.

BROWNLOW: *And you got yours for?*
KEATON: Being one of the five male stars.

BROWNLOW: *And what is this one? [Brownlow points to an Oscar, an Academy Award.]*
KEATON: That's for making pictures that play forever. For instance, had I deserved the award for making *The Navigator* or *The General*, it would have been called the Best Picture of the Year in order to get it—or it might have been for an individual performance. But the Academy hadn't been invented yet. There weren't any Oscars yet.

BROWNLOW: *Do you have prints of all your pictures?*
KEATON: They're in Munich.

BROWNLOW: *Oh, with Beta Films, yes.*
KEATON: They made dupe negatives of everything I got.
MRS. KEATON: Don't give an unequivocal *yes* to that because there are a couple of shorts we've never been able to find.

BROWNLOW: *Yes, if you can tell me the titles, you never know what crops up. Do you have* One Week, *for instance? Because I found that recently.*
KEATON: I'm pretty sure we have *One Week.*

BROWNLOW: *There's another one, a sound one. The sheriff—it's got a French title on my version. The one where you're a sheriff in a ghost town [The Gold Ghost (1934)]. Do you remember this? Do you have that one?*
MRS. KEATON: We don't have any sound, but we're not terribly interested in sound, only the silent ones that they're concerned with.

BROWNLOW: *You couldn't have the* The Saphead, *do you have that one?*
MRS. KEATON: Yes, he does. I believe so.

BROWNLOW: *You haven't got* The Round Up, *of course?*
KEATON: No.

BROWNLOW: *That little scene in* The Round Up *would be great to have, wouldn't it?*
MRS. KEATON: He's [Raymond Rohauer has] got an awful lot of Keaton-Arbuckle pictures, though, that he found not too long ago. Buster hasn't seen them since they were made in 1918, and I've never seen them at all. They're in Paris or somewhere. He's got them over there in a vault somewhere.

BROWNLOW: The Butcher Boy, Coney Island, *all those things.*
MRS. KEATON: Yes.

BROWNLOW: *Before you got the poker face . . . have you seen the* Coney Island *one, have you?*
MRS. KEATON: No.

BROWNLOW: *With Buster grinning in it? Incredible! He gets up on a lamp post and he grins.*
MRS. KEATON: Did you know that, Buster? In *Coney Island*, he says you scrambled up a lamp post and then grinned . . . with a big silly grin on your face.
KEATON: I did. Yes.
MRS. KEATON: That's how old that is.

BROWNLOW: *Amazing!*

Keaton at Venice

JOHN GILLETT AND
JAMES BLUE/1965

SATURDAY, SEPTEMBER 4, 1965, was Buster Keaton day
at the Venice Festival. At the press conference after the preview of *Film*
(in which Keaton interprets a Beckett script), the appearance of the
familiar stocky figure determinedly stumping on to the platform was
the signal for a standing ovation of wild affection from the press. "Caro
Buster . . ." said somebody happily, after a long pause while Keaton
blandly seated himself among a line of fussing officials, and went on to
ask what he thought of the Beckett film. "I don't know what it was all
about," the hoarsely grating voice promptly replied, "perhaps you can
tell me." A hand waved expressively in the air: "The camera was *behind*
me all the time. I ain't used to that."

What was he doing in Italy? He was making a comedy called *Two
Marines and a General*—"I'm The General." Loud cheers made it clear
that the audience agreed, and an attempt by the young lady valiantly
struggling with three languages to translate this as "Il Marasciallo" was
drowned by roars of protest.

Keaton was obviously warming to his task. He stood up and started
talking without waiting for questions and spoke of the new Dick Lester
film he was shortly joining in Spain. "I've had several other offers, but
couldn't take 'em. No time to spare"—and there was a certain satisfaction
in the way he said these last words, as if his present activity made up a
little for the waste and neglect of the last twenty years. One notes that,

From *Sight and Sound*, vol. 35, no. 1 (Winter 1965–66): 26–30. Reprinted by permission of
Sight and Sound.

unlike certain comedians, Keaton does not need to keep up a stream of wisecracks. Buster himself had taken over the Palazzo, in full command of his audience once again.

At the evening gala show, more unexpectedly, the smart Venetian audience also rose to their feet with delighted applause as the celebrities took their places. Somebody in the next seat poked Keaton. He looked surprised. "For me?" one could almost hear that dead-pan eyebrow exclaim; and he got up and bowed, beautifully.

Next day, thanks to the cooperation of Mr. Raymond Rohauer, we were able to interview Keaton at the Excelsior Hotel. Several other papers and television networks also had the same idea, and we had to wait a little while. Eventually we saw him peering through a door off the main foyer, apparently wiping down the glass panel with his hand-kerchief for the benefit of a lady admirer. It was only when he put his head through the space and started cleaning the "glass" from the other side that we realized that it was a beautiful Buster gag.

Keaton started talking almost before we got our equipment ready and insisted on giving us the most comfortable chairs. He sat bolt upright on the other side of the table, large eyes staring straight ahead, with the Great Stone Face set throughout in expressive immobility except for one charming moment duly noted in the interview. Our questions triggered off an immediate response, precise down to the last little detail, almost as if his films were parading before him as he talked. And in his mind, Keaton the director seemed quite inseparable from Buster the actor.

JG

BUSTER KEATON: I ought to do something about the new release print of *The General* that was shown in London. When the film was to be revived in Europe we brought over as many old prints as we could find, in order to pick out the best reels—to find the ones that hadn't faded, or been chewed up by the machine. We gave them to the outfit in Munich who were handling the film, and they made a duped negative. They did a beautiful job of it. The first thing they wanted to do, as an experiment, was to translate all the English titles in German so that they could release the film in Germany. It did a beautiful business there, so immediately they made some more prints with French titles for release in France. Now they must have lost the original list of English titles, so they put them back again into English from their own German translation.

I happened to see a print of this new English version in Rome last week—the same version you had in London—and the titles were misleading. For instance, when I'm trying to enlist and I'm asked, "What is your occupation?" I say, "bartender." Well, that type of man gets drafted into the army immediately. In the new version the title reads "barkeep"—that means you own the place. And it doesn't sound as funny anyway in English: it might in German, I don't know. Then they put "sir" on to the ends of sentences because I'm talking to an officer, but there's no "sirring" at all in our titles. Some of the explanatory titles were changed or dropped as well. Do you remember, for instance, the scene where we all got off the train and while we were away the engine was stolen? We actually stopped off there for lunch: the conductor comes into the car and says "This is Marietta: one hour for lunch." But they left that title off, and without it you'd think the train had emptied out because it was the end of the run. In which case there's no reason to steal the engine then: they could have waited until everyone had gone and the place was deserted.

JG: *Apart from the comedy values, the most impressive thing about all the features you made during the twenties is their distinctive visual style. They all have a kind of look which one associates with a Keaton film. How did you work with your various co-directors to achieve this? Who actually did what?*
BK: Number one, I was practically my own producer on all those silent pictures. I used a co-director on some of them, but the majority I did alone. And I cut them all myself: I cut all my own pictures.

JG: *What exactly would the co-director do?*
BK: Co-direct with me, that's all. He would be out there looking through the camera, and I'd ask him what he thought. He would maybe say "That scene looks a little slow"; and then I'd do it again and speed it up. As a rule, when I'm working alone, the cameraman, the prop man, the electrician, these are my eyes out there. I'd ask, "Did that work the way I wanted it to?" and they'd say yes or no. They knew what they were talking about.

JG: *You would choose the actual camera set-ups yourself?*
BK: Always, when it was important for the scene I was going to do. If I had an incidental scene—someone runs in, say, and says, "here, you've

got to go and do this"—the background wasn't important. Then I generally just told the cameraman that I had these two characters in the scene, two full-length figures, and asked him to pick a good-looking background. He would go by the sun. He'd say, "I like that back crosslight coming in through the trees. There are clouds over there right now, so if we hurry up we can still get them before they disappear." So I would say "Swell" and go and direct the scene in front of the cameraman's set-up. We took pains to get good-looking scenery whenever we possibly could, no matter what we were shooting.

JG: *What about the visual idea of the films? Take, for instance, a picture like* Our Hospitality, *which has a beautiful period feeling.*
BK: We were very conscious of our stories. We learned in a hurry that we couldn't make a feature-length picture the way we had done the two-reelers; we couldn't use impossible gags, like the kind of things that happen to cartoon characters. We had to eliminate all these things because we had to tell a logical story that an audience would accept. So story construction became a very strong point with us.

Our Hospitality (1923)

BK: On *Our Hospitality* we had this one idea of an old-fashioned Southern feud. But it looks as though this must have died down in the years it took me to grow up from being a baby, so our best period for that was to go back something like eighty years. "All right," we say. "We go back that far. And now when I go South, am I traveling in a covered wagon, or what? Let's look up the records and see when the first railroad train was invented." Well, we find out: we've got the Stephenson Rocket for England and the DeWitt Clinton for the United States. And we chose the Rocket engine because it's funnier looking. The passenger coaches were stage coaches with flanged wheels put on them. So we built that entire train and that set our period for us: 1825 was the actual year of the invention of the railroad. Now we dress our people to the period. And that was fine because we liked the costumes: you've got away there from the George Washington short pants and into the more picturesque Johnny Walker type of costume.

JG: *One of the best gags in the film is the moment when you swing out by a*
rope from the riverbank and catch the girl almost in mid-air as she goes over
the big waterfall. How did you stage this very tricky shot?
BK: We had to build that dam: we built it in order to fit that trick. The
set was built over a swimming pool, and we actually put up four eight-
inch water pipes with big pumps and motors to run them, to carry the
water up from the pool to create our waterfall. That fall was about six
inches deep. A couple of times I swung out underneath there and
dropped upside down when I caught her. I had to go down to the doctor right there and then. They pumped out my ears and nostrils and
drained me, because when a full volume of water like that comes down
and hits you and you're upside down—then you really get it.

JG: *How long did it take to shoot the scene? How many takes were there?*
BK: I think I got it on the third take. I missed the first two, but the
third one I got it . . . And it's hard to realize that it was shot in 1923. It
sounds like going back to ancient history.

JB: *But it still works. Two weeks ago in Paris I saw* The Three Ages, *which*
is also forty-two years old, and the audience were rolling in the aisles.
Presumably you did this as a take-off on films like Intolerance?
BK: I was thinking of *Intolerance* when I made it. I told the three separate stories the same as Griffith did; and of course in that film I did take
liberties, because it was more of a travesty than a burlesque. That's why
I used a wristwatch that was a sundial, and why I used my helmet the
way I did. Fords at that time had a safety device to stop people from
stealing the cars: a thing with a big spike which you locked on the back
wheel and which looked just like my Roman helmet. So I unlocked my
Roman helmet off me and locked it on to the wheel of my chariot. At
that time the audience all compared it with the safety gadget for a Ford.

JB: *This seems to lead to the question of how you find your gags. Do you*
get them from the set, things in the décor . . . ?
BK: Yes, props, and characters, and everything, and then look for the
simplest things to go wrong. And that leads to bigger things. But there
is nothing worse with us than a misplaced gag. Someone may suggest a
good gag, or even an excellent one, but if it doesn't fit the story I'm

doing and I try to drag it in, then it looks dragged in on the screen. So it's much better to save it, until some time when it does fit what I'm doing.

JB: *Quite often you start off a film rather slowly, and the camera movement increases as the action builds up.*
BK: Deliberately, I always do that. I use the simplest little things in the world, and I never look for big gags to start a picture. I don't want them in the first reel, because if I ever get a big laugh sequence in the first reel, then I'm going to have trouble following it later. The idea that I had to have a gag or get a laugh in every scene . . . I lost that a long time ago. It makes you strive to be funny and you go out of your way trying. It's not a natural thing.

JG: *In the short films it was different, of course, because you had to make it funny all the way. Playhouse—the one about the theatre in which you play almost every part—is absolutely packed with jokes. Was it in some ways easier to think up these separate gags for the short films, or did you prefer to have time to work out a story?*
BK: We didn't rush. When we thought we had what we wanted, we went ahead and ordered the sets built. But I made one very bad mistake with that picture *The Playhouse.* I could have made the whole two-reeler just by myself, without any trouble. But we were a little scared to do it, because it might have looked as though we were trying to show how versatile I was—that I could make a whole half-hour picture all alone, without another soul in the cast. That's the reason why we brought other people into the second reel, and that was a mistake.

Seven Chances (1925)

JB: *By the time you came to the features, the action was no longer just the basis for the gags but thoroughly integrated with them. Do you consistently look for a gag that will help advance the action?*
BK: Take one from a picture that I am about to re-release, *Seven Chances.* I am running away from a batch of women who are chasing me. A friend has put it in the paper that I'll marry anybody so long as I can be married by five o'clock—it has to do with inheriting an estate or

whatever. So all the women in the world show up to get married. They chase me out of the church, and so on. I went down to the dunes just off the Pacific Ocean out at Los Angeles, and I accidentally dislodged a boulder in coming down. All I had set up for the scene was a camera panning with me as I came over the skyline and was chased down into the valley. But I dislodged this rock, and it in turn dislodged two others, and they chased me down this hill.

That's all there was: just three rocks. But the audience at the preview sat up in their seats and expected more. So we went right back and ordered fifteen hundred rocks built, from bowling alley size up to boulders eight feet in diameter. Then we went out to the Ridge Route, which is in the High Sierras, to a burnt mountain steeper than a forty-five degree angle. A couple of truckloads of men took those rocks up and planted them, and then I went up to the top and came down with the rocks. That gag gave me the whole final chase, and it was an accident in the first place.

JG: *The great thing about that chase is that a lot of it is shot from a long way away, so that you get the effect of the tiny figure with the rocks all round. You often seem to prefer to work within a rather large shot, rather than using a lot of close-ups.*

BK: When I've got a gag that spreads out, I hate to jump a camera into close-ups. So I do everything in the world I can to hold it in that long-shot and keep the action rolling. When I do use cuts I still won't go right into a close-up: I'll just go in maybe to a full figure, but that's about as close as I'll come. Close-ups are too jarring on the screen, and this type of cut can stop an audience from laughing.

If I were going to show you this hotel lobby where we are now, for instance, I'd go back and show you the whole lobby on that first shot and then move in closer. But the main thing is that I want you to be familiar with the atmosphere, so that you know what my location is and where I am. From then on I never have to go back to the long shot again unless I get into action where I am going to cover space in a hurry.

Steamboat Bill, Jr. (1928)

JG: *Could you please tell us something about* Steamboat Bill, Jr., *with the big cyclone at the end when you get the impression that the whole set is being systematically destroyed? It must have been one of the most elaborate of all of your films to stage.*

BK: The original story I had was about the Mississippi, but we actually used the Sacramento River in California, some six hundred miles north of Los Angeles. We went up there and built that street front, three blocks of it, and built the piers and so on. We found the river boats right there in Sacramento: one was brand new, and we were able to age the other one up to make it look as though it was ready to fall apart. My original situation in that film was a flood. But my so-called producer on that film was Joe Schenck, who at that time was producing Norma Talmadge, Constance Talmadge, and myself, and who later became president of United Artists. Then later on Twentieth Century–Fox was Joe Schenck, and his brother Nicholas Schenck was head man of Metro-Goldwyn-Mayer. Schenck was supposed to be my producer but he never knew when or what I was shooting. He just turned me loose.

Well, the publicity man on *Steamboat Bill* goes to Schenck and he says: "He can't do a flood sequence because we have floods every year and too many people are lost. It's too painful to get laughs with." So Schenck told me, "You can't do a flood." I said, "That's funny, since it seems to me that Chaplin during World War I made a picture called *Shoulder Arms*, which was the biggest money-maker he'd made at that time. You can't get a bigger disaster than that, and yet he made his biggest laughing picture out of it." He said, "Oh, that's different." I don't know why it was different. I asked if it was all right to make a cyclone, and he agreed that was better. Now he didn't know it, but there are four times more people killed in the United States by hurricanes and cyclones than by floods. But it was all right as long as he didn't find that out, and so I went ahead with my technical man and did the cyclone.

JG: *How about the technical side? The marvelous shot, for instance, of the front of the building falling on you, so that you are standing in the window as it hits the ground. What were the problems in staging that scene?*

BK: First I had them build the framework of this building and make sure that the hinges were all firm and solid. It was a building with a tall V-shaped roof, so that we could make this window up in the roof exceptionally high. An average second story window would be about twelve feet, but we're up about eighteen feet. Then you lay this framework down on the ground, and build the window around me. We built the window so that I had a clearance of two inches on each shoulder, and the top missed my head by two inches and the bottom my heels by two inches. We mark that ground out and drive big nails where my two heels are going to be. Then you put that house back up in position while they finish building it. They put the front on, painted it, and made the jagged edge where it tore away from the main building; and then we went in and fixed the interiors so that you're looking at a house that the front has blown off. Then we put up our wind machines with the big Liberty motors. We had six of them and they are pretty powerful: they could lift a truck right off the road. Now we had to make sure that we were getting our foreground and background wind effect, but that no current ever hit the front of that building when it started to fall, because if the wind warps her she's not going to fall where we want her, and I'm standing right out front. But it's a one-take scene and we got it that way. You don't do those things twice.

The General (1927)

JB: *Your usual method was to start with a story and then look for the gags. Where did you begin a film like* The General?

BK: I took that first page out of the history book. Disney did it about nine years ago and called it by its original name—*The Great Locomotive Chase*, with Fess Parker. But he made a mistake and told it from a Northern standpoint. And you can always make villains out of the Northerners, but you cannot make a villain out of the South. That was the first mistake he made.

In *The General* I took that page of history and I stuck to it in all detail. I staged it exactly the way it happened. The Union agents intended to enter from the State of Kentucky, which was a neutral territory, pretending that they were coming down to fight for the Southern cause. That was an excuse to get on that train which takes them up to an army camp. Their leader took seven men with him, including two locomotive engineers and a telegraph operator; and he told them that if anything went wrong they were to scatter individually, stick to their stories that they were Kentuckians down to enlist in the Southern army, and then watch for the first opportunity to desert and get back over the line to the North. As soon as they stole that engine, they wanted to pull out of there, to disconnect the telegraph and burn bridges and destroy enough track to cripple the Southern army supply route. That was what they intended to do. And I staged the chase exactly the way it happened. Then I rounded out the story of stealing my engine back. When my picture ended the South was winning, which was all right with me.

JB: *How did the plot develop apart from the historical story line—the involvement with the girl and so on?*
BK: Well, the moment you give me a locomotive and things like that to play with, as a rule I find some way of getting laughs with it. But the original locomotive chase ended when I found myself in Northern territory and had to desert. From then on it was my invention, in order to get a complete plot. It had nothing to do with the Civil War.

JG: *What many of us like about your films is the treatment of the women. These poor ladies, like Marion Mack in* The General, *are subjected to all kinds of humiliations and yet they battle on. They get pulled and pushed around, but they always stand by you. Did they mind at all?*
BK: No, no. They didn't mind at all. Oh God, that girl in *The General* had more fun with that picture than any film she'd made in her life. *(At this point Keaton's face, hitherto frozen as usual, eased into a wide, knowing smile.)* I guess it's because so many leading ladies in those days looked as though they had just walked out of a beauty parlour. They always kept them looking that way—even in covered wagons, they kept their leading ladies looking beautiful at all times. We said to thunder with that, we'll dirty ours up a bit and let them have some rough treatment.

JB: *There is a moment of almost pathetic beauty, which is a gag at the same time, when you are both sitting on the steering rod of the wheel and the train starts to move. Not at the very end, but towards the middle of the film.*
BK: I was alone on it when it moved. We were afraid to put her on it, or I would have moved it at the finish.

JB: *Can you remember how that gag came to you, out of the film's situation?*

BK: Well, the situation of the picture at that point is that she says "never speak to me again until you're in uniform." So the bottom has dropped out of everything, and I've got nothing to do but sit down on my engine and think. I don't know why they rejected me: they didn't tell me it was because they didn't want to take a locomotive engineer off his duty. My fireman wants to put the engine away in the round-house and doesn't know that I'm sitting on the cross bar, and starts to take it in.

I was running the engine myself all through the picture: I could handle that thing so well I was stopping it on a dime. But when it came to this shot I asked the engineer whether we could do it. He said: "There's only one danger. A fraction too much steam with these old-fashioned engines and the wheel spins. And if it spins it will kill you then and there." We tried it four or five times, and in the end the engineer was satisfied that he could handle it. So we went ahead and did it. I wanted a fade-out laugh for that sequence: although it's not a big gag it's cute and funny enough to get me a nice laugh.

JG: *It's also beautiful: it has another quality than just a laugh. On this question of emotion, there is the difference between your films and those of Chaplin, who sometimes seems to go into a sequence with the intention of milking it for all the emotion it can stand. You are rarely deliberately pathetic. In* Go West, *however, there is a slight element of conscious pathos. Did you feel you needed something more emotional there than in the other films?*

BK: I was going to do everything I possibly could to keep that cow from being sent to the slaughter-house: I only had that one thing in mind. And I ran into one disappointment on that film. One of the most famous Western shows ever seen in the United States was called *The Heart of Maryland*, in which these two guys are playing cards, and one guy calls the other a name, and he takes out his six-shooter and lays it down on the table, pointing right at this fellow's middle, and says, "When you call me that, smile . . ." Well, because I'm known as frozen face, blank pan, we thought that if you did that to me an audience would say, "Oh my God, he can't smile: he's gone; he's dead." But it didn't strike an audience as funny at all: they just felt sorry for me.

We didn't find that out until the preview, and it put a hole in my scene right there and then. Of course I got out of it the best way I could, but we run into these lulls every now and then.

JB: *And you look for a gag to get yourself out of a situation: the pole-vault gag with the spear for instance in* The Three Ages. *There you were in a situation where you had to get the girl out of the hands of Wallace Beery. How did you work your way to the spear vault from that?*
BK: I couldn't just run over a batch of rocks or something to get to her: I had to invent something, find something unexpected, and pole-vaulting with a spear seemed to be it.

Sherlock Jr. (1924)

JG: *You very often use gags which couldn't be managed except in films. For instance the scene in* Sherlock Jr. *where you are dreaming yourself into the picture, and the scenery keeps changing. How did you get the idea of this scene?*
BK: That was the reason for making the whole picture. Just that one situation: that a motion picture projectionist in a theatre goes to sleep and visualizes himself getting mixed up with the characters on the screen. All right, then my job was to transform those characters on the screen into my (the projectionist's) characters at home, and then I've got my plot. Now to make it work was another thing: and after that picture was made every cameraman in Hollywood spent more than one night watching it and trying to figure out just how we got some of those scenes.

JG: *How did you actually do the sequence where you are near a tree, and then you are on a rock in the middle of the ocean. Was it some kind of back projection?*
BK: No, that hadn't been invented then. We call it processing, but back projection is correct. But it hadn't been invented. We used measuring instruments for that sequence. When I stood on that rock I was going to jump into the ocean, but as I jumped the sea changed to something else. As I looked down I held still for a moment, and we ended that scene. Then we brought out tape-measures, put a cross-bar in front of the camera to square it off, and measured me from two angles. That

made sure that I was in exactly the same spot as far as the camera was concerned. We also used surveyor's instruments to get me the same height, so that when we changed the scene and I went back on the set I was in exactly the same place as in the first shot. Then the cameraman just starts to crank and I jump; and when I jump I hit something else. I don't remember what I hit, but I hit something. This was all done just by changing the sets. But I on the screen never changed.

Keaton: Still Making the Scene

REX REED/1965

FEDERICO FELLINI WAS THERE. Jean-Luc Godard and
Michelangelo Antonioni and Luchino Visconti and several hundred
bikini-clad starlets were there. But just before the 1965 Venice Film
Festival ended, a silent fellow from the silent era stole the limelight.
Film buffs jammed the exits to get his autograph, the Italian photogra-
phers watched the pier night and day for a sign of his boat, and inside
the Cinema Palais on the Lido a hardboiled audience of international
critics waited with their pencils poised.

Then suddenly Buster Keaton was there, looking for all the world like
the kind of man dogs kick. His pants were a little baggy in the seat and
he had forgotten to bring a tux; his hat was a bit brushed around the
edges and his floppy, bow tie struggled crookedly for support on his
Adam's apple. But it didn't matter. Keaton was there and that was
understood in every language. He had come to show *Film*, an arty
twenty-two minute silent he made in New York in 1964, and when the
projector stopped they stood and cheered for five minutes.

"This is the first time I've ever been invited to a film festival," he
said, fighting back tears, "but I hope it won't be the last."

It probably won't be. On October 4, Buster Keaton reached his seven-
tieth birthday. At an age when most people are out buying graveyard
plots, his career is taking on new life. In Europe he is almost as popular
on the list of American exports as Coca-Cola. His films are shown at the

Cinémathèque Française in Paris and the British Film Institute in London. In Berlin there's a Buster Keaton Film Festival. In France funnyman Jacques Tati is such an admirer of his that he has composed a new musical score for the old Keaton evergreen, *The Navigator*, which will be reissued this fall. "That picture was made forty-two years ago," Buster says, "and it still holds up. I said they could add music, but that's all. Best not to tamper with the old ones." He owns all of his old films and keeps them in a vault in Los Angeles. He's lost track of the exact number but says it's "more than a hundred."

In America, a whole new generation of teenagers has "discovered" him on TV and in such real gone opuses as *Beach Blanket Bingo* and *How to Stuff a Wild Bikini*. And this winter, when eleven more of his film classics are revived throughout the world in a Buster Keaton package, new audiences will get a chance to see the still-fresh magic of hand-cranked cameras in such sad-sack history makers as *Steamboat Bill, Jr.*

Not that Keaton is relying on the old-timers to keep his flame going. This year alone he has completed six films ("I work more than Doris Day," he says). Recently, for nearly three months he was living in Rome, playing a wacky German general in *War Italian Style*, but now he has joined Zero Mostel and Phil Silvers in Madrid for the movie version of *A Funny Thing Happened on the Way to the Forum*.

One reason Keaton is so popular the world over is that in his work there has never been a language barrier. Most of the time there's been no language. "With a face like mine, I guess they figure who needs dialogue? When I was a baby my folks were in vaudeville. One day my Dad looked at me and said, 'Son, you better get into show business,' 'cause with a face like that you'll never get a job any place else.' I got my first paycheck when I was four and made my first picture in 1917. They didn't let me talk for more than thirty years after that." Mike Todd let him say a few words in *Around the World in Eighty Days*, but he figures his talkiest scene was the telephone conversation with Spencer Tracy in *Mad, Mad World*. He doesn't know about *Sunset Boulevard*. He never saw it.

Keaton doesn't like what's happened to comedy. "They'll do anything for a laugh today. But people aren't laughing. I think it's because the comics are all alike. There's no originality. In the old days, when

Chaplin and I were great friends, Charlie would give me gags right out of his own pictures if they didn't seem right, and I'd do the same for him. They don't trade anymore. They just steal."

His taste for humor may have changed, but his sense of humor hasn't. In *Film* he shows his tragic side, but he still had fun shooting it. "Heck, I'd be the last one in the world to comment, because I didn't know what those guys were doing half the time. The director, Alan Schneider, just told me to keep my back to the camera and be natural. Just try acting natural with a camera crew aiming at your back. And as for Samuel Beckett, I took one look at his script and asked him if he ate Welsh rarebit before he went to bed at night."

He admits he thinks about the old days sometimes, but not with sadness. "He cried like a baby when De Mille died," says his wife, Eleanor. "Yes, but I'm not sentimental by nature," he is quick to correct. "Sure I miss the Keystone Cops and Mack Sennett and Stan and Oliver and the rest, but I don't moon over the past. I don't have time."

When he's not working, he takes care of the garden on his acre and a half of farmland in Woodland Hills, California. His son owns a tourist lodge on Lake Tahoe and sometimes he gets in a bit of hunting there. He is an avid bridge player and stays up all night watching the late movies on television. "We're twenty-five miles from Hollywood, so we gave up driving into town to go to the movies. The only time I see my friends is on the late show."

Most of his old friends have either passed on or live in the Motion Picture Relief Home, about a mile and a half from his farm. "I drive by sometimes and talk to some of the old-timers, but it makes me so sad I don't do it often. They live in the past, I don't. One Easter Sunday I went to a party at Mary Pickford's house. Everybody from silent films was there. I tried to have fun, but I discovered we had nothing to talk about. Some of them had never heard a Beatles record. They haven't kept up with the times."

He stays young, he says, through hard work and nothing else. He doesn't eat nutburgers or drink spinach juice, has never read Gayelord Hauser, and refuses to take vitamin pills. He has so much energy, his wife says, that the neighborhood kids ring the door bell constantly, wanting to know "Can Buster come out and play?"

Buster Keaton is already a legend in his own time, and shows no sign of slowing down. "I had four friends who retired at the age of sixty-five and they were all dead within a year. They simply had nothing to do, nothing to occupy their minds. I have so many projects coming up I don't have time to think about kicking the bucket. People are always telling me I'm immortal. I just might prove them right. Hell, the way I feel, I just might live forever."

CONVERSATIONS WITH FILMMAKERS SERIES
PETER BRUNETTE, GENERAL EDITOR

The collected interviews with notable modern directors, including

Robert Aldrich • Woody Allen • Pedro Almodóvar • Robert Altman • Theo Angelopolous • Ingmar Bergman • Bernardo Bertolucci • Tim Burton • Jane Campion • Frank Capra • Charlie Chaplin • The Coen Brothers • Francis Ford Coppola • George Cukor • Brain De Palma • Clint Eastwood • Federico Fellini • John Ford • Terry Gilliam • Jean-Luc Godard • Peter Greenaway • Howard Hawks • Alfred Hitchcock • John Huston • Jim Jarmusch • Elia Kazan • Stanley Kubrick • Fritz Lang • Spike Lee • Mike Leigh • George Lucas • Sidney Lumet • Roman Polanski • Michael Powell • Satyajit Ray • Jean Renoir • Martin Ritt • Carlos Saura • John Sayles • Martin Scorsese • Ridley Scott • Steven Soderbergh • Steven Spielberg • George Stevens • Oliver Stone • Quentin Tarantino • Andrei Tarkovsky • Lars von Trier • Liv Ullmann • Orson Welles • Billy Wilder • John Woo • Zhang Yimou • Fred Zinnemann

INDEX